JANE AUSTEN'S NOVELS

JANE AUSTEN'S NOVELS

The Art of Clarity

ROGER GARD

1992
Yale University Press
New Haven and London

Set in Linotron Sabon by Best-set Typesetter Ltd, Hong Kong
Printed and bound at The Bath Press, Avon, Great Britain

Library of Congress Cataloging-in-Publication Data

Gard, Roger.
    Jane Austen's novels: the art of clarity/Roger Gard.
      p.   cm.
    Includes bibliographical references and index.
    ISBN 0-300-05494-7
    1. Austen, Jane, 1775–1817 – Criticism and interpretation.
I. Title.
PR4037.G37   1992
823'.7—dc20   91-38044
                                           CIP

To my friend
KIT PRICE

"When I knew Jane Austen I never suspected that she was an authoress ... I did not know that she was addicted to literary composition."

Sir Egerton Brydges, 1834.

Contents

Acknowledgements

Grateful acknowledgements are due, whether they know it or not, to Sydney Bolt, Warren Chernaik, Martin Dodsworth, the late John Dow, Beryl Gray, Simon Gray, Barbara Hardy, Paul Keegan, Ian MacKillop, Leonee Ormond, the dedicatee, Victoria Rothschild, Stephen Wall and Gordon Williams.

For special support I must thank Liza Shaw and Maisie Gard, and the former also for putting up with being asked to read chapter on chapter.

No publisher could be warmer, more adept or more thoughtful than Gillian Malpass of the Yale University Press.

But my greatest thanks are for the informed, warm, prompt, intelligent, logical and generally invaluable readings – and marking – given at my request over the years by Katie Fullbrook.

References in the Text

All references in the text to Jane Austen's works are to the standard edition: *The Works of Jane Austen*, ed. R.W. Chapman, Oxford, 1923–54, illustrated, 6 vols., revised Mary Lascelles, 1965–7. This includes, as vol. 6, the 'Minor Works' in which *Lady Susan* and *Sanditon* are printed (abbreviation: MW).

This edition retains the original two- or three-volume form. For economy and neatness I have employed the following numbering system: volume (arabic) e.g. 3; chapter (roman) e.g. xiii; page (arabic) e.g. 431. Thus: 3, xiii, 431 (Mr. Knightley's proposal in *Emma*).

However, since many other reprints number the chapters straight through without reference to volumes, it will clarify things to note here the number of chapters in each volume (in roman):

Northanger Abbey   1: i–xv; 2: xvi–xxxi
Sense and Sensibility   1: i–xxii; 2: xxiii–xxxv; 3: xxxvi–l
Pride and Prejudice   1: i–xxiii; 2: xxiv–xlii; 3: xliii–lxi
Mansfield Park   1: i–xviii; 2: xix–xxxi; 3: xxxii–xlviii
Emma   1: i–xviii; 2: xix–xxxvi; 3: xxxvii–lv
Persuasion   1: i–xii; 2: xiii–xxiv

Chapter One

Introductory: Jane Austen's Ease – and Criticism

.

It may sound absurd to say that a novelist sometimes needs to be preserved from her admirers. Nevertheless, the underlying purpose of this book is to stem the tendency in criticism and scholarship – or the series of tendencies – to take Jane Austen out of the common realm and into that of historical or theoretical specialisms alone. My feeling, manifest again and again in detailed commentary on the novels, is that she is still, and ought therefore still to be, the common property of any basically qualified reader of English. So I shall start by outlining what I think might be elementary positions for a critic, before going on to talk generally about more substantive issues concerning her.

Jane Austen's works used, fondly, to be thought of as the sponta- neous effusions of a vicarage parlour: as little systems of light and energy, full of delicate, decisive love comedy and miraculously in- dependent of any hampering local circumstances. If these are classics, we thought, then classics are fun. Their nature encouraged us to feel about them somewhat as we might feel about lyric poems conceived in the same way – the song of a witty skylark perhaps. It is a mistake to sneer. Such a response is a response to some perennially fresh quality in the novels which if we miss we miss everything. Henry James wanted to patronise rather than to sneer, apparently, but he makes the point with characteristic breathy eloquence:

> The key to Jane Austen's fortune with posterity has been in part the extraordinary grace of her facility, in fact of her unconsciousness: as if, at the most, for difficulty, for embarrassment, she sometimes, over her work-basket, her tapestry flowers, in the spare, cool drawing- room of other days, fell a-musing, lapsed too metaphorically, as one may say, into wool-gathering, and her dropped stitches, of these pardonable, these precious moments, were afterwards picked up as

1

little touches of human truth, little glimpses of steady vision, little master-strokes of imagination. ("The Lesson of Balzac", 1905)

This is an attractive picture, and I do not sympathise with the pleasure, the animus even, with which more recent, no doubt very hard working, commentators point up its inadequacy. The "grace of facility" is exact. Nevertheless, such genteel inadvertence has never been the whole story ... and now perhaps, with the advent of modern heavy – ever heavier – weight academic criticism, such a vision of innocence is gone for ever.

i

Perhaps. Of course specialisms are often valuable; and I have tried – as it were incidentally – to unfold in what follows a reasonably comprehensive, though still selective, picture of the climate obtaining around the study of the novels in the latter half of this century. For I do not want to propose a new brand of sprigged-muslin escapism, a new way of being a Janeite, or merely a Miss Austen fan. On the contrary, it is a theme of this book that Jane Austen is obviously one of the most challenging moralists in European fiction and one of its most brilliantly accomplished creative practitioners. But I do want to discourage any and all of the ways in which readers of would-be enlightened research evidently feel able to assent to such propositions as:

...only now have a few readers begun to realise the explosive qualities embedded in her fiction.

And:

She obviously fooled her male relatives and her neighbors; the miracle she performed was that she fooled almost two hundred years of the reading public as well.[1]

It is the reading public I wish to defend.

It is certainly felt by some recent writers, possibly looking at each other in some embarrassment, that general books are nowadays not at all, at least academically, required. Marilyn Butler remarks scornfully in 1987 that in 1975:

Academic studies of Jane Austen were multiplying prodigiously, virtually all in the same format: a short introduction proposing that the Austen novels were a pinnacle of human achievement, followed by six chapters which read each of the six finished novels in loving detail.

2

Professor Butler's detail, in her large and distinguished historicising enterprise (see below, *passim*), is not, it is true, particularly loving: in her account Jane Austen is one who obeyed the (masculine) "injunctions to silence and obedience" in politics, to the benefit of her reputation with posterity; has "many lacunae", especially in sexual matters; avoids women "as active free spirits" in "novel after novel"; "hardly exploits the more positive aspects of the Tory tradition of thinking about women"; – and more. But such an unease with the ordinary does not depend on holding such bleak views. Alistair Duckworth sounds equally scathing or amused in 1983 when referring to the common "legitimist" fare of "six chapters of explication preceded by a brief introduction providing a hypothesis". So it is quite easy to imagine that in turn Michael Williams's opening disclaimer in 1986 that "It is no longer necessary to defend Jane Austen from the charge that she achieved her art unconsciously . . ." might be prompted by an awareness of the shadow cast by such formidable forward characterisations of what he, after all, might be said to be offering – as well as by the very evident truth of his proposition.[2] I am certainly so aware: but though the present work is not exactly in the six-chapter form, it would not *mind* being described in that way.

Of course, any new writer on the subject is going to feel self-conscious. So no wonder it is often found rhetorically sound, if implausible, to pretend that without one's own approach Jane Austen would remain un-understood. Even Professor Butler, reviewing what she considers to be the very considerable impact that feminist studies should have on her own work, insists that "to participate with Austen, we have to re-learn the code [of generic expectation] her first readers already knew".[3] But surely such notions and motions – radically opposed to each other as they often are – show an alarming lack of confidence in the communicative powers of their subject, as well as an implicit dismissal of the non-academic, or even non-specialist or enthusiast, reader? Do we really have to read a lot of eighteenth-century novels, or at least some books about them, in order to "participate with" Jane Austen? I shall be discussing this in some detail in chapters two to four in the light of the early fiction. But meanwhile – really?

It must depend upon who we are. And here I take up my defence of an intelligent, ordinary, alert audience for the books. The idea of a common reader has always been a vexed one. My impression is that, like Virtue and civic probity and the organic community, it is one of those desirable concepts usually thought to have existed in the time of our fathers, but never now (this kind of reverence – at least as old as Homer in the matter of heroic boulder throwing – being the interesting obverse of an equally predictable patronage of the past by the then modern). Richardson, for example, was at tremendous pains to create a public; the identity of the common reader in *Northanger Abbey* is, as we shall see, at least dubious (Jane Austen being so characteristically intelligent on the issue); and Henry James lamented that he had just missed the epoch in which serious art was widely appreciated. Instances could be multiplied. But the received commonplace wisdom of the late twentieth century, often of an amused and head-wagging kind, seems to be that there never was such a thing as an educated and sensitive common reader – as distinct, perhaps, from a populist culture and popular literature, which is much studied, and often in terms of the novel. And indeed this may be simpler and less painful than assuming, or trying to prove, that there was once, but is no longer. It is nice to feel that we have lost nothing, even if the nothing that we have lost was, should it have existed, implicitly not worth very much in any case. On the other hand, if there is a wide readership capable of appreciating Jane Austen (for instance), why is it not likely to exist, especially, now?

To invoke a little impressionistic sociology: It is another modern commonplace, running counter to the first, that the basic conditions likely to nurture common readers are unprecedentedly present in the more prosperous parts of the world today – and this in spite of the distractions, vulgarisations and imperfections to which they are liable. Social critics and journalists in the nature of the case prefer to batten on imperfections: but is it complacent, absurdly idealistic or optimistic, or anything other than realistic, to observe that, in fortunate societies, widespread literacy and the availability of books render their members *potentially* part of an historical *élite* whether they like it or not? (To the less fortunate the critic of Jane Austen can have, in that rôle, alas, nothing to say.) It is impossible, of course, to establish how many people do like it; and depressing, the cultural and spiritual grossness and apathy everybody habitually deplores. But it is equally impossible to deny the probability of some, relative, light. To anyone who looks around at modern bookshelves, or who ponders the significance of so many paperback editions (of *all* the works) at a time, or who notices the undemanding popular company kept by Jane Austen in recordings for one's Walkman, it must be obvious that in her case the privilege conferred by widespread literacy is massively taken up. I am privately, but reliably, informed that one of the large paperback houses sells around 80,000 copies of each of the novels each year – and only a smallish fraction of these could be accounted for in the (semi-compulsory) student market.

4

ii

So, whilst one respects, as I say, the virtues of single-minded specialists, recognises from experience the exigencies sometimes enforced by the disciplines of a complex subject, and recognises even more vividly the difficulties of penetrating the alienness and due distance of the past – roughly, but not always, the more difficult the further back one goes – I nevertheless think it is the serious duty of professionals to try to speak as far as possible to the common reader. And with Jane Austen this is easy, because she is so clear. Because the relationship with the reader is so spontaneously pre-existent, and ready to be taken up. By which I do not, of course, mean – very much do not mean – that either Jane Austen or her common reader are to be taken as simple, cosy, entities. To make the novels food for slack fantasies about a past conceived of as *merely* comforting, is to misrepresent both them and it. As I hope we shall see.

There is an acute passage about distance from the past in a letter of Henry James's:

> You may multiply the little facts that can be got from pictures and documents, relics and prints, as much as you like – *the* real thing is almost impossible to do, and in its essence the whole effect is nought: I mean the invention, the representation of the old CONSCIOUSNESS, the soul, the sense, the horizon, the vision of individuals in whose minds half the things that make ours, make the modern world were non-existent. You have to *think* with your modern apparatus a man, a woman – or rather fifty – whose own thinking was intensely other-wise conditioned, you have to simplify back by an amazing *tour de force* – and even then it's all humbug... (to Sarah Orne Jewett, October 1901)

But he is here talking about recreating a past consciousness in a mod-ern fiction, whereas all the difference he so powerfully and rather beautifully evokes is, of course, redeemed, made present and embodied in ravishing detail in fine imaginative work from that past itself. It is the special, and indeed unique, attribute of imaginative art to make us close intimates of whole different modes of being, past or present. If we are led by dramatic and poetic representation to feel and think even somewhat *like* Tom Jones, or more remotely – but not finally remote – like Aeneas or Achilles, then the externals James mentions – documents, relics and prints – are by-passed or transcended. Work like that of Jane Austen is exactly the beneficent medium which puts us into fruitful connection with the past and allows it to constitute part of our present.

And I think it is the proper province of the critic to enhance and organise this process so far as possible, for as many people as possible.

Of course, it does no service at all to the past, or to us, to deny it its appropriate distance – a denial that leads too easily to patronising it. So it is only a slight necessary qualification of the above to say that we should be simultaneously aware that the very ease and vividness with which Jane Austen is available to most readers may make us forget – formally – the definite small unstated ways in which she *is* distanced, exactly, by being in fact of the past. Everybody at all attentive to foreign or old language will know that the difficult parts are not where the words are strange – they will be looked up – but where they are familiar but have a slightly different meaning.[4] So – in a precisely parallel way – while we know very well that a phaeton is not a Ford, those beliefs that are not stressed and not so very different from our own, but which underlie the novels, may escape a reader and yet be a part of, and subtly influence, the taken meaning. Jane Austen's firm, though unobtrusive, Anglicanism is an example – very few readers today, even Anglicans, are likely to have the same habits of faith. Yet we are scarcely made aware of this – especially in comparison with the insistently religious or moral protestations in other writers of the period – except perhaps in *Mansfield Park*, and scarcely even there. And so on. Similarly, even if one does not agree with Marilyn Butler – or her many opponents who propose diametrically opposite views but in the same terms (see below, *passim*) – about the probabilities, in the form proposed, of Jane Austen's conservatism and/or feminist radicalism, it is useful to be aware of the available ideas.

I consider that – ignoring physical presence – we need to and can comprehend the past in exactly the same mode as we need to and can comprehend other people who are our contemporaries. In a quite plain sense all are ultimately subject to a necessary isolation of minds – living or dead. But otherwise I think the last thing most serious readers of Jane Austen are likely to want to do is to contemplate her in relation to her time, or any particular time except the present, the now of the reader in front of the novels. So if religious and political beliefs and assumptions are not more than close, acceptable and unobtrusive sub-strata in the novels, then they may remain just that. Great artists take what they need actively, critically and creatively: and we cannot accept a version of Jane Austen – of all people – that characterises her, as some scholars come perilously close to doing, as a mere inert reflector of the commonplaces of her age – as one who, to take an example often trotted out, took the female conduct books of Gregory, Fordyce, Gisborne etc. with a kind of paralysed seriousness.[5] The Jane Austen present in the novels is present in a way qualitatively different from the way in which she may as a person have been present in her life and times, in relation to her predecessors in literature, or in relation to the thought of the age. And it is the ambition of critics of literature to try to put us into a fresh relation with what still so vividly speaks there, in literary creation.

This is so much the case regarding criticism that I would add that the hypothesis of a common reader, even if it could be shown that no such one existed or would read your book even if she did, is actually a rhetorical advantage – bordering on a necessity – for the writer. One writes partly, always, for one's other self – for that person, with several clinical and poetic names, who hovers somewhere above the back of any author's preoccupied head. But a demand for clarity by a notional real other person, and thus for a tone divested both of patronage and of learned collusion; for coherence if not strict logic; for accuracy without display; for a real illumination of the subject; and for interest and even entertainment – such a demand ought to determine the critical form, however difficult the material, and however imperfectly it is met. Otherwise the writer on humane matters (and ultimately, if much less directly, on scientific ones) deserves little respect and no gratitude from fellow citizens.

iii

In just this connection arises the question of 'literary theory', which seems as forbidding and potentially invasive of the enterprise – and ideal – as are the historicising or theorising exclusivities alluded to just now. Literary critics who want to get on with their loved calling of exegesis, commentary and evaluation, often nowadays feel a duty to shore against the sapping tide of 'theory' with a parenthesis of the following sort – though not always so grandly expressed:

> I believe that post-structuralist and deconstructionist hermeneutics and theories of insignificance are fundamentally erroneous. I take them to be the satyre [*sic*] play and epilogue after the great motions of nihilism in Nietzsche and Freud. But such a belief must be argued, and argued stringently ... [as they are not in a book on Vergil under review]. (George Steiner)[6]

It will later become apparent in some detail, especially when it comes to the questions surrounding realism in art, that I agree with Professor Steiner about the erroneousness of the greater part of these theories;

and the implication that modern employees of universities are in danger of re-deserving that their activities be called 'academic' in the vulgar sense of useless, fruitless, unreal, pedantic, logic chopping, peripheral – or, most aptly, *merely* theoretical ("an academic point. Meaning a bit of nonsense", as a character in Julian Symons unkindly but symptomatically puts it) is surely very telling. Materially secure scholars perhaps needlessly imitate the ingenious codified obscurities evolved by some intellectuals – victims of less benign or neutral climates than ours and hence glamorous models – to deal with situations in which common sense has become dangerous: the *estetica del guino* (wink) of Pinochet's Chile, for instance. On the other hand I do not think it a good idea to make a pre-emptive move, as it were in the dark, and as Steiner seems to want. The full implementation of such a strategy would involve – would it not? – writing an extensive gloss, or a book around a book – about why procedures that one thinks futile are not followed every time that criticism is attempted.[7] (This as opposed to merely incorporating any few benefits to be derived from conscious modernity – or post-modernity.) To do so would be a contradiction within the form. It would also be a defeating concession. Imagine the tiresomeness of having every time to argue one's right to speak – "but when it comes to the question of dependence or independence!", as Mr. Knightley says of a different matter. Or, as Jacques Lacan himself remarked in a comparable dilemma, "To suppose . . . that everything that is not Sartrian need first define itself as not being Sartrian is more than debatable . . . ".

Besides which it seems to me seriously the case that the genuine benefits to be derived *in practice* from Structuralism – and, after it, from the less extreme forms of Deconstruction – are to be looked for in their pedagogical effect, when by elaborating and bringing to the surface the hidden or implicit they render the subtle half-obvious, and available. Interpretative niceties and kinds of approach which were previously the rewards only of taste and hard striving are now explicit and, in a rather gawky and thin but refreshing manner, learnable.

This optimistic remark will seem insufficiently approbatory to theorists – and insufficient to their opponents in being approbatory at all. But the lack of fundamental confict with older traditions which is apparent in the usual outcomes of even quite radical arguments over many areas (e.g. about questions of impersonality and the status of the author in literature) is another reason why I feel able to pass 'theory' by (following Nietzsche's advice in *Zarathustra* on how to deal with some disagreements) and instead offer simple literary criticism. In addition, of course, anyone who knows anything about the technical terminology involved in this type of theoretical discourse will recognise that a major effort of re-translation would also be involved – for to address the common reader one must use the common, proper, language.

Another reason for this stance is that it is an almost inevitable feature of many theoretical approaches that one, or maybe two, linked lines of self-limited argument are isolated, described, defended and then applied to the matter under discussion. So that whatever the advantages of focus and demonstrability proposed, there seems to be a loss of sophistication and richness. Or, to put it another way, since it is impossible to *read* a novel properly while simply holding oneself to being an adherent of some creed or other (though one may also be that), as opposed to as a complicated individual with a past, the theoretical critic is arbitrarily subduing or ignoring part of his whole response, and thus that of the reader. Naturally what anyone writes is constructed on their imlicit assumptions about deity, decency, language, the likelihoods of psychological patterns, the nature of politics – or even natural history: but these are the assumptions we have to – and do naturally – use for the greater part of our transactions, and without which communication would be blunted, stifled. The assumptions may well be questioned: but they can hardly be described on each instance. To use them freely may be more ambitious than the theorist wants to be: but it is likely to be truer to the experience of reading.

However, Steiner is right about the need for some such apologia today.

iv

It is time to outline what I *do* hope to accomplish in this book. One of Dr. Johnson's (five) definitions of EASE in the *Dictionary* is "Unconstraint; freedom from harshness, formality, forced behaviour, conceits". He quotes Pope:

> True *ease* in writing comes from art, not chance;
> As those move easiest who have learn'd to dance.

And, of course, a lot of what I shall have to say is about the illumination to be derived from our recognition of, and pleasure in, the artistic methods evolved by Jane Austen to ensure the powerful swift tripping grace offered to any attentive reader. This sophisticated achievement is the product of much labour and genius, as Pope says. The resulting literary ease has been, for very complex reasons – some of them good – infrequently a priority, or even popular, with twentieth-century *avant garde* artists and intellectuals. So I have approached it in as many ways as I can.

I wish to present then, as I have said, no one theme or theory — save for Jane Austen's divine ease and clarity, which are phenomena, not theories — upon which her works are supposed to hang, or which they are supposed to illustrate; though I hope that various leading ideas will be found to interrelate and converge. I hope also to have traced in an interesting and coherent way her growth as a novelist. The succeeding chapters offer accounts of the novels singly and in turn, starting early with *Lady Susan* and ending, as late as possible, with *Sanditon*. Each chapter contains new interpretations and notions about the book in question.

In chapters two to four I have focussed on Jane Austen's creative relation to her literary past while tracing her early, and very various, development. Here, also, I initiate what becomes a series of discussions and definitions of the nature of her characterisation, and her unique kind of realism. In these discussions, as elsewhere, I have felt at full liberty to bounce off fellow workers in the field, but have put a large amount of the detail of this into (the necessary evil of) endnotes in order not to repel the common reader, on whose existence I so seriously insist, and whose enjoyment and suffrage I so earnestly desire.

In chapter five I have, to change the tone, tried a mild critical experiment in tribute to the nature of *Pride and Prejudice*. I have attempted to revive the critical form of the *aesthetic dialogue* — a method that has at least the advantage for me of economically meeting some possible cruder, but real, attitudes towards Jane Austen, especially those which equate the serious with the solemn.

In chapter six I have returned to a more level and conventional critical-scholarly mode of interaction with other critics (much of it again in endnotes) — but on an even larger scale than before because of the new modern grandeur of *Mansfield Park*. This chapter also has my most sustained effort at defining Jane Austen's great stature in relation not just to the English but to the European novel, and to other forms and kinds of art: a necessary effort it seems to me, and one to which I return to with pleasure at intervals throughout the book. The comparison here is to Flaubert's art, though a little also, and a bit surprisingly, to some of his attitudes.

Chapters seven and eight set out to be freer from the academic habit of always citing and considering other commentators. The argument tries to flow more freely around *Emma* in its character as masterpiece, and *Persuasion* as culmination and wonderful regression. So that arguments with others are more — though not completely — implicit or even unconscious.

Finally, chapter nine returns to the experiment of chapter five in an appropriately reduced and relaxed, but I hope happy, form.

v

I do not think it needful in these preliminaries to chew over in a systematic routine way the obvious topics involved with Jane Austen's having so deliberately limited her subject matter. Readers will perhaps be over familiar with the playful modesties about bits of ivory and families in villages,[8] and with the many ingenious critical disquisitions on this subject. The genuine, functional, limitations will be considered in specific terms in the detailed – i.e. the real – contexts within the novels in which alone they are accurately seen. Nevertheless, it would be rash not to acknowledge and explore a little some of the boundaries of her art at once – and even to amplify the usual description.

Henry James is obviously right, and sensitive, in his famous insistence that it should be elementary in the criticism of fiction that the artist be granted his or her *donnée*. At the very end of time, I suppose, when the trumpets sound, we shall have to say that the greatest artist is the one who has taken on the largest subjects and succeeded – a relatively uncontroversial choice in those circumstances will be Shakespeare. Meanwhile we are content to give – let alone the allegiance of the heart – the highest kind of objective praise to writers who occupy what at first appears a very small ground. James himself is one of these, and so, of course, is Jane Austen. Conversely, the choice of a large subject – the late Cold War, say, or the grandest of passions or the politics of the chemical industry – is obviously no guarantee at all of intellectual or spiritual quality and depth. And accordingly, intense admiration of Jane Austen usually co-exists with a quite explicit acknowledgement on the part of readers, and rarely a regretful one, that the revolutions of her age (French and Industrial), its wars and empires, and indeed much of its everyday life and people (e.g. servants) are simply not present, or present only by implication, in her novels. (See below, *passim.*) But there are more drastic recognitions to be made – the absence of which from a lot of commentary is probably to be attributed to their (the recognitions', I mean) really crashing obviousness.

Still on the larger questions of subject matter, it is sometimes asserted, for instance, perhaps with the grand Continental masters in mind, that great art must treat of Death. Yet death is only in the unstressed past, and on the peripheries, of Jane Austen. There is little one can do with such a fact in criticism other than note it – quite probably with a view to revising one's opinion of the assertion.

Turning to the nature and terms of the apparent intention, expression and implicit valuation in the novels, there is none of that penumbra of vagueness – doubts and uncertainties – that is much admired in other, mainly later, prose fiction. Wickham, for example, may charm at first, then disgust, then be lightly tolerated – but there is no ultimate doubt as to what he is like. There is no *ambiguity* in Jane Austen: the reader is never long unsure about what has happened, and never finally unsure as to how to take it.

Again, in the page-by page texture of the fictional world, there is an absence of the ordinary life of the body – eating, running, sleeping, sweating. They are marginal in the novels for themselves, if there at all, and only present when, with a typical economy, they are significant of something else as well. I am sure the reader will be able easily to extend the list of such absences. But the really interesting – the crucial – places where boundaries can be detected require a little more attention.

vi

First there is something that is perhaps by historical accident a limitation, but also has to be classed as a first-class, characterising, virtue. Jane Austen is a great national figure.

It is certainly *infra dig.* in some circles to emphasise this fact, but she has already been on stamps and looks set fair, if we continue to emulate the admirable French practice, to appear on banknotes: and few true admirers will hesitate, much, to admit to the possession of a mug or a tea towel from Chawton. To do so is not necessarily latter-day Janeiteism. It is clearly at the least harmless (an underrated quality): and I refuse to believe it necessarily superficial. Perhaps only that perennially worried, modest and irreplaceable type among the British themselves, who would have been called Bonapartist in Jane Austen's day, will be likely to find it suspect at all. At any rate, most of her readers, whatever their nationality, are likely to be mildly pleased by being told, quite often, that she is very English. Insofar as this is a result of the general good taste of her works, their rigorous wit and refined beneficent energy, the description allows the gratifying feeling of being part of discriminating community of readers. And of course the *mise en scène* of the novels flatters the imagination perfectly – how very pleasant indeed to be a proxy part of that green, happy, bustling, elegant, semi-pastoral land – even if on closer examination a great many of its inhabitants turn out to be unpleasant people against whom one has even more pleasingly to discriminate – in company with the author, who like most satirists encourages a sense of exclusive collusion with the reader (often a delusive sense). It is difficult not to feel sometimes, as Henry James's Morris Gedge in 'The Birthplace' feels about Shakespeare, that "It would be prodigious that of this transfigured world" – "peopled with vivid figures, each of them renowned" – "*he* should keep the key".

However, this observation has a concomitant difficulty. Why is it that an artist who is justly compared in some of her powers with Shakespeare is so markedly *un*-international? Admittedly there are no statistics here: but I have the strong impression, confirmed by questioning students year after year, and re-confirmed by questions asked in the bookshops of Paris, Rome and Munich, that Europeans – of course, particularly the French – think of Jane Austen as really like a stricter earlier version of *Cranford* (see below, chapter four). Think of her as an English provincial miniaturist with all those familiar genteel, class-ridden ways – just as *we* used to think of her, in short, but without the affection. Accounts of translations into Chinese, German, (Mexican) Spanish, Romanian, Russian and Swedish all stress the simplifications, distortions and dulling her prose undergoes, often necessarily, in the process of cultural and linguistic transmission.[9] So Jane Austen becomes what the English 'Miss' traditionally was: a fount of propriety, limited, respectable, intensely national, and with a faint tinge of the ludicrous – and therefore something of an English fad and a long way from the strenuous generosities of the great artist, *Maître*, *Maestro*, or *Meister*, or their female equivalent.

Why? It cannot be because there is anything repulsively nationalistic or Charlotte Bartlett-like about her novels. Unlike, for instance, Smollett or Shakespeare there is no explicit xenophobia presented in the work: unlike Charlotte Brontë or Dickens there is no parody of strange speech or customs which could alienate a foreign person. To come closer to her period, there is nothing comparable to the fierce absurdity of Madame Duval in Fanny Burney's *Evelina*, and nothing resembling the (Anglo–Irish) national consciousness displayed in Maria Edgeworth's *Patronage* – where a good German sets off a bad Frenchman and a balance of affectations is ridiculed in the pair of dandies, English Clay and French Clay. And incidentally, there is nowhere in Jane Austen that casual semi-humorous, semi-derisory mention of 'the Jew' which in a post-Hitlerian age so embarrasses the admirer of all these authors (and most others – the only exceptions among great artists who spring to mind in English are George Eliot, Henry James and Joyce) – even when this admirer realises that hard usury is usually the context, and the specially painful feeling, usually –

not always – an anachronism. The nearest Jane Austen comes to hearts of oak is in the warm and properly grateful admiration of the navy in *Persuasion* (backed up by what most people know of Admirals Francis and Charles Austen); the slight disapproval possibly projected over the Crawford's too ready use of French phrases in *Mansfield Park* (where, incidentally, admiration for the navy establishment is much less in evidence); and Mr. Knightley's heart-warming distinction in *Emma* – *vis-à-vis* Frank Churchill of the idea of whom he is jealous – between being *aimable* and having that true "English delicacy towards the feelings of other people" (1, xviii, 149) which makes one amiable. This should not lead to complacent feelings about a sunny Austen world – it should rather make the reader reflect how regularly fine and sharp discrimination is a feature of it. But a reader of other English fiction of the Revolutionary and Napoleonic period will find these instances moderate indeed – and it is worth letting the imagination play for a moment on what one might have been tempted to feel and say with the Grand Army of the virulently hostile and subversive Great Nation thundering on the other shore, and one's brothers at sea. I doubt whether a writer's patriotism or even chauvinism ever puts readers of other nations off, for it is so easy to share. (Shakespeare and Tolstoy are good arguments against its doing so.) But if it did, Jane Austen would be the last to cause offence.

It is, however, not with offence that I am primarily concerned, but with the lack of ready sympathy. An obvious resort from this difficulty is the observation that Jane Austen's effects are brought about by such subtle, decisive uses of language that while the native English speaker finds them easy, piercing and natural, foreigners, whether reading in translation or in the original, see little or nothing outside – or rather inside – competent observation of a limited fictional sphere. (See, again, the observations on translations by Andrew Wright, mentioned above.) Jane Austen would have to be broader, like Balzac perhaps, to be welcomed abroad. This argument clearly has some advantages – it would account for her popularity not only in North America (where today she has her largest constituency), but in less likely places that were once part of the British Empire such as Australasia, Singapore or even, surprisingly, Egypt. It also accords with the impression that, of otherwise intelligent British students of literature, it is those with the weakest natural feel for the language (and therefore the worst taste in poetry) who like her least – whose enthusiasm, if any, is the most merely dutiful. This explanation goes some of the way. But as a complete solution it is vulnerable to the objection (among others) that if true, foreign readers of any given language would only ever readily appreciate writers who dealt mainly in broad effects — or at least the broader parts of those who have subtler and deeper repertoires. Clearly this would lead to the despair of the monoglot — and to the despair, for example, of most English-speaking would-be readers of any or all of Tolstoy or Thomas Mann or Galdos — and of all readers of Homer.

There must be something else beside the general problems attending cultural and linguistic transmission. Why is the *feel* of Jane Austen — so far as we can imagine it dissociated it from her language — still so peculiarly English? Conscious that it may sound *naïf*, fatuous, or wildly generalising in the mode of Taine in the nineteenth century or Foucault in ours, I wish to offer a speculation that will eat, so to speak, the tail of Jane Austen's deliberate limitations in subject matter.

She is remarkably unpolitical for a novelist — except, of course, in the rather tiresome sense, which modern critical theorists are eager to point up on almost any occasion, that everything is in a wider way implicitly political. But *equally* unpolitical, I think, is a dominant part of Anglo-Saxon culture.[10] In the novels the only function of the few men who are, incidentally, politicians (i.e. M.P.'s — and it would be a mere penetrating quiz question to ask the reader to name them) is to frank or not to frank letters. That kind of thing is all that most of us still think most of them would be any good at. In life and in Jane Austen politics are either absent, or not for real, serious people. And her indifference is not to be explained by saying, rather banally, that she is a novelist, an artist. On the contrary, most nineteenth- and twentieth-century European fiction of any stature is informed by politics. Quite apart from the obvious, the explicit, subject matter of much of Balzac or Stendhal, Tolstoy or Fontane — and so on — those whose reputation would at first suggest an in-turning to the sensitive, the private, life, are often full of a political critique lying very near the surface. *Madame Bovary* is a great novel of the frustrated soul — but the frustration is enacted within the sphere of the obvious ambitions of M. Homais (whose *croix d'honneur* crowns, as it were, the tragedy) and the heavily satirised speeches of the *comices agricoles*. Turgenev's novels, loved by Henry James for their poetry of late-romantic indeterminacy, are correspondingly vivid with magistrates and revolutionaries and land reform. Even Proust (most of all Proust?) builds up a picture of the movement of the structure of wealth and power in his time. These may well reflect European life. But the life selected and reflected in Jane Austen is also real and recognisable (it obviously continues to be reflected on and off in the English novel, though never with quite such purity).

To embroider the point with a little further speculation: it is my impression that modern Anglo-Saxon civilisations, and to a lesser extent those civilisations determined by Anglo-Saxon assumptions which bear the traces of them, are historically very unusual in being peopled with those who, even during continental or world wars, on the whole contrive to evince a *positive* disregard for politics and power, and a disesteem for the hucksterings and manoeuvrings and trappings that go with them. (Which is no doubt why politically active people in Britain and parts of North America notoriously get furious about apathy rather than about fanaticism.) I think this is because of the loss of a habit of fear. Politics, with its associated ambitions and trepidations, is not allowed to impair or cramp the moral style. And reflective readers of Jane Austen will be struck – especially if they have a fresh memory of the eighteenth-century feeling that the Lord or Master (Squire Western or Mr. Harlowe) has weight *ex officio* even when judged to be tyrannous – with how an awe of the powerful, or the sense of danger surrounding riches and influence is pleasingly absent from her novels. General Tilney, Mrs. Ferrars, Lady Catherine de Bourgh, Sir Walter Elliot and even Sir Thomas Bertram may fume as much as they like – see if we care. Given (an important proviso, but granted) that there is enough to live on in a moderate way, power has no claim to a special respect, and certainly none willingly granted over virtue. Traditional subordination and duty – most evidently that of child to parent – is, of course, present (although treated very critically), but it is a private matter and not a political factor. And I guess these liberties of Jane Austen coincide roughly with an on the whole happy historical outcome in those prosperous, highly developed and politically semi-representative societies called – with a poor etymology which breeds frequent semantic disaster – democracies.

It is significant that Jane Austen's own class and the one she writes about – the upper range of the middle – is the one most associated with the capture of executive power from aristocratic oligarchy in England in the eighteenth century (late in the century according to the most recent historians[11]), and its subsequent domesticisation. The security thus generated allowed to the majority not actually involved – and still allows even if it ought not to – a consequent disregard of direct political power in everyday life (underlying economic power and influence is a different matter, and for once not to the point here). Correspondingly, the protagonists of Jane Austen's novels have sufficient – abundant – implicit confidence in themselves and their habitual social organisation to feel very rigorous and subtle demands, loyalties and dislikes to, from and between themselves and each other and the local community – but the big world of the state is taken for granted.

This is a reason, to put beside the fineness of her language, for our feeling that Jane Austen is especially, and congenially, English. She writes from and into a spiritual atmosphere which, by means of a positive absence of perceived restraint, is a real presence in English culture and those related to it. Unpolitical, she is *therefore* the realistic novelist of an evolving national democracy.

vii

Which remark naturally brings me, by a transition that is scarcely a transition at all, to a second area of possible limitation which is often found a major matter for note and discussion about Jane Austen: social class. This remains a delicate matter for modern readers – almost as much as it was when (the marxist) Arnold Kettle brilliantly raised the problem in relation to *Emma* forty years ago and defended Jane Austen's resolution of it.[12] It has to be faced: and is never more difficult to deal with than among those, unlike Kettle, whose moral or political objections to a social hierarchy, and the distinctions adjunct to it, prompt them to deny or blur its existence. Its prominence in Jane Austen can in fact lead to two of the worst possible readings: that which still delights in the contemplation of a secure and cosy world of past elegance, the world of the refined 'Miss Austen'; and that which, with a superior crassness, dismisses the whole Austen business as too trivial, limited and smug for the attention of the serious. Probably most honest readers will admit to having belonged at least momentarily to both schools.

But, although the question of class will not go away, we can clarify it. First, it is necessary to emphasise that the attitudes and structure shown in the novels existed – in a way that it is easy to comprehend – and that Jane Austen, as a realistic writer, is obliged to recognise and describe them. Second, we have at least to indicate how they are used in the structures of the novels – though a more detailed analysis must, of course, await discussion of those novels themselves.

First, then: the assumption of subordination, of the superiority, often conferred by birth alone, of some people over others, was as prevalent in early nineteenth-century England as is the assumption of the theoretical equality of humankind with us today. That both assumptions are extremely partial and rickety and frequently bogus is obvious. Equally obvious is the fact that – perhaps especially in the former case – such ideas are felt as the more *natural* the more they are challenged. The savour of naturalness in class distinctions was enhanced by the fact that they were inherited, traditional, religiously sanctioned and, above all, accepted and underwritten by the majority of all classes (not, of course, just in England). It would be silly – although tempting to the dedicated egalitarian – to view the lower orders as made up of people who felt persecuted and resentful. Everyone has observed that servants may well be more retentive of fixed distinction than their free-thinking masters. Accordingly, the characters in Jane Austen often envy the rank and status of others and in more or less comic ways aspire to share it, but nobody questions its existence and very rarely its justice as an institution.

We have no reason to think that Jane Austen was misrepresenting a society which she intimately knew. That she was severely critical of it does not mean that she did not share its fundamental values. Even Robespierre had servants. It is rather we, in the rôle of assertive democrats, who are historically eccentric. We are also the descendants of this system, and to some extent retain it. But I think any reader, any-where, is likely to grasp and have a sympathetic understanding of it – just as we have a grasp of the village system of late feudal Russia from Tolstoy and Turgenev, or of mediaeval court life in Japan from Lady Murasaki – because the nuances of such a finely articulated structure are easily felt and intelligible when they are dramatised in fiction and made analogous to any experience of distinction we do happen to have.

Arguments for and against social hierarchy are not to the point here. It would obviously be foolish to read Jane Austen with the implicit idea that she somehow endorses or negates it for future ages, both of which I have seen done. But we should note, nevertheless, two important further limits in the chosen range, which in turn must determine the width of our response. The hierarchy evoked is social, but only social. We are scarcely concerned with direct power as opposed to status. Ultimately, of course, status derives, in more or less complex ways, from the perceived ability for external domination. But this is not Jane Austen's point of focus. Similarly money gives power, but it is not necessarily linked with the suggested estimate of position. Mrs. Elton in *Emma*, for instance, is clearly not a lady in the sense in which Jane Fairfax is. Yet she attempts a financial patronage that is rightly felt to be odious. More subtly, the very wealthy Rushworth in *Mansfield Park* is three times richer than Henry Crawford – but he does not compare with him as a fine gentleman, let alone with Sir Thomas Bertram. And the grandest of Jane Austen's figures, Mr. Darcy and Lady Catherine de Bourgh in *Pride and Prejudice*, although rich, only marginally exert power through patronage in the Army and the Church. There are many other examples: but as this last emphatically suggests, both status and direct power are not at all the same thing as personal merit. There is a description of Jane Austen's novels as portraits of people learning, or failing to learn, to deserve their position, and this is not bad as a quick characterisation of their tone. Further, even leaving aside the question of personal gifts, one of the features of the tradition we encounter here was at least a residual sense of the Christian doctrine of the equality of souls in the sight of God. And although this may often seem either too hotly protested or only notional in other accounts from the period, it is implicitly endorsed in some depth by Jane Austen. So much so, and so obviously so, that it is reasonable for the distinguished psychologist D.W. Harding to claim that the Cinderella theme – with its inevitable topsey-turvey effect – is vital within her novels.[13]

The second and much more important question about class is: How, given this material, did Jane Austen exploit its possibilities? How does she use its conventions in the service of her own artistic conventions? The short answer to this is that social gradation provides one of the most fruitful opportunities for the exercise of her particular genius: it is, as it were, a ready-made system in which she can show how the fine sensitivity and intelligence of her best characters at their best operate in shades of more or less intense contrast to the blundering insensitivity of her worst. For the novelist it is a splendid framework rather than a prison.

In this – to digress slightly – it exactly resembles two other important areas (which will be discussed much more specifically later in the body of this book) in which Jane Austen is always being said to be limited: the presentation of men – never from the inside – and the presentation of the transactions of sexual attraction. Faced with these, her admirers often produce a marvellous idiotic banality to the effect that 'she wrote about what she knew'. This is true; it is also tautological. How do we know what she knew? Because she seems to know what she wrote about. The same would be true if she wrote well about the art of the lepidopterist. And further, its truth is very limited. Jane Austen clearly did not 'know', in the sense of having experienced it, what it was like to be a substantial landed magnate, a widow, an empty-headed yet scheming young girl, a prig, a lawyer or even a married woman. She had met such figures and deals with them and their like. They people her pages – and consequently English culture. But this does *not* mean that she failed to exercise her imagination. One has to ask of any writer why such and such limits were chosen – what is the artistic point? – why *those* limits? – and the answer lies not in any putative first-hand experience the author may be imagined to have had (disappointingly few people experience being of both sexes, for example), but in what use is made of them; precisely, in fact, in their expressive point. Jane Austen chose – and this is the word to be stressed – to write about those parts of experience which gave her the chance to create and analyse the areas of value that seemed to her, and seem to us, important: love, marriage, discrimination, elegance of mind, charity, wit, selflessness, taste, courage, patience, cheerfulness – and all the gradations of their opposites.

This is obvious when stated. And, to digress a little further, an example of its operation in the matter of sexual attraction is conveniently provided by a small comparison of her with the most celebrated of all realists, Tolstoy. The reticence of the conclusion of Mr. Knightley's courtship in *Emma* is often quoted – sometimes almost in disbelief by unregenerate naturalists – as entirely typical of Jane Austen's dealings with the erotic, which it is. "What did she say – Just what she ought, of course. A lady always does" (3, xiii, 431). And equally, of course, the reason for this inspired brevity – as I hope to indicate a little more fully later on – is that this is the climax and clearing of a long, intense and elegant sequence of erotically charged moments, and that we need no more than this to be appropriately moved. More reference or description – let alone the direct presentation of, for example, a kiss – would negate the whole piercing effect. Surely we expect a difference in Tolstoy, famous for the square magnificent clarity with which he takes on in fiction all sides of life, including the physical? But what about the climax of an even lengthier, though more diffuse, sequence, in *War and Peace*, which presents the – at first sight curious – growing attraction between the dashing but slightly ordinary Nicholas Rostóv and the timidly spiritual Princess Mary? Here it is:

> She turned round. For a few seconds they gazed silently into one another's eyes – and what had seemed impossible and remote suddenly became possible, inevitable, and very near. (Epilogue 1, ch. 2; trans. Louise and Aylmer Maude)

That is all. Tolstoy is comparatively wordy, of course; but both writers elect a fine economy of effect as opposed to a redundant or pointless demonstration of their knowledge of (here elementary) facts about behaviour.

So, to return with this in mind to the question of class, let us look at a few simple examples of how the massive and yet intimately felt social structure is employed in Jane Austen to express its as it were local self, but also more than itself. When, in *Persuasion*, Sir Walter Elliot learns of Anne's intention to visit Mrs. Smith instead of spending the evening with the cold-stricken Lady Dalrymple he suddenly shows an unusual concern with the doings of his least favourite daughter:

> "Westgate-buildings!" said he; "and who is Miss Anne Elliot to be visiting in Westgate-buildings? – A Mrs. Smith. A widow Mrs. Smith, – and who was her husband? One of the five thousand Mr. Smiths whose names are to be met with every where. And what is her attraction? That she is old and sickly. Upon my word, Miss Anne Elliot, you have the most extraordinary taste! Everything that revolts other people, low company, paltry rooms, foul air, disgusting associations are inviting to you . . ." (2, v, 157)

And he concludes:

> ". . . an every day Mrs. Smith . . . to be the chosen friend of Miss Anne Elliot, and to be preferred by her, to her own family connections among the nobility of England and Ireland! Mrs. Smith, such a name!"
>
> Mrs. Clay, who had been present while all this passed, now thought it advisable to leave the room . . .

This is, of course, yet another instance of Sir Walter's foolish pride. And his speeches always have a diverting comic pomp. But there is, typically, more to it than that. His stupid vanity is cruel. Cruel in an obvious way to Anne and the idea of the Smiths; but cruel also to Mrs. Clay who, as Anne is made to reflect, is not readily distinguishable in her character as a widow of about thirty with a common enough name, from the actually socially superior (in his very terms) Mrs. Smith. Cruel, too, in its dismissal of – or rather innocence of – friendship and charity as motives. And, finally even rather pathetic when the reader reflects on the declined circumstances (paltry rooms compared to Kellynch) of Sir Walter himself, and on his ludicrous inflation of the dull Lady Dalrymple and her "plain and awkward" daughter into the "nobility of England and Ireland". So here a class distinction is used to dramatise far more than class distinctions.

Much the same may be said of episodes throughout Jane Austen's work. Elizabeth Bennet's great pivotal assertion of spirit and intelligence is made, again in an atmosphere of powerfully directed comedy, through a point of class. Faced with the majestic and peremptory – "Miss Bennet, do you know who I am?" – demand by Lady Catherine that all thoughts of her – infinitely superior – nephew be forthwith abandoned, she intrepidly replies: "He is a gentleman; I am a gentleman's daughter; so far we are equal" (3, xiv, 356). This is a truth with some omissions, as Lady Catherine is swift to point out. But it wins the day and wins Mr. Darcy.

Even more telling is the irruption of the badly born and bred Mrs. Elton into the society of Highbury of which Emma, with some reason, thinks herself the queen. Here a heroine who too securely looks down and patronises is faced with a vulgarian who insists, in a spate of irrepressible pretension, on being her equal or superior. The whole of chapter fourteen in volume two should be read to appreciate the fine fury of their initial encounter. But the following will recall its flavour:

> "And who do you think came in while we were there?"
>
> Emma was quite at a loss. The tone implied some old acquaintance – and how could she possibly guess?
>
> "Knightley!" continued Mrs. Elton; – "Knightley himself! – Was not it lucky? – for, not being within when he called the other day, I had never seen him before; and of course, as so particular a friend of Mr. E.'s, I had a great curiosity. 'My friend Knightley' had been so often mentioned, that I was really impatient to see him; and I must do my caro sposo justice to say that he need not be ashamed of his friend. Knightley is quite the gentleman. I like him very much. Decidedly, I think, a very gentleman-like man."
>
> Happily it was now time to be gone. They were off; and Emma could breathe.
>
> "Insufferable woman!" was her immediate exclamation. "Worse than I had supposed. Absolutely insufferable! Knightley! – I could not have believed it. Knightley! – never seen him in her life before, and call him Knightley! – and discover that he is a gentleman! . . ."
> (278–9)

Note that Mrs. Elton is peculiarly infuriating in that she cannot be convicted of the inconsequence or foolishness that Emma wants *first* to attribute to her – that of mentioning an acquaintance unknown to her audience. It is two different kinds of snob at war – though clearly at this point Emma is in the right. And again the conventions of class are exploited by Jane Austen for her deeper purposes: – to embody a crude, clever, stupid ambition coupled with a disregard for language and people, in conflict with offended established pride – and a proper sense of value, in this case that of Mr. Knightley.

viii

In arguing that the distance between Jane Austen and a contemporary audience is negligible in terms of its difficulty and stimulating where it is felt, I have, quite naturally, been adducing some of her moral and spiritual qualities. To mention another, last, self-imposed limitation in this regard: it is rather strange, I find, that her views of marriage seem often closer to modern ones than do those of writers nearer to us in time. Everyone knows, and we have to accept, that the particular type of marriage plot that she inherited from her predecessors – which she refined and strengthened and passed triumphantly on by her evolution of its virtually perfect (yes, perfect) form – is a plot that *ends* with a wedding. This is not to say (as I shall frequently argue later) that the context of courtship excludes the study of other, contrasting and subtly interrelated, pre-existing marriages – on the contrary, this is often half the point; nor is it to say that hundreds of novels being written now have not an identical trajectory. But it is true that the great serious broken structures of subsequent nineteenth-century novels, in which a marriage is achieved early on and then its problems, and usually its dry failure, studied, is not what Jane Austen chooses for *her* intenser focus. (One thinks here first of George Eliot and Tolstoy – but then of Flaubert – and then of Thackeray and Meredith and Henry James . . .) Unless one believes that there were fewer unhappy marriages in Jane Austen's day than there were later (somehow some critics seem to imply this, flatteringly taking what they think to be the characteristics of one author for the truth of history, but insulting probability), it is obvious that, again, this is a matter of artistic choice and economy – as well make it a great point of surprise and comment that *Much Ado About Nothing* ends with marriages, or that *Romeo and Juliet* does not. Nevertheless, in the detailed texture of (finer) feeling, Jane Austen seems easier and more natural to me than most of her successors. The veil of elaborate codified *pudeur* in official Victorian relations is not yet in place. Characters blush and faint very little. It is only a very minor problem for an unmarried young woman to go for a walk by herself. Simply there seems less fuss, less false consciousness about sex. And above all, artistically, the final marriages in Jane Austen are ends, codas and resolutions (like those of fairy tales I suppose) into private happy enclosures within a society that goes on being what it – very imperfectly indeed – is. (Though, as I argue in chapter eight, *Persuasion* implies the evolution of a less protected outcome in this respect.) And, of course – for all our talk about modern changes – marriage or its equivalent is still for most people at least an epochal event.[14]

ix

If the reader does indeed feel that degree of accessibility and easy intimacy with Jane Austen's works for which I am arguing, it may be that many of the above remarks will appear superfluous. If so I apologise. I am haunted, naturally, with the implications for culture of such a remark as the following, made as of course by Adam Mars-Jones: we encounter, he says, as though it were routine, ". . . a feeling of trespass on to other people's territory, and a male critic who wants to deal with the subject of women's writing faces particular difficulties".[15] Well, bluntly, I do not feel anything of the kind. And is a woman critic to feel, *vice versa*, the same? Genuinely to do so would be to deny the imagination – let alone the possibility of lesser kinds of communication.

Perhaps this implication of rigid little compartments of the spirit is merely casual. But consider what is at stake. It is essential to prevent Jane Austen being separated off; made quaint; made part of a dead, past past whose thought and feeling has to be explained and annotated, and merely *consciously* understood. She was of an identifiably different time, naturally: but she is still one of us. At the moment it takes only responsiveness, intelligence and goodwill on the part of a reader to understand her – to recognise with ease that her novels are at the very least, in John Bayley's light, elegant phrase, "beautifully finished comedies of art and simple and natural comedies about life". But the critic must attempt as earnestly as possible to articulate and strengthen understanding of the points worth discussing, and offer a vocabulary to facilitate the reader's proper, own, perceptions.

I am assuming that anyone reading this work will already have a high valuation of Jane Austen as an artist and a moralist. Valuation is the most vital critical act as well as the most primitive one.[16] Nevertheless, I dread that moment, especially for the serious minded, when a natural delighted esteem might give way to the limitation of her appeal by arguments that are *only* historical, marxist, freudian, generic, feminist etc. Specialising Jane Austen, if not done with great tact and skill, might, however great the reverence, end up by re-placing her in a limiting context – one oddly resembling the old Janeite cult in being confined and partial, but far more exigent and less yielding. How little one wants to cease to be able to re-echo with something like the warmth of Q.D. Leavis:

> . . . If one thinks of it, it is *only* Jane Austen (no longer Charles Lamb to the same extent or even Dickens, and we don't *love* Dr. Johnson though his life is incessantly being investigated) – only Jane Austen who is loved and esteemed by her readers as a *person*. Isn't it because, through her writings alone, we acquire the impression of a delightful personality and an admirable character, in spite of the impersonality of her novels?[17]

Chapter Two

Early Works, Traditions, and Critics I: *Lady Susan* and the single effect

i

In his *Biographical Notice* of 1817 Henry Austen said of his sister's working methods that "some of these novels had been the gradual performances of her previous life". This emphasis has, as I have indicated, been taken up with the greatest energy over the last decades – as against that of spontaneity in the vicarage. The newer image, at least since Mary Lascelles's *Jane Austen and her Art* (1939) and Q.D. Leavis's 'A Theory of Jane Austen's Writings' (1941–2), is much nearer to that of a professional writer than of a miraculously gifted amateur. It may have less charm, but it is equally, if not more, touching. Tapestry stitching is in fact quite a serious business. In the manuscript of *The Watsons* (1804–5), for instance, (which I have occasion to notice almost every week[1]), one can see – amongst hundreds of precise corrections of detail and rulings out and writings between – exactly where Jane Austen pinned with her own three sewing-pins a carefully cut half-page to cover a neatly cancelled paragraph. Materials from the work-basket imagined by Henry James no doubt: but scarcely consonant with mere inspired musing. And *The Watsons* is only a start for a novel, a fragment never prepared for publication.

One result of Jane Austen's scrupulosity, her authorial hard work, is that – if we want to identify and isolate the early works in order to consider the growth of a novelist's mind – we find that they are difficult to date; or, rather, that the relative dates are difficult to pin firmly into a mental pattern. Which exactly *are* the early works? To answer this a little close detail is necessary.

Apart from the *Juvenilia*, written roughly between 1787, when she was twelve, and 1793, when she was eighteen, we know that *Elinor and Marianne*, a novel in letter form, was drafted in or before 1796, to be revised drastically into *Sense and Sensibility* in 1809–10; and that *First Impressions*, possibly also in letters,[2] was written in 1796–7, to be revised into *Pride and Prejudice* in 1809–10, 1811, and 1812. Of the first trio of famous novels this leaves only *Northanger Abbey*, which was written in 1798–9, lightly revised for publication under the title *Susan* in 1803, and again probably lightly (there can be no certainty here) under the name *Catherine* in 1817. It was re-titled and published after Jane Austen's death by her brother Henry in 1818.

But of early completed substantial work there is also *Lady Susan*, of which a draft survives in a fair copy made around 1805. This is the date once assigned to its composition, but in spite of the reluctance of some modern critics – it in many ways feels later – it now seems that 1798 or 1793–4 are better guesses.[3] It too was named and published by a relative, her nephew the Revd. J.E. Austen-Leigh in his *Memoir of Jane Austen* (1871).

Such detail may seem tedious, or at best peripheral to the interests of the serious reader who cares more for art than for the dust of elementary literary history. In fact, there is much more that could be said, both in the way of speculation – once the biographical mind is abandoned to it – and of adducible evidence. Very well; dating is in itself dull; but what emerges from the thicket of conjecture is interesting and potentially valuable to criticism: – that if we want to look at the early efflorescence of Jane Austen's genius in fully articulated forms (as opposed to the *Juvenilia*), we had best go to *Lady Susan* and then to *Northanger Abbey*. And, further, that it is through them that we most conveniently come at the perplexed but necessary questions about her relationship with the literary past. A lot of her writing, in spite of its brilliant and increasing originality, can usefully be compared with that of her contemporaries and predecessors – though this can be stultifying if differences in quality are lost, as they sometimes are, in the celebration of superficial resemblances.[4] (Some of the difficulties *Sense and Sensibility* presents could be described by saying that it too easily lends itself to being thought of as an eighteenth-century novel.) That *Northanger Abbey* positively *has* to be considered in an *imagined* relation to other books is the most obvious thing about it; but *Lady Susan*, relatively slight and lacking in a final polish as it is, also repays consideration in this manner – though in a different way. The results turn out to be surprisingly complicated and enlightening.

It is important to get very clear the *quality* and *manner* of the early Jane Austen's interaction with the literature of her age. And this I intend to attempt. This main purpose does not demand that I should, except incidentally, take on the complex subject of her relationship with her culture. Fortunately, in many ways, the undertaking would be thoroughly redundant. As I argued in the last chapter, it has been done, seriatim and at large, by others. The active dialogue in her works with political and large-scale social phenomena, with past novelists and poets, with philosophers and political thinkers, and with – particularly since the 1970s – feminist and anti-feminist writers of her age is the subject of many scholarly and critical studies, some of them interesting.[5] Gone are the days when a few pleasant references to Johnson and Richardson, Fanny Burney and Maria Edgeworth, Cowper and Crabbe (and, of course, Shakespeare) would suffice. And there are able general summaries available.[6] But we are here concerned with what gives point and significance to all this activity. We are concerned with literary value.

Every reader creates a personal version of what is read. A reader such as Jane Austen makes a new art from it. This is often the very opposite of what might at first blush be expected: but on consideration it is exactly the way in which a writer of genius should – we perhaps suddenly realise – respond. It is, in short, creative rather than passively parallel, and a matter of unobtrusive decisive omissions followed by the flow of new matter, of demarcation rather than of imitation.

ii

Taking then the more difficult, probably earlier, and certainly lesser work first. *Lady Susan* has been an embarrassment to lovers of Jane Austen. Its chiselled brilliance and evident amorality, whether the product of an eighteen, twenty-three, or twenty-nine year old, are unlikely to recommend it in any way to admirers of 'gentle Jane' or "their 'dear', our dear, everybody's dear, Jane" (as Henry James exasperatedly put it). From the very first: – "entirely unworthy of Miss Austen's hand . . . thoroughly unpleasant in its characters and details" (E. Quincey, 1871)[7] – to nearly the very last: – it is "hard to make a real response to a story so clearly focussed on a female monster who becomes increasingly artificial and unreal" (Douglas Bush, 1975)[8] – there have been readers who have found it difficult to take, difficult, one almost gathers, to grant the real existence of. Like so many things in life, like the letters one has not sent or the Venetian shirt with scarlet piping, it would be better out of the way. And even where Jane Austen's gentility is discounted in favour of the acutely stern critic and moralist of human nature and society, unease lingers. Often the steely little thing is not mentioned. Or it is grouped with the *Juvenilia* of which it is perhaps the last salvo. Or it is indirectly accommodated into the

27

account – "a necessary sketch for the very likeable, assertive Elizabeth Bennet a little later" is a recent and rather astonishing tribute.[9] But, whatever the attitude, two – in a way contrasting – aspects should be made prominent.

First, that it is indicative of the very free sense in which Jane Austen was a child of her time that it is a short story, or *nouvelle*, at all. Modern easy, intense familiarity with the short story as a type may blind us to the obvious fact that it was only really with Hawthorne and Henry James and Maupassant and Turgenev in the mid- and late nineteenth century that a shorter prose fiction, not dominated by the tradition of the moral tale as exemplified by Johnson and Voltaire, blossomed and fertilised itself by interaction. When Jane Austen was beginning, and produced so accomplished a work, the form was very little practised. Crabbe was shortly to write admirable stories, but they are some of the best things in a tradition of verse narration. Otherwise there are prose fragments and sketches such as Jane Austen's own; moral essays that flower at the verge of the fictional but remain there; occasional burlesque outbursts such as Fielding's *Shamela*, which is short because its purpose is quickly accomplished; and there was soon to be an interesting development, to which Jane Austen no doubt attended, in Maria Edgeworth's *Moral Tales* (1801), *Popular Tales* (1804) and *Tales of Fashionable Life* (written from the early 1800s; published from 1809) – although here, especially in the former, the fiction is still almost avowedly subordinate to a simple maternalistic instructive purpose. But perfect short work which is irresponsible in Henry James's sense – i.e. freely exploratory? I cannot think of anything good enough to have survived, even supposing it to have been written, since Aphra Behn laid down her pen at the end of the seventeenth century. Even if the reader can instance with what would be proper indignation some neglected masterpiece, Jane Austen was certainly not contributing to a well-founded tradition. And *Lady Susan* is not accidentally short. It is evidently designed from its opening to be a limited action concerned with a key period in the life of its heroine, whose past is quickly established, and an action, moreover, not amenable to the kind of enclosed moralisation characteristic of the fable or even folk tale from which (with wicked witch perhaps included) it might be thought ultimately to derive. Critics of Jane Austen are often tempted to deploy the description 'modern', with more or less unease (see below, chapter six). Perhaps it is better – and related to the problem of fixing its date in the mind – to say that in this respect *Lady Susan* seems curiously independent of any particular period, and seems just to shine there alone, attractively indifferent to a context.

In that respect perhaps. But the second aspect I want to stress, equally obvious as an external fact, takes us squarely back into literary history and critical argument about that. *Lady Susan* is the sole extant example of a work by Jane Austen which she allowed to remain in letters, and thus offers the clearest field for studying her remarkable response to a vital part of her inheritance, spiritually as well as technically. (Detecting and discussing the epistolary bedrock of *Sense and Sensibility* is a much more speculative affair which must remain mainly the interest of scholars – let alone doing the same for the, notional, basis of *Pride and Prejudice* and *Mansfield Park*.[10]) What Jane Austen did with the letter form is very illustrative: it is a matter of daring reductions, of discipline for a confident limited purpose. Epistolary novels are virtually as old as novels themselves. At least a fifth of eighteenth-century prose fiction is in this form.[11] But Richardson is the master, the obvious comparison, the outstanding initial *point de repère* both for the modern reader and for Jane Austen herself. He was that with which modern writers then had to reckon, and Jane Austen was not alone in trying and then moving away from letters as a compositional principle. Fanny Burney, for instance, had notably replaced the lucid and entertaining first-hand reports of her skirmishes with the world by *Evelina* (1778) with the sober, often ponderous, narratorial voice of *Cecilia* (1782). Jane Austen's admiration for, and immersion in, Richardson is one of the best-known facts about her. Henry Austen alludes to it, though he does not mention the slight amusement, due no doubt to the private consciousness of a superior genius, that peeps out of her talk in later letters of "Harriot [*sic*] Byron's feather" and Harriet Byron's "Gratitude".[12] And there are numerous references in the novels themselves – beside the tradition that she knew *Sir Charles Grandison* by heart and the fact of a dramatic sketch lightly based on that novel.[13] So what can she be said to have done with this model in *Lady Susan*? Leaving aside for the moment questions of weight and maturity, the answer is that she selects with great rigour from the resources offered by the Richardsonian letter, in the service of a single effect. It is Lady Susan who matters in *Lady Susan*, and very little, technically or morally, is allowed to hamper her. This is not a question of who writes the letters – only sixteen out of forty-one are by Lady Susan whereas almost all in *Pamela* and *Evelina* proceed from the heroines, well over half from Clarissa in *Clarissa* (though she has a mighty counterweight in Lovelace, and there are many lively lesser voices) and the most important part of *Grandison* is carried by Harriet Byron. It is rather a question of the other characters being subdued to Lady Susan's nature, whether in protest or in admiration (or both).

In order to get this effect a great deal of possible expressive matter
has to be jettisoned, or, rather, remain uncreated. The difference between Jane Austen and other epistolary writers is teasing and takes
some pondering. But the solution is actually quite bold and simple. It is
that she uses letters in *Lady Susan* only *as* letters – reports of happen-
ings, the news relevant to the acts of Lady Susan, and the writer's
response to it – whereas in the extended ordinary form they are put as
well to practically every other use a novelist, a moralist and a narrative
may require.[14] (Hence the unwieldiness and implausibilities of the
method, the cause of frequent complaint and satire, and no doubt one
of the reasons why Jane Austen dropped it in later books – in addition
to her more obvious motives for developing a subtly directive narrative
voice.)

An impression of lightness and economy is part of Jane Austen's
special exhilaration. It is always felt: but its nature is difficult to demon-
strate. Who wants a list of negatives? It is easy (and essential) to note
that in *Lady Susan*, and in the Jane Austen of the future, much of what
a young writer especially might have been expected to include, what
her contemporaries did include, silently but definitely goes. A lot of
the clatter of novels – violent dramatic action, low-life comedy – is
nowhere. There are, as I shall emphasise later in a related context (that
of chapter six on *Mansfield Park* – which also contains very worldly
people), no duels, no challenges of the externally exciting kind. But
also, in *Lady Susan* there is no requirement for one of Richardson's
much finer resources: the close, nervous, subtle introspection of some of
his most interesting letters. Such incursions into the presentation of the
living consciousness were later to be achieved in, among other things,
the creation of free indirect speech (of which, again, more later). For the
moment it may be useful to consider an example of Richardson at his
best to illustrate what must have tempted Jane Austen, and what she
was soon to do in her own way, but which is eschewed in *Lady Susan*.
This is the creation of complicated, crowded and public scenes. There
is little of the scenic in *Lady Susan*. The drama is rarely directly
presented, and this allows the effects of the actions, the temperament of
Lady Susan and thus the point of the tale to operate unimpeded.
Compare with its manner the following from *Sir Charles Grandison* –
full of vigorous comic polyphony, tending to redundancy. Mr. Greville
and Sir Hargrave Pollexfen are the frenetically assertive contenders for
Harriet Byron's hand, and the scene is set in the company of her
relations. Mr. Greville has just described himself as desperate, and
Harriet speaks (it is necessary to quote at length):

The man's mad. O my cousins, let me never again be called to this man.

Mad! – And so I am. Mad for *you*. I care not who knows it. Why don't you hate me? He snatch'd at my hand; but I started back. You own that you never yet loved the man who loved you. Such is your gratitude! – Say, you hate me.

I was silent, and turned from him peevishly.

. Why *then* (as if I had said I did not *hate* him) say you love me, and I will look down with contempt upon the greatest prince on earth.

We should have had more of this – But the rap of consequence gave notice of the visit of a person of consideration. It was the Baronet.

The devil pick his bones, said the shocking Greville. I shall not be civil to him.

He is not *your* guest, Mr. Greville, said I – afraid that something affronting might pass between two spirits so unmanageable; the one in an humour so whimsical, the other very likely to be moody.

True, true, replied he. I will be all silence and observation. – But I hope you will not *now* be for retiring.

It would be too particular, thought I, if I am. Yet I should have been glad to do so.

The Baronet paid his respects to every one in a very set and formal manner; nor distinguished me.

Silly as Vain! thought I: handsome fop! to imagine this displeasure of consequence to me!

Mr. Greville, said Sir Hargrave, the town I understand is going to lose you.

The town, Sir Hargrave, cannot be said to have found me.

How can a man of your gallantry and fortune find himself un-employed in the country, in the winter, I wonder?

Very easily, when he has used himself to it, Sir Hargrave, and has seen abroad in greater perfection than you can have seen them here, the kind of diversions you all run after, with so keen an appetite.

In *greater* perfection! I question that, Mr. Greville; and I have been abroad, tho' too early I own, to make critical observations.

You may question it, Sir Hargrave; but *I* don't.

Have we not from Italy the most famous singers, Mr. Greville, and from thence and from France, for our money, the most famous dancers in the world?

No, Sir. They set too great a value in Italy, let me tell you, upon their finest voices, and upon their finest composers, too, to let them turn strollers.

Strollers do you call them? Ha, ha, ha, hah! – *Princely* strollers as we reward them! And as to composers, have we not Handel?

There you say something, Sir Hargrave. But you have but one Handel in England. They have several in Italy.

Is it possible? said every one.

Let me die, said the Baronet, with a forced laugh, if I am not ready to think that Mr. Greville has run into the fault of people of less genius than himself. He has got such a taste for foreign diversions, that he cannot think tolerably of those of his own country, be they ever so excellent.

Handel, Sir Hargrave, is not an Englishman. But I must say, that of every person present, I least expected from Sir Hargrave Pollexfen this observation.

He then returned the Baronet's laugh, and not without an air of mingled anger and contempt.

Nor I this taste for foreign performances from Mr. Greville; for so long a time as thou hast been a downright country gentleman.

Indeed, thought I to myself, you both seem to have changed characters. But I know how it comes about: Let one advance what he will, in the present humour of both, the other will contradict it. Mr. Greville knows nothing of music. What he said was from hearsay: And Sir Hargrave is no better grounded in it.

A *downright country gentleman*! repeated Mr. Greville, measuring Sir Hargrave with his eye, and putting up his lip.

Why, pr'ythee now, Greville, thou what shall I call thee; thou art not offended, I hope, that we are not all of one mind; Ha, ha, ha, hah!

I am offended at nothing you *say*, Sir Hargrave.

Nor I at any-thing you *look*, my dear; Ha, ha, ha, hah.

Yet his looks shewed as much contempt for Mr. Greville as Mr. Greville's did for him. How easily might these combustible spirits have blown each other up! Mr. Reeves was once a little apprehensive of consequences from the airs of both.

Mr. Greville turned from Sir Hargrave to me . . . (Vol. 1, Letter 22)

We notice how much more interested and interesting Harriet is than she would admit, or her explicit commentary allows. It is like Restoration comedy, but vastly widened and enhanced.[15] It would be amusing to set beside it the first dance – with Mr. Lovel and Sir Clement Willoughby in alternation – in *Evelina*; or the oddly disturbing masked ball in

Cecilia; or, indeed, the Pump-room scenes in *Northanger Abbey*. The private life led willy-nilly in public, and often to the excruciation of the more sensitive parties, is a constant element in eighteenth-century English fiction – and life? – and leads naturally into the much subtler orchestration of comparable events in Jane Austen's later novels. But my point here is that it is precisely this kind of dramatisation that is left out, abstained from, in *Lady Susan*. It would get in the way. For example: a recent editor (John Davie) is right in calling Letter 24 "climactic". It is not from Lady Susan. It is full of important reversals and an unusual amount of directly reported speech – of a kind of drama in fact. But it is more interestingly true for the present argument that this is accomplished by a string of conversations between individuals rather than by a complex single structure composed of many of them. It is, so to speak, melodic rather than harmonic. And the melody consists of the repercussions of Lady Susan's actions, and then a restatement of her charm, unmodified by an interest in anyone else for their own sake. To remind the reader: Mrs. Vernon writes to her mother, Lady De Courcy, of talking to her husband about the state of affairs – she is delighted that Reginald is to part angrily from Lady Susan. She then meets Frederica on the stairs who shyly informs her of a letter *she* has written to Reginald about her aversion to Sir James Martin, and of Reginald's awesomely sympathetic reception of this:

> "He was so good as to take it immediately; I dared not look at him – & ran away directly. I was in such a fright that I could hardly breathe. My dear Aunt, you do not know how miserable I have been."

Mrs. Vernon is fired by this:

> "Frederica, said I, you ought to have told *me* all your distresses. You would have found in me a friend always ready to assist you. . . . In such a point as this, your Mother's prohibition ought not to have prevented your speaking to me on the subject. She has no right to make you unhappy, & she shall *not* do it."

But this reassuring conjunction is immediately shattered by Reginald himself appearing out of, of all places, Lady Susan's dressing-room:

> My heart misgave me instantly. His confusion on seeing me was very evident. Frederica immediately disappeared. "Are you going? said I" . . . . "I am *not* going. Will you let me speak to you for a moment?"
> We went into my room. "I find, continued he, his confusion increasing as he spoke, that I have been acting with my usual foolish impetuosity. I have entirely misunderstood Lady Susan, & was on the

point of leaving the house under a false impression of her conduct. There has been some very great mistake – we have all been mistaken I fancy. Frederica does not know her Mother – Lady Susan means nothing but her good . . ."

He asks Mrs. Vernon to go to Lady Susan; and she does this, only to be baffled by a pose of correct argument and politeness which she knows to be meretricious but cannot successfully combat:

"Did I not tell you, said she with a smile, that your Brother would not leave us after all? . . . I was resolved to lose no time in clearing up these mistakes as far as I could. The case was this. Frederica had set herself violently against marrying Sir James. . . . had Frederica possessed the penetration, the abilities, which I could have wished for my daughter, or had I even known her to possess so much as she does, I should have not been anxious for the match." "It is odd that you alone should be ignorant of your Daughter's sense." "Frederica never does justice to herself; her manners are shy & childish. She is besides afraid of me; she scarcely loves me. During her poor Father's life she was a spoilt child; the severity it has since been necessary for me to shew, has entirely alienated her affection; neither has she any of that Brilliancy of Intellect, that Genius, or Vigour of Mind which will force itself forward." "Say rather that she has been unfortunate in her Education." "Heaven knows my dearest Mrs. Vernon, how fully I am aware of *that*; but I would wish to forget every circumstance that might throw blame on the memory of one, whose name is sacred with me."

Here she pretended to cry . . . (MW – to which all subsequent references – 285–8)

Mrs. Vernon – herself no stranger, incidentally, to disingenuity – cannot win against such mightily correct sentiments; and is forced outwardly to concur with more variations on them, which justify Lady Susan's ban on Frederica's complaints and the, now affectionately resolved, quarrel with Reginald. As she retires worsted – "My heart sickens within me" – she meets Sir James about to depart on Lady Susan's orders: "How easily does her Ladyship encourage, or dismiss a Lover!" The little episodes advance the action with great spirit. But they are a sequence, not an *ensemble*.

iii

So why is this? Why, on top of the primary, obvious abstention from a controlling narration, is there a further abstention in favour of a single effect from some of the richest resources offered to the author by the English epistolary tradition? At least a vagrant thought must be that it is because of an understandable unripeness. That Jane Austen was too young, or too uneasy with the larger effect, or too modest, to write more than a satirical fragment which she then polished off with a dismissive narrator's summary at the end – often taken, plausibly but wrongly I think, as an attack, in eagerness to resume control, on the epistolary method itself[16] – and which after all she did not publish. But this is not nearly good enough. Readers have often been surprised by the tale; but no one thinks it feeble. Rather its power to disconcert lies in the uncontradicted contempt expressed by and through Lady Susan for the mediocre world in which she finds herself. This world is outwardly respected, but is inwardly the subject of an undisguised scorn to which the reader can oppose but little, because little, in this short fiction, is supplied with which to oppose it.

The concentration on Lady Susan I have described means that figures who are undeniably decent in the abstract, as it were – the responsible Vernons, the quite spirited Reginald, and poor Frederica, who, with her "artless" charms and accomplishments is the very type of a normal novel heroine – are seen as thin, vain, ineffective. In fact, a good reason for thinking *Lady Susan* the work of a very young genius lies precisely in its non-contrapuntal nature. "All the brains allotted to the bad side and diffused scorn directed at the good people" as Mrs. Leavis said. It is surely a sign of real immaturity to deny, as people in their twenties often do, that late adolescence is that creative time of life when we feel most intensely, painfully, and, probably, accurately. This transitory fire – notoriously bliss to be alive in – is commonly associated with romantic love, religious intensities, or political idealism. Even the most ordinary young person feels some dissatisfaction with adult arrangements, if only to identify more or less at random with some minority group or some, perhaps tedious, exotic ideological stance. People in their teens are as inspiritingly given to unmitigated gloom as to unmitigated delight. (That idealists in later life seem childlike in some respects is a *cliché*.) So Jane Austen's early perception of the dullness and vanity of much of the world, which runs side by side with a vast sense of its comicality through all her work, finds expression in the at least implicitly admiring portrait of a stylish female rake.[17]

Such a view is not new, exactly. The "cold unpleasantness of 'Lady Susan' is but the youthful exaggeration of that irreconcileable judgement which is the very backbone of Jane Austen's power" said Reginald Farrer in his centennial obituary for the *Quarterly Review*;[18] and this is one of the most intelligent remarks ever made upon the work, except

that it is necessary to deny its premise. It is hard to see any unpleasantness except formally – in the subject – or just possibly in the older
Victorian reviewer's usage of "unpleasant" to mean "having to do with
sexual relationships" (as in E. Quincey, above). On the contrary, the
whole movement of the tale seems suffused with a shared delight in the
successful deployment of manipulative skills, as illustrated by such
high points from the first half as the following: Lady Susan arrives at
Churchill, heralded by her initiating *comme il faut* remark "I long to be
made known to your dear little children, in whose hearts..." etc.
(243–4); her true nature is then wittily displayed to her ally Mrs.
Johnson in Letter 2d which begins, with a decisiveness we come to
consider characteristic, "You were mistaken, my dear Alicia, in supposing me fixed..." (244). Then follows swiftly her campaign to keep
Charles Vernon sweet enough for convenience, thereby arousing his
wife's jealousy without letting her indulge it (Letter 6). Her total rout
of Reginald's rash would-be worldly attempt to "witness and detect"
her (Letter 4), which is effected by making him fall in love with her
purity and thus provide the "exquisite pleasure in subduing an insolent
spirit, in making a person pre-determined to dislike, acknowledge one's
superiority" (Letter 7, 254). Her brilliantly modest dissembling of this
(reflected in Letter 6 and *passim*); her handling of what she pleasantly
labels "the sacred impulse of maternal affection" in her toughly rational
treatment of "the greatest simpleton on Earth" – and near contemporary of the *author* – the tender Frederica (Letters 17 to 19, 269–75);
and her generalship upon the unexpected arrival of Sir James (Letters
20 and 22, 275–83). All these firmly align the reader on her side at the
expense of the virtuous ciphers around her. It is only on reflection,
abstracted from the texture of the work, that we are liable to feel it
dubious to have gone along so far with an adulterous schemer; only
then see harm in what we have been led to admire as courage, wit and
dash.

Neither does *Lady Susan* feel *cold*. It is possible to scheme with animation. The frank easy uncensored upper-class diction of Lady Susan's
letters to her ally Mrs. Johnson tend toward the enjoyably drastic
epigram: "I... look with a degree of contempt on the inquisitive &
doubting Fancies of that Heart which seems always debating on the
reasonableness of it's Emotions" she remarks of the "sort of ridiculous
delicacy" in Reginald; and of Manwaring in the same Letter (16), "Poor
Fellow! he is quite distracted by Jealousy, which I am not sorry for, as I

know no better support of Love" (268–9). Throughout she seems possessed of a sort of knowledgeable zest in life so free from inner scruple as to make later, more complex villainesses in good fiction – Becky Sharp or Kate Croy in *The Wings of the Dove*, for example – appear positively guilt ridden. "I really have a regard for him, he is so easily imposed on!" she pleasantly says of Mr. Vernon in Letter 5 (250). Her most ruthless remarks are the product of an exasperated contempt for failures in style. What really riles about her daughter is not her persistence in virtue but her lack of wit. Frederica makes a mess of running away from school – she "had really got as far as the length of two streets" – and her mother is moved to the mock-heroic:

> Such was the first distinguished exploit of Miss Frederica Susanna Vernon, & if we consider that it was atchieved at the tender age of sixteen we shall have room for the most flattering prognostics of her future renown. (Letter 19, 274)

The feeling behind this is similar to that with which Dr. Sloper in *Washington Square* greets his poor Catherine, overdressed in crimson and gold fringe: "Is it possible that this magnificent person is my child?" Parental impatience at ineptitude regardless of moral quality is sympathisable with if not sympathetic, and it is this that leads to another characteristic piece of Lady Susan's creed: "Artlessness will never do in Love matters, & that girl is born a simpleton who has it either by nature or affectation" (*ibid.*).

But is such literary, stylised, hard wisdom really to be endorsed? Where do the reader's sympathies finally come to rest, if they do? Marvin Mudrick, easily the ablest and most determined defender of both the *nouvelle* and its heroine, sees Lady Susan as:

> The ultimate, tragic victim . . . the beautiful woman who must waste her art in pretense, her passion in passing seductions, her will on invertebrates like her daughter and Reginald. . . . The world defeats Lady Susan, not because it recognizes her vices, but because her virtues have no room in it.[19]

Striking as this is it seems to veer off the point as much, though in an opposite direction, as those who see in an adverse depiction of the brilliant London 'smart set' merely a preliminary run for Mary Crawford in *Mansfield Park*. The trouble with both ideas is that far from being ill at ease in any context, a tragic heroine leaving us with a sense of waste, or a reject in the fiction, Lady Susan is quite triumphant, and correct in being so. She has no art *but* in pretense, and she enjoys seductions. She rides events with panache, and gets her pleasure precisely from this process. In spite of the accident which upsets her scheme for playing Reginald along she is convincingly confident in her last Letter, while accepting that Mrs. Johnson will have to cut her for a while:

> I never was more at ease, or better satisfied with myself & everything about me, than at the present hour. . . . Have I not reason to rejoice? Manwaring is more devoted than ever. . . . I am tired of submitting my will to the Caprices of others – of resigning my own Judgement in deference to those, to whom I owe no Duty, & for whom I feel no respect. I have given up too much – and have been too easily worked on; Frederica shall now find the difference. (Letter 39, 307–8)

Perhaps it is necessary to be thus brave with Mrs. Johnson, and there is an element of rationalisation, as well as what one feels to be a genuine independent courage. "This Eclaircissement is rather provoking" as she has earlier admitted; and she has had to re-group and attack another way, eventually abandoning Frederica and Reginald to one another's virtue. But although it is fatuous to talk of this realistic tale as an "extended fantasy of sexual reversal" placing "women-on-top",[20] it is entirely consistent that in the Conclusion Lady Susan is discovered by Mrs. Vernon annoyingly "easy & chearful", completely un-guilty and unembarrassed, and in "excellent spirits" (311). She easily faces out the Vernons and even manipulates them into taking Frederica, while giving Mrs. Vernon the impression that *she* is doing the persuading. She then marries lots of money and a nonentity in Sir James Martin. As usual we are given no material with which to work up sympathy for those she manipulates – one hesitates to call them 'victims' (I am not sure that it would be too bad to be Sir James Martin in spite of his "harder Lot"). Could the tone of pleased teasing in the book's penultimate paragraph possibly apply to a tragic victim or to the strangely punished Mary Crawford (rather it sounds *like* Mary Crawford)?

> Whether Lady Susan was, or was not happy in her second Choice – I do not see how it can ever be ascertained – for who would take her assurance of it, on either side of the question? The World must judge from Probability. She had nothing against her, but her Husband, & her Conscience. (313)

The scorn in the tale is not directed at Lady Susan, but by her. She manifests an impatience with the commonplace which is nowhere countered or neutralised or judged. We are liable to sympathise with her even when (in Letter 22) she is comically outraged by Reginald's failure to love her in his mode, the mode he proposes but she despises –

"Where was his reliance on my Sense and Goodness . . . ?" etc. (282). And it is surely to achieve such intimate comic effect that the texture of other people's lives and dramas and motives is calculatedly absent.

iv

Being content to state that a work of art not only has no explicit moral point, but also that no criteria are offered within it which would assist at a judgement of its morality, is probably quite acceptable nowadays. The reluctance to moralise may even lend *Lady Susan* a certain *kudos* now, just as predictably as it produced unease in former readers. But such a bland attitude is second rate because it amounts to denying the power of the work to move. It makes our response to it like that to mild pornography which, properly, says 'Oh, how (slightly) shocking, but really how remote, how ultimately harmless.'[21] I want to modify or at least refine it by pressing further, slightly speculatively, the idea of the novel's being an adaptation of the Richardsonian mode.

Henry Austen comments not only on his sister's admiration for Richardson but on her having eliminated "the errors of his prolix style and tedious narrative". He was talking of her subsequent novels, but, as we have seen, the process is even more nakedly evident in the corresponding form of *Lady Susan*. The most prolix feature of Richardson's manner, unfortunately outweighing for some modern readers his profound dramatisations of consciousness and the social scene, is the habit of seemingly obligatory moralisation of the action at nearly every point.[22] Little goes by but we must listen to some pi, predictable, antiquated stuff (though excellent sense usually) about the *finesse* of the right attitude to be adopted. Modern readers plead that they do not read him because he is so long: in fact, he is not long compared with Dickens or many contemporary blockbusters. They do not read him first because they are told to read *Pamela* which, although shorter, a work of some genius and vastly influential, is as inferior to the two later novels as *Pickwick* is to *Bleak House* and in something of the same way; but largely because his real work is cluttered with and impaired by chunks of eager sententiousness. Even Lovelace, descendant of the awful Lord Rochester and prototype of all future aristocratical rakes in literature including Lord Byron, is constantly observed brilliantly justifying himself not only to Clarissa but to his companion in rakehood, Belton. "Dost thou not understand me, Jack?" or the like is the repeated accompaniment of his scintillating accounts of deeds and schemes, and eventually gives off the impression of something like pleading. There is nothing at all resembling it in *Lady Susan* – though it can be argued that there might have been in Jane Austen at the other end of her career had she been spared to elaborate the libertine character of Sir Edward Denham in *Sanditon*. Was it just Jane Austen's youth and her "irreconcileable judgement" that allowed such drastic economies with morality?

I think quite probably not. There is another epistolary novel which could well be relevant. The resemblances between *Lady Susan* and Laclos's *Les Liaisons Dangereuses* (1782) have been noted in passing by a few writers[23] but never, so far as I know, been accorded any explanatory force. They could do a lot to account for the eruption of *Lady Susan*'s calm immoralism into English life. Although the idea does sort oddly at first sight with the idea of the happy late-Augustan vicarage, it is far from unlikely that the young Jane Austen would have read the sophisticated French shocker, which was even discovered hidden at around that time in plain binding in the library of Marie Antoinette. Critics have speculated extensively on whether her brilliant and attractive cousin and subsequent sister-in-law Eliza de Feuillide might or might not be the model for Lady Susan/Mary Crawford;[24] by comparison, the idea that Eliza might have imported from Versailles in 1787 or later the wonderful novel that "all Paris read and discussed" is innocuous. It is also completely feasible. There is nothing more obscene in *Les Liaisons Dangereuses* than there is in *Pamela*; it is well known that the Austen family devoured novels; they "loved French culture" (as, incidentally, Laclos loved Fanny Burney's novels); and, more importantly, the tragic *Les Liaisons Dangereuses* is the most impressive European book to have derived from the Richardsonian example (possible rivals in influentuality being *La Nouvelle Heloïse* and *The Sorrows of Werther* – the second of which is guyed by Jane Austen in 'Love and Freindship').[25]

The big French masterpiece and the little English tale have a lot in common. Both present the schemes and deeds of brave idle unscrupulous plotters through their own letters and letters from those upon whom they work. What particularly distinguishes them is that this is done not only without authorial comment except of the most peripheral, incidental and even sarcastic kind, but also with any moralising that is going allotted to the inferior stupider characters – who are themselves mainly concerned with themselves. (For this purpose Mrs. Vernon, Reginald and Sir Reginald can be aligned with Mme. de Volanges, Mme. de Rosemonde and Danceny, Frederica with Cecile de Volanges –

although admittedly the comparison does no justice to the moving figure of La Présidente Tourvel in the larger book.) Moreover, Lady Susan shares with Valmont and the Marquise de Merteuil a kind of heroic code, perhaps that of a debased chivalry.[26] Although none of them is supposed to be at all above physical rewards – certainly not the French pair – it is the game itself and its heady ethos that matter. They know already what Lovelace comes so bitterly, and more deeply, to realise at the end of *Clarissa*: that the delights of the intellect and spirit are what really count for them. It is remarkable how the metaphorical vocabulary concurs in the two works. Military terminology for amorous matters is common enough in literature; in love poetry sieges and assaults are regularly the order of the day. And so, echoing this in action, these three figures are members of a caste, part born, part self-appointed, the function of which is to conduct civil campaigns against their contemporaries. They are presented as equipped for strenuous activity, and probably compelled to it, by superior gifts of intelligence and language – "If I am vain of anything, it is of my eloquence. Consideration & Esteem as surely follow command of Language, as Admiration waits on Beauty" asserts Lady Susan (Letter 16, 268). And they feel justified by the arbitrary notion of a high-strung obligation of revenge for real or imaginary offences. Mme. de Merteuil opens her correspondence with a scheme for Valmont "digne d'un heros: vous servirez l'amour et la vengeance" (Letter 2); Lady Susan thinks Mrs. Vernon conscious of "deserving every sort of revenge that it can be in my power to inflict" (Letter 10, 258); and "conquérir est notre destin, il faut le suivre" (Letter 4) announces Valmont at his first appearance. Every reader of Laclos will recall that his characters constantly describe their exploits in terms of an almost tyrannical desire for "gloire" until with Mme. de Merteuil's celebrated "Hé bien! la guerre" (annotation to Letter 153) the conflict becomes internecine and their world destroys itself. It is worth comparing the diction of Letter 10 of *Lady Susan* where she is describing her first encounter with Reginald:

> I have made him sensible of my power, & can now enjoy the pleasure of triumphing over a Mind prepared to dislike me.... It has been delightful to me to watch his advances towards intimacy.... My conduct has been equally guarded from the first, & I never behaved less like a Coquette in the whole course of my Life, tho' perhaps my desire of dominion was never more decided. I have subdued him entirely by sentiment & serious conversation... (257–8)

"Power... pleasure of triumphing.... advances.... guarded... desire of dominion.... subdued" are ordinary enough in solution, I suppose;

but together their martial effect is strikingly similar to Valmont's and Mme. de Merteuil's habitual terms of campaign. "Manoeuver" is one of Lady Susan's favourite words. Indeed, the vocabulary is even more apt than it usually is in erotic literature – and apt to both actions. It is used to sustantiate an ideology of unprovoked aggression as irrational as anything undertaken by Napoleon (one of whose generals the engineer Laclos became). The young Jane Austen is giving a neat undiluted account of an aggravated impulse which in other books finds more disguised, complex, displaced and even benign forms. It is plausible that she was helped to it by an experience of the subtle, hard discipline of Laclos's extraordinary novel.

To leave it there would, however, be lurid. *Lady Susan* is an English book. The society it depicts can be sophisticatedly cruel in speech – readers seem divided as to whether Lady Susan's complaint about Mr. Johnson being "too old to be agreable, & too young to die" (Letter 29, 298) and her wish "May the next Gouty Attack be more favourable" (i.e. fatal – Letter 39, 308) are to be taken seriously or not – but it is hardly an equivalent in drastic refined debauchery to the desperate last flower of the *ancien régime*. There is nothing in it of the seduction and training to libertinage of schoolgirls or the planned ruin to death of rivals. One feels that there are plenty of things at which Lady Susan would baulk; even that she, charming as she is, is at just the other side of virtue, and therefore plausibly an ancestress of some aspects of some later Jane Austen heroines. Moreover, there is nothing in *Lady Susan* of the deeper concern about the constitution of society which emerges from *Les Liaisons Dangereuses* and makes it an undermining book. As I have noted of Lady Susan, all these villains emphatically accept the judgement of "the World" – in a sense. They are precursors of Sir Willoughby Patterne in *The Egoist* or Gilbert Osmond or Grandcourt or Hélène in *War and Peace* in that their contrivings take place under, depend on, an appearance of social respectability of the first water. "Those women are inexcusable who forget what is due to themselves & the opinion of the World", says Lady Susan (Letter 16, 269): and Valmont and Mme. de Merteuil are finally, if not altogether convincingly, destroyed by scandal. Virtuous appearances are one of the exciting rules of the game, and that Lady Susan is able to sidestep and face out the unfortunate intrusion of the truth – "Facts are such horrid things!" (Letter 32, 303) – is a tribute to how well she has played it as well as to her flexibility and courage. But she is never in it for such high stakes as the others are. Discontent bred of idleness they may share: but Lady Susan's is local and temporary whereas Valmont is a soldier without a war and Mme. de Merteuil, a woman of capacity with nothing whatever to do. The brilliant autobiographical letter (81) in which she explains with elegant ferocity the origin, progress and degree of her triumph over socially imposed handicaps on women, how facile are Valmont's victories compared to her's, and how superior she therefore is – a "Nouvelle Dalila" – is at the core of the novel. Anything like it even the most predisposed feminist search in *Lady Susan* is unable to uncover.[27]

I think it is this lack of radical disquiet, together with the absence of a concomitant voluptuousness in realisation, that illustrates why *Lady Susan* is a comparatively comforting, little, book. After all, a young genius, however sophisticated and well read, cannot be expected to imagine everything. Having gone along pleasantly with Lady Susan as a ruthless Flirt for a time it is disconcerting to have to ask what precisely and substantially she can mean when, going back to London, "the fairest field of action", she proposes to herself the reward of "a little Dissipation for a ten weeks' penance at Churchill" (Letter 25, 294)? Similarly with Manwaring: we are pleased with observations on his "polished ... insinuating" powers, his habit of "saying those delightful things which put one in good humour with oneself & all the world" (Letter 10, 258) and with his being "impressed with the deepest conviction of my merit ... satisfied that whatever I do must be right" (Letter 16, 269). He sounds ideal. But the imagination glances away at the idea of the substantiation of a real lover, a real adulterer. In spite of the fact that Lady Susan's beauty is described in unusual detail for Jane Austen (in Letter 6), there is no physicality and no question of the bedroom is felt – let alone of the exotic kind of bedroom described in *Les Liaisons Dangereuses*. In his review of the first publication in 1871 the tough Victorian intellectual R.H. Hutton very acutely objected to the use of letters, that to realise this wicked subject properly we "absolutely need to have [Lady Susan's] relations with her daughter and with her admirers freely described in language other than her own".[28] This is debatable in view of other eighteenth-century fictions; and that we do not get it is, I have argued, consonant with its uncluttered focus and clarity compared to the Richardsonian model (we should note that Hutton could not be expected to be very familiar with the idea of a short story). Nevertheless he is in a way right. How far does the tale accommodate what is suggested about its heroine's depravity? The real fault, if we must find one, and if we care to press hard and perhaps discover why after all Jane Austen did not publish it (it takes a very confident author not to publish such fine work), is that we cannot imagine anyone so demonstrably intelligent as Lady Susan really wanting to go in for Dissipation, sexual or otherwise. Without Valmont's and Mme. de Merteuil's lust for "gloire" in action, what could it be but merely gross? Her masterful manoeuvering spirit would surely soon get bored even with sporting with Manwaring and with tormenting Frederica. A similar question is posed by Henry (not Mary) Crawford – more of which in due course. For the moment we have a spirited transposition of the epistolary form, the substance of which is not real licentiousness as in its possible French model, but the expression of a youthful, lively, short-cutting impatience with, and scorn of, the commonplace – specifically of the commonplaces of routine virtue. A powerfully attractive thing and certainly an essential part of Jane Austen's genius.

Chapter Three

Early Works, Traditions, and Critics II: *Northanger Abbey* and other Novels

i

There are some areas of agreement about Jane Austen that seem to contradict one another.

Most ordinary readers of *Northanger Abbey* agree that it is delightful, funny, and easy to take in, perhaps even at a sitting. One of the pleasant things for them is that they thus behave like the heroine and her friends. Most scholars, on the other hand, imply that full understanding of the novel requires a great deal of knowledge from outside. This, too, offers an obvious pleasure, that of solidarity with equally knowledgeable people, and with the satirical voice of the book. How are these pleasures to be balanced? Even more than *Lady Susan, Northanger Abbey* is the ideal novel of which to ask the general question 'how far does reading Jane Austen's fiction *demand* knowledge of other literature?' If we require it anywhere we would require it here, for it so patently depends for its point on the point of other novels — is so literary in the nicest possible way, and is so explicit about its own form.

Of course, it is my general argument that Jane Austen's works are, besides being close to us spiritually, not commonly thought of as needing much special learning or proposing special stringencies of application — unlike, for example, some of those of Milton, Crashaw or James Joyce — but only little pieces of information about Regency dress, dances, and so on. Yet the importance and ubiquity of reference to previous literature in *Northanger Abbey* may seem to present a problem. And considering it is an excellent way in to approaching the novel as a whole.

First, however, as a preliminary to talking about novels, I want to note something bound up with the question, yet also worth celebrating on its own account. As with Jane Austen's transposition of Richardson this is a matter of her resisting temptation – in this case a powerfully specific one, Dr. Johnson's prose.

ii

There is something portentous for literature about:

> To begin perfect happiness at the respective ages of twenty-six and eighteen, is to do pretty well; and professing myself moreover convinced, that the General's unjust interference, so far from being really injurious to their felicity, was perhaps rather conducive to it, by improving their knowledge of each other, and adding strength to their attachment . . .

This could be from near the – felicitous – end of any eighteenth-century novel. But what follows is unmistakable:

> I leave it to be settled by whomsoever it may concern, whether the tendency of this work be altogether to recommend parental tyranny, or reward filial disobedience. (2, xvi, 252)

This is the voice of Jane Austen. Or, more correctly because the distinction can be useful in analysis, her narrator's voice. (Whether or not this voice corresponds exactly with the historical author is a theoretical question, both interesting and tedious, which it is not necessary to decide in order to read the novels, though I expect everyone would be surprised, in some future existence, if it did not.) The unique quality is far easier to recognise than to describe; but one characteristic is suggested, negatively, by the reference to Johnson – that looming presence of the time just past (he died when Jane Austen was eight), and himself a great encourager of women novelists. For *unconscious* imitation is obviously inimical to the self-aware and gifted parodist; and 'Johnsonese' – which has only a tangled relation to its source – was one of the literary scourges of her age, a fact of which she showed herself brilliantly aware when putting chunks of it into the mouth of the fatuous and foolish Mary Bennet in *Pride and Prejudice*.

Johnson himself was quite famously "dear" to Jane Austen. But his unique trenchancies are so clearly the product of the conflict and union of his vast information and intellectual power with his possibly even greater humanity and wit that it could be no part of a first rate genius to imitate him, however infectious the grand, masculine(?), manner. Rather he, and what Lady Davenant in Maria Edgeworth's *Helen* (1834) calls his "tripod sentences", are irresistible to lesser talents.

When serious sentiments and dignity are called for in late eighteenth-century novels Johnsonese often supplies at least the tone in which to elaborate the correct view. Here, for example is a heroine, Miss Burt, refusing a grand proposal in Lady Mary Hamilton's *Munster Village*:

> "I can neither", said she, "adopt the virtues, or the vices of the great; the former are too conspicuous, the other too obscure. A round of peaceable employments, proper to satisfy the mind, and to soothe the heart is a kind of happiness for which I find myself inclined.
>
> With such principles and inclinations, I could not be happy in the great world, where the general way of life is solely calculated, to flatter the senses, and where superior genius is contemned, or at least only permitted to exhibit itself in sallies or smart repartees."[1]

Such deliberative pomp is anxiously correct – and lifeless. It is an unexceptionable re-cycling of *Rasselas* or the *Rambler*, though with none of the urgency or ironic context of the former, none of the candid moral purpose of the latter. It is death to the *dramatic*. One cannot imagine it in the mouth of a Jane Austen heroine, except possibly Emma at her most obtuse and self-satisfied or Fanny Price at her most prim and insecure. Fanny Burney is its most talented victim. In his amused and amusing pages on the imitations of his friend, Boswell quotes a passage from *Cecilia* (1782) which is actually, typically, rather fine in itself and ends with gloomy authority:

> "I dread, therefore, to make a trial where I despair of success; I know not how to risk a prayer with those who may silence me by a command."[2]

It is quite likely that Johnson himself oversaw *Cecilia*: but readers of that novel and to a lesser degree of *Camilla* (1796)[3] will remember how this magnificently turned rhetoric overcharges and obscures the otherwise sympathetic, lively and poignant little actions of the books. The influence is "either Sam Johnson or the Devil" as Macaulay remarked.[4] The change from *Evelina* (1778) – that sparkling work which is the nearest thing there is outside Anna Howe in *Clarissa* to a predecessor of *Pride and Prejudice* – is striking: but even there the reverend guardian, Mr. Villars, adopts the tone and sometimes the substance of the great moralist. His abstract scenario based on the clash of personified qualities –

> ... he [the virtuous Lord Orville] seemed as unconscious of his power as you of your weakness; and therefore you had no alarm, either from *his* vanity or *your own* prudence.
>
> Young, animated, entirely off your guard, and thoughtless of con-

sequence, *Imagination* took the reins, and *Reason*, slow-paced, though sure-footed, was unequal to a race with so eccentric and flighty a companion. How rapid was then my Evelina's progress through these regions of fancy and passion whither her new guide conducted her! (Letter 68)

– (and so on) has the air and the imagery, though not the power, of "The Vanity of Human Wishes":

> Ye nymphs of rosy Lips and radiant Eyes
> Whom Pleasure keeps too busy to be wise, . . .
> What Care, what Rules your heedless Charms shall save,
> Each Nymph your Rival, and each Youth your Slave? . . .
> Against your Fame with Fondness Hate combines,
> The Rival batters, and the Lover mines.
> With distant Voice neglected Virtue calls,
> Less heard, and less the faint Remonstrance falls;
> Tir'd with Contempt, she quits the slipp'ry Reign,
> And Pride and Prudence take her Seat in vain . . .

The resemblance is not surprising, for as Boswell remarks, the "strength and animation" of Johnson's style made his imitators so "numerous" as to defy a full citation, although:

> . . . every good judge must see that they are obviously different from the original; for all of them are either deficient in force or overloaded with its peculiarities; and the powerful sentiment to which it is suited is not to be found.[5]

By contrast, when reflections of the tolerant pessimistic conservative Johnsonian kind *are* found in *Northanger Abbey*, the phrasing tends to be very much the author's own – as when, for example, the happiness caused by the kindness of the younger Tilneys leaves Catherine "only just so much solicitude as the human mind can never comfortably do without" (2, xiii, 221).

iii

Jane Austen is not alone in resisting this temptation, of course: other admirable contemporaries, Maria Edgeworth or Mrs. Inchbald or Charlotte Smith, are also more or less free of it. But it is time to turn from what she avoided to what she inimitably achieved – and thus back to her relations with the fiction of her age.

Her thought is in its own way as complex, as much a matter of organising disparate or even conflicting truths into language as Dr. Johnson's, and clearly often more subtle. But she makes complexity into limpidity. If we look harder at the end of *Northanger Abbey* the manner is as usual clear and precise:

> I leave it to be settled by whomsoever it may concern, whether the tendency of this work be altogether to recommend parental tyranny, or reward filial disobedience. (2, xvi, 252)

– but something not at all simple has occurred. The effect of calm tongue-in-cheek irresponsibility is the result of three things happening at the same time. We realise, first, that there can be no genuine question of the solemn balancing and judgement evoked by the parodied legal tone of "whomsoever it may concern" because – second, neither 'moral' could be seriously offered, or would adequately sum up the preceding action, even if we thought that novels should do this, which – third, we do not because, and this is the immediate point, we have been reading a novel which has evolved into a novel from being a pastiche of one.

Jane Austen was clearly irritated to death by the contemporary tic of anxiously concluding creative fiction – perhaps in order to lend an irrelevant respectability to what might otherwise be stigmatised as lies – with a burst of simplifying virtuous protestation. To take a few examples from different kinds of novel: *Sir Charles Grandison* ends with a eulogy of the "TRULY GOOD MAN" and·a three-page pseudo-editorial note about his practical excellence as an example. The sight of Harley's grave in Mackenzie's *The Man of Feeling* (1771) is "worth a thousand homilies". *The Old English Baron* (1777) by Clara Reeve leaves us with "the certainty of RETRIBUTION". *Cecilia* has a passage, often noted by scholars of Jane Austen, about PRIDE AND PREJUDICE, the ebb and flow of evil and human "cross purposes" and DISOBEDIENCE, and then proceeds to a Johnson-type "MORAL about putting up with "partial evil". Mrs. Inchbald's distinguished *A Simple Story* (1791) lapses into an explicit demand at the end for "A PROPER EDUCATION" for young women. Mrs. Radcliffe concludes *The Romance of the Forest* (1791) with the assurance that it is "an example of trials well endured . . . of virtues well rewarded"; *Udolpho* (1794) itself protests "Oh! how useful it is to have shown . . ." etc. – and so on.

It is too easy to persuade the modern reader to feel superior to all this overt moralising, and to judge the habit as below the dignity of art. One wonders whether, in fact – after Richardson set the powerful example – it was usually much more than an amiable convention of the "husbands, wives, babies, millions, appended paragraphs, and cheerful remarks" kind which later so amused and annoyed Henry James in Victorian fiction. And it is noticeable that other novelists besides Jane Austen sometimes make great play out of joking about what they were supposed to do: that Sterne does little else goes almost without saying; but straighter writers enjoy the same game: Robert Bage in *Hermsprong* (1796) – which we know Jane Austen also to have read – rather heavily and extendedly teases the "dear ladies" as to how he should end; and the last chapter of *Belinda* (1801), called 'The Dénouement', has Maria Edgeworth's characters – less tiresomely than it may sound – self-consciously composing a stage group in order to deliver:

> . . . a moral – a moral! Yes
>
> "Our tale contains a *moral*; and, no doubt,
> You all have wit enough to find it out." (xxxi)

Yes. So Jane Austen was not alone – except in her concision.

But my point about literary culture is at once more obvious and more elusive than the mere observation of precedents. It is that the reader who has never heard of any of the novels mentioned – save through allusions to them in *Northanger Abbey* – will understand this joke about endings as readily and completely as someone soaked in eighteenth-century literature. Why? Because good satire or parody or pastiche *always creates its own object*. It is only inferior anger directed at the local and ephemeral that dates. This point can be equally easily illustrated from the first sentence of *Northanger Abbey*:

> No one who had ever seen Catherine Morland in her infancy, would have supposed her born to be a heroine. Her situation in life, the character of her father and mother, her own person and disposition, were all equally against her. Her father was a clergyman, without being neglected, or poor, and a very respectable man, though his name was Richard – and he had never been handsome. (1, i, 13)

The tone of this is, like that of the end, calm, drained of pomp, and somehow outrageous. There is a bizarre air of factuality, which is nevertheless not that of whimsy. A heroine who is not a heroine – and "Richard". Why Richard? No one knows why. Or why he is funny. He seems merely a wild extrusion of (youthful) imagination, and is certainly not defused by John Davie's persuasive editorial conjecture that he "may be an Austen family joke". In a text thoroughly revised for publication there should be no place for private jokes; but there is a place for Richard, and no explanation would improve him – neither Jan Fergus's that Jane Austen is reversing the absurd Yorkist *parti pris* in her sprightly young 'The History of England'; nor my own that the name, or collocation (which evidently so amused the author that it reappears in the "poor Richard" of *Persuasion*, 1, vi and viii), has a remote resonance with the title of Benjamin Franklin's popular collections of satirical maxims, *Poor Richard's Almanack* (1732–57). Instead we *sense* that there is a background, just as we sense the background to the jokes at the end of the novel – and to many in between. The fact that we are logically *bound* to be ignorant in this particular case illuminates the nature of all of them, including those whose reference scholarship can easily plumb. We are taken into a pleasant conspiracy about the ludicrousness of the name – there must be some persecuted, dashing scoundrelly vicar somewhere – and, as with many jokes, can share the amusement not because there are any facts of the case (as there are facts we can learn, if we please, about the endings of contemporary novels), but simply because we are invited to. A comparable effect occurs at another important point of structural punctuation in the book. The last sentence of the first volume ends with Mrs. Allen's absurdly random and unexplained "kind compliments to all the Skinners". The Skinners? Admittedly Mrs. Allen has mentioned them twice before as her predecessors as visitors to Bath; but here we are approaching the charmingly random territory of William Coxe in – or, rather, not in – *Emma*.

This goes some way towards illuminating the problem about special knowledge with which I began. All the literary jokes for which *Northanger Abbey* is noted need no other explanation than that given within its pages. It is importantly *untrue* to say that "some of its value disappeared with the vogue of Mrs. Radcliffe's romances".[6] As I argued in chapter one: knowledge of contemporary fiction – of what is known in computing circles as the 'authoring environment' – of course does no harm, or, rather, could only hamper reading if it were to incline anyone to see the novel as possessed by its period and to be reaccessed solely by experts. But it is distasteful as well as banal to desire to think of a good work of art as substantially dependent on anything but common skills, or, where any such dependence does exist, to maximise this into a limitation of the circle of interest that specialism necessarily involves. Imagine being told that we have to listen to Schütz in order to appreciate J.S. Bach, or that Johann Strauss is a delicate case because we no longer waltz or polka, but dance to – whatever is currently danced to.

This general truth is particularly important to *Northanger Abbey* because one of its exemplary features is its simple accessibility. The usual, more or less accurate, account is as follows: the book starts,

like much of the *Juvenilia* and a bit like *Shamela*, from the impulse
to juxtapose a literary ethos with real life, the high-strained literary
with the mundane, the artificial with the true. But Catherine and her
acquaintances at Bath take on an independent life and become interesting in themselves. So Catherine's love story – although the satire of
novels and Gothick in particular is sustained in counterpoint to it – is
soon much more substantial than mere pastiche could be – as *Joseph
Andrews* is much more substantial than *Shamela/Pamela*. The climax
comes when the worldliness of the world, as embodied in the mercenary
General Tilney and the vulgar fortune-hunting Thorpes, is revealed as as
much of a threat to happiness, in its way, as anything Gothick imagin-
ings could evoke. But then Catherine's candour wins through. Although
a few commentators want, implausibly, to intensify this happy effect by
claiming that Henry Tilney also is not so delightful as he seems,[7] this is
the commonly accepted description, and there is no reason to modify it
here. Only a very poor reader indeed could fail to appreciate what is
going on. What is interesting is to look at the way it is realised in detail.

The satire on the education of a heroine in the opening chapter is
unremitting. How much do we need to know about other heroines to
see the point? Catherine is not very proficient, and shirks her lessons:

> What a strange unaccountable character! – for with all these symp-
> toms of profligacy at ten years old, she had neither a bad heart nor a
> bad temper . . . (14)

Her literary education is a delightful string of miscellaneous gems from
the poets; but a little later she fails at polite art:

> . . . she had no notion of drawing – not enough even to attempt
> a sketch of her lover's profile, that she might be detected in the
> design . . . (16)

For – worse as it were –:

> She had reached the age of seventeen, without having seen one
> amiable youth who could call forth her sensibility; without having
> inspired one real passion, and without having excited even any
> admiration but what was very moderate and very transient. This was
> strange indeed! But strange things may be generally accounted for if
> their cause be fairly searched out. There was not one lord in the
> neighbourhood; no – not even a baronet. (16)

It is plain enough what this, and its surrounding, depends on. Not on
knowledge of other novels, but merely on the implication that there are
some. The humour posits works in which heroines are precociously

virtuous, are likely to be detected sketching (amiable) youths, have "sensibility" and inspire aristocratic passions. The act of positing is sufficient. We need only an ordinary imagination able to deduce, for instance, the existence of some form of epistolary fiction from its being called "remarkable" that Mrs. Morland does not demand a letter from Catherine describing her experiences when she goes to Bath. And all this is done with the greatest good humour – unlike political satire, literary parody is usually the tribute of love, or at least affection. The evolution of a heroine is presented in fetching contrast to the everyday, to Catherine's "rolling down the green slope at the back of the house" or remarks such as: "To look *almost* pretty, is an acquisition of higher delight to a girl who has been looking plain the first fifteen years of her life, than a beauty from the cradle can ever receive." In this case the undermining suffered by the higher mode, the mock in the mock-heroic, is engaging and pleasant rather than dowdy, severe or disillusioning.

Where one requires more exact information about the object of parody than the non-specialist reader of eighteenth-century novels could provide, the book supplies it. Supplies it most notably in Henry Tilney's own parodies of the Gothick – especially that of 2, v, complete with the exotic creation of the housekeeper Dorothy – the explicit nature of which recalls the large pieces of fantasy Romance spouted by the (nevertheless charming) Arabella in Charlotte Lennox's *The Female Quixote* (1752), which gave Jane Austen "very high" amusement; but supplies it strongly also in Catherine's excited reflections before and after her arrival at Northanger.

This is not to deny that a slight additional pleasure is felt – the pleasure of finding things quite insignificantly cohere, as in a crossword puzzle – when the reader can spot a submerged reference or structural similarity. For example: the fortunate transience of Catherine's "severe mortification" at having to refuse Henry Tilney because she is pre-engaged to dance with the boorish John Thorpe (that Regency pre-figuration of a sports-car enthusiast, 1, vii–ix), perhaps echoes and contrasts with the blushing, paralysing, confusions of Evelina when she makes a *faux pas* in dancing mutely with Lord Orville after refusing Mr. Lovel at her first dance, and later compounds this at the *ridotto* by refusing Sir Clement Willoughby in the hope that Lord Orville will reappear. Or more likely all these embarrassments are based on life? In any case, only a learned smile is at stake. Even when the satire feels as though it is 'literary' in a wider sense, it cannot be said to depend on any other specific piece of literature. A characteristic narratorial remark occurs when Catherine first meets Isabella and quickly, temporarily, forgets about Henry Tilney: "Friendship is certainly the finest balm for the pangs of disappointed love" (1, iv, 33). (She has met Henry once.) The first impression of this sub-acid implied proverb is that it is merely a sarcastic rebuke to Catherine for her silliness. But obviously it also invokes ("certainly") a climate or convention of feeling in which such things could pass as wisdom. It looks like an adage from a book. And actually, as adages go, it is quite sensible. So it can only be silly as applied to those who think of friendship and love as the products of five minutes. Which means Catherine – Which means girls who read the kind of book in which such things occur or are said and who proceed to think of their own passing emotions as illustrating such certainties – and so on. It is a mistake to understimate the ease with which such conventions are understood.

Similarly when Eleanor Tilney fails to resemble her dead mother we would realise a joke even if we did not know how much Evelina's fate – or, for that matter, later, Maud's in Sheridan Le Fanu's magical Victorian Gothick *Uncle Silas* (1864) – depends upon genetic inheritance. Literariness is being proposed at the same time as it is being exposed, and this effect of the simultaneous recreation of the satirised form in relation to the present action is familiar from – for a much earlier example in the relevant English literature – *The Rape of the Lock*. On Belinda's dressing table/altar:

> This casket India's glowing gems unlocks,
> And all Arabia breathes from yonder box.
> The tortoise and the Elephant unite
> Transformed to combs, the speckled and the white.
> (Canto 1, 133–6)

Here domestic luxury is described in epical terms. It is very much the same order of exotic creation as Catherine's linen-chest/mysterious cabinet (closer to it, really, than anything in *Udolpho* or *The Romance of the Forest* in richness of effect). Yet no one would seriously propose that a knowledge of Vergil and Milton, of Homer and Ariosto is a *prerequisite* for reading Pope. Good satire always creates *enough* anyway of its object for its further, more interesting purposes.

It is the same with the central thematic material: Catherine's launch into Bath or "our heroine's entrée into life" (1, ii, 20) probably echoes the sub-title and subject of *Evelina*, "the history of a young lady's entrance into the world". But this is as much the history of Juliet or Miranda or, *caeteris paribus*, Tom Jones. Actually it is the history of literally hundreds of novels. Henry James called "the conception of a certain young woman affronting her destiny" the "cornerstone" of *The Portrait of a Lady* – which is a shade too grand for Catherine who is more like Daisy Miller. But again we may reflect that the shape of such a history is written into everyone's life.

Where the satire bites in *Northanger Abbey* it bites on the real. General Tilney, the cold father and eager *arriviste*, John Thorpe, the braggart whose selfish puffs cause real harm, Isabella, the hollow sexy flirt (not villainess), are the obvious figures whose deeds recoil upon them. The touch is light, and it is quite possible to find something mitigating, even appealing, in the General's excessive compunction over the health of an heiress, or in Isabella's wide, roving eyes. However, what they have in common with the heroine is an ordinary humanity which it does not take other books to enable us to recognise.

I hope I have not hectored the reader on what – when insisted upon – sounds merely a plain man's point.[8] Actually I feel I am trying to describe and recover a sense of what an ordinary sophisticated reading would be like. The recreation of parodied objects in works of literature is of the same order of phenomena as their power to evoke with an astonishing precision (which it is easy to take too much for granted) the essential mundane: the facts and values, from the most banal to the most exalted, of people and societies remote to us in time or place. From realistic novels, for example, we not only learn, but feel the vivid force of, the rule that it is vulgar for Frenchmen's coats to have more than four buttons on each sleeve under Charles X; that not to pray aloud in Russian in Church is the height of ostentatious piety under Nicholas l; that silence is the only proper response to grief in Senatorial circles in Hamburg; or, for that matter, that Camden-place is not quite the best address in Regency Bath.

iv

Enough of these simple quasi-theoretical points. Before discussing the two most exciting aspects of *Northanger Abbey* – its view of itself as a novel and its extraordinary tact in the balance of characters – I want to confirm the foregoing argument by shifting it around a little and considering how it is around this very area, the parodic or nearby, that Jane Austen most shows herself an apprentice (inappropriate as this term nevertheless sounds). It is exactly where the book most wants to establish its self-sufficiency that tiny blemishes can occur. *Lady Susan*, swept on by youthful literary inspiration, eventually reveals imaginative limitations about what might satisfy the clever and vicious. *Northanger Abbey* – also a relatively short work – is by contrast completely at home with its comparatively unambitious heroine, but is sometimes a trifle too anxious to put its reader into the required relation to her experience and her surroundings.

There are sharp contrasts – for instance – in the quality of writing in the fourth chapter: when Catherine misses Henry Tilney on her second visit to the Pump-room her feelings are first rendered by an experiment in free indirect speech:

> Mr. Tilney did not appear. Every creature in Bath except himself was to be seen . . . people whom nobody cared about, and nobody wanted to see; and he only was absent. "What a delightful place Bath is," said Mrs. Allen . . . (31)

The modulation from the factual voice of the narrator into Catherine's drastic thoughts ("nobody cared . . . nobody wanted") and out again gives an innovatory foretaste of that flickering and subtle immediacy in representation of consciousness which is one of Jane Austen's great gifts to the English novel (a gift formally unhonoured for a long time – see chapter six, below). But then, as the Thorpes appear, the narratorial voice re-enters, almost as though unconvinced by its own experiment, in a more than usually conscious way. Mrs. Allen continues her excruciating commonplaces with her too familiar thought: "how pleasant it would be if we had any acquaintance here". And:

> This sentence had been uttered so often in vain, that Mrs. Allen had no particular reason to hope that it would be followed by more advantage now; but we are told to "despair of nothing we would attain", as "unwearied diligence our point would gain;" and the unwearied diligence with which she had every day wished for the same thing was at length to have its just reward . . . (31)

For Jane Austen this is clumsy. It points up explicitly what the reader already realises. And, when the two older women recognise each other in a novelistic sentimental way – "I cannot be mistaken . . . is not your name Allen?" – there follows:

> Their joy on this meeting was very great, as well it might, since they had been content to know nothing of each other for the last fifteen years. (31–2)

For the last fifteen years. This is not rich irony, but sarcasm. And, as is often the case with sarcasm, no one needs it. The tone, interestingly, is near to that of the young person who just cannot believe how *incredibly* stupid (and so forth) middle-aged people can be. It seems likely to have at least some relationship – on the wrong side of the fence as it were – with what is otherwise so lovely a feature of this part of the novel – the mastery of teenage thought and sentiment. The author of *Lolita* could well have learned something from the chatter of Isabella (though she *is* older) at her next presented meeting with Catherine (1, vi) — "I have been waiting for you at least this age . . . Oh! these ten ages. I am sure I have been here this half hour" (five minutes actually) — though I suppose this kind of *skaz* is universal, from life, like the serious heroine Evelina's phrase "For the Universe". But, again, the introduction to this hilarious conversation about horrid novels, Miss Andrews and *Sir Charles Grandison*, is rather too concerned to direct our response. It is:

> . . . given as a specimen of their very warm attachment, and of the delicacy, discretion, originality of thought, and literary taste which marked the reasonableness of their attachment. (39)

And this is too direct, marking off by strict counter truths the absurdities of would-be heroines in novels.

One of the reasons for being sceptical of the critical suggestion that *Northanger Abbey* divides into 'Bath' and 'Northanger' sections written at different times[9] is that such petty falterings — but any fault in Jane Austen tends to be remarkable — persist throughout in much the same form; and are, of course, related to the qualities heroines should or should not have. Isabella's awfulness is often underlined. After her charade about paying no attention to the "odious young men" in the Pump-room it seems superfluous to learn that she "looked back at them only three times" while pretending to escape (1, vii, 47); and her nicely caught vulgarity — "you men" this and "you men" that (they are lazy, too curious and never stick at anything) — is certainly over-produced (for Jane Austen, though it might do well in Fanny Burney or Dickens) by the time of "you men think yourselves of such consequence" to the duffer James Morland in 1, xi, 90. This tendency towards redundant emphasis is not confined to cases where we are to feel hostile. After Catherine's appealing eager harping on Henry Tilney during her conversation with Eleanor in 1, x the narrator adds, what we already know:

> . . . they parted — on Miss Tilney's side with some knowledge of her new acquaintance's feelings, and on Catherine's, without the smallest consciousness of having explained them. (73)

These are episodes at Bath. But much later Catherine's first impression of her room at Northanger exhibits a comparable anxiety on the author's part to spell out the humour, this time in direct enforcement of the Gothick parody. We are plunged straight into an account of what she says to herself, or might be supposed to say in literary speech — a far cruder device for the presentation of the working of consciousness than the free indirect speech mentioned above:

> ... these thoughts crossed her: –
> "This is strange indeed! I did not expect such a sight as this! – an immense heavy chest! – What can it hold? – Why should it be placed here? – Pushed back too, as if meant to be out of sight! – I will look into it – cost me what it may, I will look into it – and directly too – by day-light. – If I stay till evening my candle may go out." She advanced ... (2, vi, 163)

The trouble with this – amusing as it is – is that it is too stupid. The Catherine who interests Henry and Eleanor Tilney is too human, too really naïve, to carry on to herself in this Gothick fashion. Only in *novels* do people say "cost me what it may" – unless *they* are the parodists. Here the jokes – even to the extent of taking up the hint about the self-extinguishing candle from Henry's preceding mock fantasy – intrudes and smudges what has become the genuine, everyday, interest of the book. The mistake is one of register – everything has led up to this point and everything depends on some such reaction – but the direct transposition of Catherine's determined fright into the language of stilted extremity jars compared to the framed and filtered versions provided by the avowed satire of the narrator and Henry. The same is true a little later when General Tilney suddenly calls "Eleanor", "giving to his daughter the first intimation of his presence, and to Catherine terror upon terror" (2, ix, 191–2). Terror? This is from the narrator, but again the pounding in of Gothick excess rings slightly false. It is a question of slight faults in a voice which the later Jane Austen so perfectly commanded.

v

What is the relation of all this – the evolution of a personal style and ethos through a parody which quickly becomes more than a parody – to the explicit statements about novels and their nature for which *Northanger Abbey* is also renowned? There are five passages that use fiction as a yardstick by which the action is judged. I shall concentrate on the one most often quoted and discussed: the direct narratorial defence in 1, v. It is an extended polemic in which the author seems to turn round on the hypocrite reader with humourous exasperation, and may be considered yet again in full:

Yes, novels; – for I will not adopt that ungenerous and impolitic custom so common with novel writers, of degrading by their contemptuous censure the very performances, to the number of which they are themselves adding – joining with their greatest enemies in bestowing the harshest epithets on such works, and scarcely ever permitting them to be read by their own heroine, who if she accidentally take up a novel, is sure to turn over its insipid pages with disgust. Alas! if the heroine of one novel be not patronised by the heroine of another, from whom can she expect protection and regard? I cannot approve of it. Let us leave it to the Reviewers to abuse such effusions of fancy at their leisure, and over every new novel to talk in threadbare strains of the trash with which the press now groans. Let us not desert one another; we are an injured body. Although our productions have afforded more extensive and unaffected pleasure than those of any other literary corporation in the world, no species of composition has been so much decried. From pride, ignorance, or fashion, our foes are almost as many as our readers. And while the abilities of the nine-hundredth abridger of the History of England, or of the man who collects and publishes in a volume some dozen lines of Milton, Pope, and Prior, with a paper from the Spectator and a chapter from Sterne, are eulogized by a thousand pens, – there seems almost a general wish of decrying the capacity and undervaluing the labour of the novelist, and of slighting the performances which have only genius, wit, and taste to recommend them. "I am no novel reader – I seldom look into novels – Do not imagine that *I* often read novels – It is really very well for a novel." – Such is the common cant. – "And what are you reading, Miss—?" "Oh! it is only a novel!" replies the young lady; while she lays down her book with affected indifference, or momentary shame. – "It is only Cecilia, or Camilla, or Belinda;" or, in short, some work in which the greatest powers of the mind are displayed, in which the most thorough knowledge of human nature, the happiest delineation of its varieties, the liveliest effusions of wit and humour are conveyed to the world in the best chosen language. Now, had the same young lady been engaged with a volume of the Spectator, instead of such a work, how proudly would she have produced the book, and told its name; though the chances must be against her being occupied by any part of that voluminous publication, of which either the matter or manner would not disgust a young person of taste: the substance of its papers so often consisting in the statement of improbable circumstances, unnatural characters, and topics of conversation, which no longer concern any one living; and their language, too, frequently so coarse as to give no very favourable idea of the age that could endure it. (37–8)

This is brilliant – what a marvellous literary critic Jane Austen would have been. But it is also polemic in the sense of being not quite straightforward.

As *scholars* we can note that although it does indeed refer to a common eighteenth-century attitude – the common attitude of Fathers and Mentors which is recreated in the phrase "the trash with which the press now groans"[10] in just the same way as the novels parodied are elsewhere recreated – it also disguises the extent to which such a defence was itself a part of the heritage into which Jane Austen was, as it were, writing herself. The writer's treasons implicit in such a contrast as the following are certainly familiar to readers of early novels:

> ... the young ladies were lolling upon a settee, with each, a volume of a *new novel* in her hand. Mrs. Taddington, a good-looking grave faced woman, was sitting at her needlework ... (Elizabeth Blower, *George Bateman*, 1782, 2, 222)

But far from its being the universal practice of heroines to denigrate the works that sustain them, there was also a lively practice of what has been elegantly called "positive self-evaluation". "Can one help wondering ..." asks Francis Coventry as early as 1751 when dedicating his *History of Pompey the Little; or the adventures of a Lap Dog* to Fielding, "at the contempt with which many people affect to talk of this sort of composition? they seem to think it degrades the dignity of their understandings to be found with a novel in their hands, and take great pains to let you know that they never read them."

And in general accord with this mood of counter-attack, the grave doctor who dispels Arabella's illusions about the real truth of Romances at the end of *The Female Quixote* willingly concedes that:

> Truth is not always injured by Fiction. An admirable writer of our own time [Richardson], has found the way to convey the most solid Instructions, the noblest Sentiments, and the most exalted Piety in the pleasing dress of a novel [*Clarissa*], and, to use the words of the greatest genius in the present age [Johnson], "has taught the passions to move at the command of virtue". (9, xi)

This is part of a weighty discussion which rounds off the fantastical humour of the book. But the subject is frequently glanced at. The dedication and preface to *Evelina* are full of the kind of bashfulness pinned down so wittily in *Northanger Abbey* – the defence is conducted by "the humble Novelist" offering "frivolous amusement" which has been "the trifling production of a few hours".[11] (It is perhaps an indication of Jane Austen's justified assurance that she never felt the need for any preface of this sort.) However, this was written, as Fanny Burney says, "with a very singular mixture of timidity and confidence", and by the time of *Cecilia*, four years later, the latter had prevailed to the extent that it is the insufferably pompous and dishonest Delvile senior who disapproves of young ladies reading and says:

The Spectator, Tatler, and Guardian, would make library sufficient for any female in the Kingdom, nor do I think it like a gentlewoman to have more. (9, ii)

In these novels sympathetic characters typically like novels. Henry Tilney has forbears. The lively curate Mr. Woodcock in *Hermsprong* would write them if he knew more about "human life and character" – and if they were not "pretty generally considered as the lowest of all human productions". And in *Belinda* itself Lady Delacour, one of those racy witty women dear to Maria Edgeworth, and who is really a heroine in spite of her fast *chic*, teases Belinda with:

... you must be elegantly dressed, and you must not wear the same dress on the birthnight... You are thinking you are like Camilla, and I like Mrs. Mittin [i.e. a character absurdly intrusive about getting clothes]. Novel reading – as I dare say you were told by your governess, as I was told by mine, and she by hers, I suppose – novel reading for young ladies is the most dangerous – ...Do, pray, Clarence [to Clarence Hervey, the hero, who has just entered] help me out, for the sake of this young lady, with a moral sentence against novel reading: but that might go against your conscience, or your interest... (v)

There are many other examples.[12] Jane Austen's defence of novels is not a sudden counter-attack on an otherwise benighted world – as she would half have us believe with "almost a general wish of decrying the capacity and undervaluing the labour of the novelist" – but the most scintillating and cogent contribution to a debate already in progress in the best circles.[13] There is a pleasant doubleness in this fact.

Does not this knowledge seem to contradict my general contention that external, specialised, knowledge need not be possessed by a good reader of Jane Austen? If it did it might be a very useful reminder that in order to produce light on their subjects literary arguments not only need not but should not pretend to scientific exactitude, though, of course, they should aspire to rigour. They deal in truths more difficult to phrase and more difficult to enforce, though perhaps easier to apprehend. Disappointingly, however, the chief interest – and the chief reason why the common acceptance of this passage as straightforward 'Jane Austen' is wrong – lies, as we might now expect, not in external literary historical considerations but within the tone and structure of the argument itself and its place in the novel. We should quickly understand that we are being lectured in a manner as exaggerated as Isabella Thorpe's, though with a charm she only looks for, when implausibly told that abridgers and anthologisers "are eulogized by a thousand pens" – and it is wonderful that the dramatisation (and hence the thought) is so thorough that even the young lady caught guiltily reading borrows a tone of sarcastic dismissal: "It is really very well for a novel". More fundamentally the alert reader is likely to question the logic of the relationship claimed with other novelists. "Let us not desert one another; we are an injured body." But who are these (sister?) novelists, and who are the heroines who should patronise them? The novelists are those whose silly works mislead their silly girlish readers, Catherine and Isabella. So at this stage the narrator, despite her decisive manner, is in a way pretending to be at one with the subjects of a great deal of the surrounding parody. However, after the amusing little detection scene, this fine teasing tone changes to produce praise of Fanny Burney and Maria Edgeworth in the highest terms – "the greatest powers of the mind . . . the best chosen language" etc. I do not believe that this could be read as ironical or tongue-in-cheek, even if the description is flattering and might be thought better reserved for Jane Austen herself. (One feels a little annoyed with Maria Edgeworth – who was never sufficiently appreciative of Jane Austen and had found *Emma*, which she could not read beyond the first volume, insipid – for saying, albeit modestly, that *Northanger Abbey* is the "most stupid nonsensical fiction".[14]) This is only a pseudo-problem: no reader is likely to be in doubt of the over-all effect which easily accomplishes a switch in voices from mocking (several things) to sincerity and back again. But airing it might also help to smooth the disquiet occasionally felt over the stringency of the vigorous attack on the *Spectator*. For in a similar way we do not have to think that Jane Austen herself, as opposed to this witty polemicist, held the gossip's view that topics "which no longer concern any one living" are therefore automatically of no interest or importance.[15]

This fine oscillation of meaning in what really is too often blithely welcomed as "one of her own rare outbursts of opinion" is in strict parallel with the more obvious, though usually delicate, oscillation in the way we are invited to respond to Catherine. The silly novel reader is the same person as the honest, courageous and good little adventurer into the world; the vision of one easily alternates with and at the same time informs the vision of the other. And here another problem – and thus another source of possible illumination – presents itself. Everyone agrees, everyone must, that *Northanger Abbey* works through constant reference to other novels. But after this vagueness may overtake the commentator. Is it an attack on them or a defence? On the one hand they are the fantasy works beloved of Isabella and Miss Andrews with their glutinously horrid titles (1, vi) and their preposterous ideas of existence which lead to Catherine's shaming interpretation of every-day life at Northanger and her tender humiliation by Henry Tilney's famous rebuke "Dear Miss Morland, consider the dreadful nature of the suspicions you have entertained..." etc. (2, ix). This is obvious. But on the other hand they are the works explicitly defended as well as joked about in the passage just discussed and which are, in a familiar way, touchstones of taste. Similarly it is obvious that Isabella's dismissal of *Sir Charles Grandison* ("horrid" to her in a sense different from her erotic/melodramatic staple, 1, vi) shows her to be as insincere a reader as she is a lover. John Thorpe's stupidly masculine Oxford-undergraduate "Oh, Lord! not I; I never read novels; I have something else to do" (1, vii, 148), his contradictory admiration for the lurid, if amusing, porno-mystical trash of *The Monk*, and his in every sense Chauvinistic description of Fanny Burney – "that woman they make such a fuss about, she who married the French emigrant" – with his failure to read *Camilla* – "such unnatural stuff" (this from a reader of 'Monk' Lewis) – merely deepens our sense of his boorishness; and Henry Tilney's admiration, even passion, for novels might almost be thought too pat a contrast were it not for the elder brother/lover-like charm with which he expresses it.

What is interesting is that the reader does not have to, indeed should not, settle blandly for either alternative. The novel is everywhere, albeit light heartedly, raising the question of what fiction is like; of how much we learn through imaginative apprehension and how much by direct exposure to the General Tilneys and Isabellas of life – and nowhere settling it except by making credibly happy the heroine who can move from one mode of experience to the other without breaking. This is the point: it is because Catherine is such a believable, silly, candid young person that the idea gets light and air. All readers enjoy the sequence at Northanger in which the bemused creature, who has earlier spiritedly described History as "torment", treats what she has read in the Gothick as fact. We laugh when she half expects to "wait shivering in the cold" in the night until "a faithful old servant frighten[s] one by coming in with a faggot!" – as so many poor girls have been obliged to do" (2, vi, 167); when beginning to suspect murder, she reflects on "how many were the examples to justify even the blackest suspicions" (2, viii, 186–7); when "She could remember dozens" hardened enough in Evil to erect a monument to their murdered wives and yet remain outwardly calm (2, ix, 190) – and so on through the whole comical delusion. It is easy to laugh. Yet – and here the reader must try to be as candid as Catherine is – is this so very far from the way in which fiction is habitually and legitimately taken as part of experience? Granted that she has picked the wrong *genre* for judging likelihoods in "the Midland counties of England", or indeed anywhere real, and is a very naïve reader, is she essentially different from anyone who judges through what they read as well as what they directly experience? Obviously not. Eleanor Tilney acutely says of historians: "In the principal facts they have sources of intelligence ... which may be as much depended on, I conclude, as any thing that does not pass under one's own observation" (1, xiv, 109). And most of us would not know of the existence of China or Peru, for example, and almost nothing of the past, if we did not rely on such intelligence from the outside – constantly – including the special kinds of intelligence yielded in various ways by works of art. It is the highly respectable epistemological category of "knowledge by description" proposed by Bertrand Russell.

This question, to which I alluded earlier when discussing the creative powers of parody, is both so clear to common sense and so laden with philosophical difficulty, that I may rest it here. But on the subject of Catherine's absurdities, could it be that our liking for and intimacy with her, and the consequent warm ease with which every reader will feel entitled, with the Tilneys, to patronise her might lead us to some private admissions? Who can really say – with hand on heart – that a creak in the passage, or a billowing curtain at the suggestible hour, has never caused a moment's unease? – especially after a book or a film, and even if, as with Catherine, any fancies are dismissed with confident scorn until the next gust? Only those perhaps for whom *Northanger Abbey* will have in any case no charm.

Catherine's final disillusion with the Gothick in 2, x beginning: "Charming as were all Mrs. Radcliffe's works ... " is her first act of strict literary criticism. It ends with what might be an optimistic receipt for the subject matter of the realistic[16] novel Jane Austen was learning to write in *Northanger Abbey*:

...among the English she believed, in their hearts and habits, there was a general though unequal mixture of good and bad. Upon this conviction, she would not be surprized if even in Henry and Eleanor Tilney, some slight imperfection might hereafter appear; and upon this conviction she need not fear to acknowledge some actual specks in the character of their father, who, although cleared from the grossly injurious suspicions which she must ever blush to have entertained, she did believe, upon serious consideration, to be not perfectly amiable. (200)

This *is* optimistic, of course. It is quickly followed by the severer shocks of James's and Isabella's letters and the General's real-life ungentlemanlike nastiness. But as a critical view of likelihood, achieved by the first of Jane Austen's wonderful series of abashing, remorseful, educative crises for her heroines (the sort of development not given to Lady Susan), it is the primary immediate charming outcome of the debate about novels in *Northanger Abbey*.[17]

vi

If this is so, if the success of those parts of the novel devoted to literary self-definition (by both protagonist and author) are bound up so integrally with our finding Catherine a genuine heroine as well as a 'heroine', then we should look lastly at an area which is traditionally, even banally, one of the great strengths of the novelist: characterisation. Here, though it is also in the deepest way obvious, there is a revealing and daring piece of work which should in a way be a surprise. Catherine, as well as being unheroic for the purpose of satire and parody, and despite being at the centre of the action in that it is entirely her experience we follow (there is no other), is very unusual indeed in not being even potentially the finest mind or source of judgement in the book. Henry James very influentially elevated the idea of an intelligent central consciousness almost into a structural principle. He even found one in Tom Jones: and most protagonists of novels, however naïve, perverse, misguided or obscured in their beginnings, have at least the abilities for some form of pre-eminence. Even Madame Bovary has this – let alone Emma or Anne Elliot or Fanny Price (in her way). Even Evelina, even Hans Castorp – even, if we let ourselves go, K. More generically local the deluded Arabella of *The Female Quixote* will clearly be a wonderful person once she throws her library of Romances instead of her self into the river. But there is no sense in which even the educated and improved Catherine is seen as being the intellectual core of anything. And although, of course, every reader recognises this and is duly charmed by it, I do not think that Jane Austen's feat of positively celebrating the undeniably vapid, of making the silly modern girl so sweet and lovable – and without the benefit of great attributed beauty either – is sufficiently recognised. It is surely a remarkably sophisticated enterprise for a young novelist, and very original. Even when the feat is brought off elsewhere, as in *Daisy Miller* or with one of the central figures in *War and Peace*, Natasha, it seems to me not quite so calmly, almost provokingly, successful. If we think of "Cecilia, or Camilla, or Belinda", all are exceptionally serious and intellectual young women, even though they are subjected to far more trying adventures (being thought a bastard, going mad and so on).

There is no need to illustrate this point in much detail. The whole novel consists in it. But there is appropriate confirmation in J.F. Burrows's useful *Computation into Criticism*. A relevant graph (No. 14) shows Catherine's voice as being one of the furthest divergents from the "general norms of Jane Austen's dialogue" and as exceeded only by Harriet Smith in *Emma* in "garrulousness and intellectual indiscipline" – whereas Henry Tilney is the most formal speaker in all the novels.[18] In compensation, perhaps, the narratorial voice, which can elsewhere be so famously sharp, is, like Henry, very noticeably tender in its handling of Catherine's youthfulness – almost as tender as it is to "my Fanny" in *Mansfield Park*. When she learns, for example, that she is going to be near the Tilneys for "another three weeks, and her happiness being certain for that period, the rest of her life was at such a distance as to excite but little interest" (2, ii, 138), we feel the charm of truth to nature much more strongly than (what is usually more gratifying) the opportunity to be wise. But the closeness encouraged by Jane Austen's development of free indirect speech, mentioned earlier, more plausibly accounts for a lot of the affection felt for Catherine.

Limited outward developments in her character are easily noticeable: that, for example, it is not only the artless candour of her prattle to those she admires that endears, but also her increasing ability to discriminate in general, and even be firm with those who would exploit her. After enduring with her the galumphing persecutions of John Thorpe and wondering how she can be allowed to put up with them – modest George III young lady and second-cousin to Evelina though she is – it is gratifying to find her quite remarkably distant in her pre-occupied unconsciousness (while he thinks he is intimating marriage to an heiress) in the comedy of misunderstanding in 1, xv, on the occasion of their goodbyes – "'... *you* will not be sorry to see me.' 'Oh! dear, not at all. There are very few people I am sorry to see.'" (123). Her instincts are reliable one feels, so that she is forthright, even to Henry, in her defence of her conventionally swainly brother in 2, iv; and she is quick enough to see through Isabella's letter in 2, xii – "such a strain of shallow artifice could not impose even upon Catherine" (218) – though this *is* after her literary education. Such advances are very clear, even if they testify to a beautifully good nature rather than to intellect. But, more inwardly, our sympathy is involved and confirmed by the intimacy achieved in those innovative passages where we are taken into her mind as she experiences things. I have already discussed the charm generated by the use of her own vocabulary to convey her disappointment in the Pump-room. Now compare the awkward literariness (in 2, vi) that was analysed above – when Catherine first contemplates her room at Northanger – with its continuation in the same chapter later that night. It is a different mode entirely:

> Henry's words, his description of the ebony cabinet which was to escape her observation at first immediately rushed across her; and though there could be nothing really in it, there was something whimsical, it was certainly a very remarkable coincidence!... It was not absolutely ebony and gold; but it was Japan, black and yellow Japan of the handsomest kind; and as she held her candle, the yellow had very much the effect of gold. The key was in the door, and she had a strange fancy to look into it; not however with the smallest expectation of finding any thing, but it was so very odd, after what Henry had said. In short, she could not sleep till she had examined it. So, placing the candle with great caution on a chair, she seized the key with a very tremulous hand and tried to turn it; but it resisted her utmost strength. Alarmed, but not discouraged, she tried it another way; a bolt flew, and she believed herself successful; but how strangely mysterious! – the door was still immoveable. (168)

(She has locked the cabinet.) Here the parody is present in the same terminology and with the same sensation as before, but it is much more powerful – and funnier – because the thoughts really do 'rush across her' within the prose. We are made to dip in and out of Catherine's domestic consciousness. Idioms we must attribute to her rather than the narrator – "certainly a very remarkable coincidence... of the handsomest kind... not... with the smallest expectation of finding any thing... but it was so very odd... how strangely mysterious" – are mixed up with, integral to, the objective account of the action. The effect (including perhaps her allowance for Henry's slight, masculine, mistake about the gold) is very different from being given a humorous version of a Gothick heroine's supposed self-communings *in* Gothick. It is a subtle matter – perhaps I bear too heavily on the first passage – but the result of this kind of writing is to align the amused reader on the side of, inside, the character as opposed to seeing her only as the object of sympathetic farce.

But since Catherine is nevertheless not an *especially* intelligent girl, certainly not a prototype for James's flawed but lucid centres of consciousness, it also follows that the novel must rely to a proportionate extent on the figures surrounding her. Here the art is very strong. Every reader will have an account of the abounding touches, delicate and broad, that serve to make the Thorpes so appalling, the General so impressively yet so pettily dominating, Mrs. Allen so null, James such a stiff booby, Henry so captivating – and so on. It would be tedious and highly unnecessary to go through the book pointing them up here and there. I shall only remark, in passing, some special points of admiration: how quickly and economically the different exuberancies of the first book-chat between Catherine and Isabella, in 1, vi, begins to differentiate the two – for the former novels are objects of genuine enthusiasm, for the latter, occasions for compliment seeking, posing, and a line in flirtatious innuendo which falls on ludicrously deaf ears; how the force of the irritation with the insincere Isabella-type is so strong that when she claims to prefer the country to Bath ("we could not live here for millions", 1, x, 71) the reader's outrage at the empty commonplace is likely to blow away any positive reactions such a correct sentiment might be expected to deserve; and how, in making Eleanor almost as agreeable as Henry, Jane Austen is playing on yet another novelistic convention – that of the contrasted or negative sibling, as in Lord Orville's sister Lady Louisa Larpent in *Evelina* or for that matter Elizabeth Elliot in *Persuasion* (this role is reserved here for the shadowy Frederick).

Furthermore, the brilliance of the secondary characterisation in *Northanger Abbey* also raises and perhaps illuminates a general question about fiction which one is often shy of, and reluctant to address directly because it can sound silly and be discussed finally only in the terms of tautology. What is involved in a work of literature when a figure 'comes alive'? It is a familiar – common in the best sense – and indeed important, casual judgement of novels to say that characters in them do or do not perform this vital act. (It is relevant to mention that some characters in life also do not – or at least that one fails to perceive them doing it.) The process is finally ineffable, a mystery; but casting the eye back over *Northanger Abbey* it seems true, if still abstract, to propose that lifelikeness here is, formally, a matter of characters' having exactly the right amount of the right kind of behaviour given to them at the right time in relation to the whole design. Ciphers, angels, extras, animals, caricatures and even Jamesian "*ficelles*" can seem alive if this condition is fulfilled. If there is too much treatment a character develops into a 'character' or disrupts his context by becoming too interesting – the notorious case being Satan in *Paradise Lost*. If too little there will be, beside the local failure, a sag in the structure where it leans on that part. This formulation is admittedly general and of course in no way supersedes the more important consideration of the quality and vigour of the experience presented. But it is more capacious than the traditional, ancient and respectable demand for 'truth to life' *per se*, which is apt for the main part of realistic novels of the highly wrought Jane Austen kind, but becomes hard to apply at the edges with figures like Lady Catherine de Bourgh or Mr. Allen – or even Sir Walter Elliot – who are in danger of being felt as comic types rather than as the people one might meet. It is also clearly more satisfactory than saying that characters in novels are *like* some other piece of history already known from other sources (proving Valmont from the Chevalier du Boufflers, so to speak); or than approving or disapproving of them, allowing them weight or not, because they embody some evident authorial wisdom or its opposite – they are in favour of being magnanimous, or strive in vain to recompense past misdeeds, for instance. It is important to say that part of Jane Austen's achievement in entering into novel writing is immediately to achieve this balance, exactly. So that Catherine is the centre of a group that gives her just the right amount of support and play, and even the kind and unimaginative Mrs. Morland lives on in the mind. But I shall return to the subject of characterisation quite frequently in what follows.

Chapter Four

Early Works, Traditions, and Critics III: Implications of the Second Chapter of *Sense and Sensibility*

i

Sense and Sensibility is the least thoroughly achieved of Jane Austen's completed novels, and it certainly seems the one furthest away in spirit from the immediate concerns of the modern reader. But it is still a striking and living work of art. To see this the first thing the reader will want to digest is the title, stiff and somewhat forbidding to some. As we know the book started off in the 1790s – written in letters, and known unexceptionably as *Elinor and Marianne*. But by 1811 it acquired, together with its present form – and in a style then current practice – its two apposed, semi-opposed abstract nouns with their hints of philosophical connotations, grander than – or at least different from – those we would naturally supply.

The titles of novels are in any case often their weakest feature. At best they give an interesting interpretation of what follows: the plural of *The Ambassadors* is significant, for instance; or the tenderly ambivalent adjective of *The Great Gatsby* (which so fortunately replaced *Among Ash Heaps and Millionaires* or *The High-Bouncing Lover* in Fitzgerald's imagination); and we can get to be pleased with the grim imposition on to Emma of her married state by *Madame Bovary*. Often titles are neutral but necessarily limited, as in all those identifying a central subject: *Tom Jones* or *Lolita* (though these works could well, if implausibly, be called *England in 1745* and *A European in the United States*). Others are thematic in a general way, such as *Great Expectations* or *War and Peace*, or more specifically and directively so, as in *The Way We Live Now*. But a large proportion are positively misleading because they elevate for attention only a part of the work, and suggest that the reader, willy-nilly, attend to this at the expense of the rest. It is surprising how hard it is, even for the experienced, to broaden out a reading from the narrowing focus imposed by *Ulysses, Nostromo,* or *La Rabouilleuse* (in their various ways). And in this class fall nearly all the psychologically or morally pointed titles of Jane Austen's period: *Patronage, Self-Control, Pride and Prejudice,* of course, and, perhaps most limiting in this respect, *Sense and Sensibility.* I shall say something later on about the slightly arbitrary entitlings of Jane Austen's post-humous published works; the fame and glitter *Pride and Prejudice* let it carry *its* way regardless: but in the present case the offer of two – antique sounding – generalities before the fiction starts can act as a deterrent (just as it is often attractive to the scholar). So I shall consider this problem for a moment, before moving in to the substance of the book.

ii

Even if a possible initial coolness is felt, it is easy enough for the reader of any period to explore and expand the suggestion in the title. Everything important can, as we have seen with *Northanger Abbey,* and as usual with Jane Austen or any really good modern writer, be obtained from *within* the novel. (A fact that becomes even more to the point in reading *Mansfield Park* – see chapter six, below.) For, as we might expect, the meaning and detail of the general qualities proposed quickly receive vivid and entertaining clarification and exemplification through their dramatic application to the evoked experience of Elinor and Marianne.

This is obvious: what is less immediately palatable is that the set and ordered nature of the process is itself an important feature. Modern readers, accustomed and inured by so many successful instances of it, tend to expect everyday realism in a novel unless they are alerted by something like (to borrow an example from Raymond Tallis) goblins in the kitchen. So they may be reluctant to recognise and praise – though they are bound to feel – the sophisticated pleasures of a formal argu-ment in which a pattern of oppositions about prudential behaviour works itself out in balances, correspondences, echoes and appropriate upshots. When if, as here, sense is put beside sensibility with a pithy regularity, in every line so to speak, our general unrecognised as-sumption that novels offer a nearly unmediated imitative account of day-to-day imagined experience begins to feel challenged. We miss what Edith Wharton called, in a different context (late Henry James) the *"human fringes* we necessarily trail after us through life" – we realise

71

that what confronts us is art, and therefore organisation, and therefore not quite the relaxed experience we had assumed.

More serious: the resulting disquiet might lead, perhaps, to a (not entirely flattering) perception that at best we usually order coherently about thirty per cent of what we perceive, and perforce let the rest go into stereotype and fuzz. So if an apparently realistic work offers something like one hundred per cent of meaning, it feels too clear and easy, too symmetrical or too pat to convince – on what we are liable to feel are the sole, or at least the familiar, terms for appreciation. Perceptual sluggishness conspires with preconceptions about the genre to tolerate, then admire, then even require, areas of obscurity (*lifelike* unclarity or profundity). Who but the arrogant or the shallow would sincerely claim that *Ulysses* was wholly clear to them? In addition, a slightly snobbish cultural idea of the desirability of complexity, whether it is actually present or not, and of the mysteriousness of art, whether it is pertinent or not, can seduce us into discriminating against too much light and balance.

Yet these tendencies are based entirely on a confusion about the actual status of novels. Because the fine and cunning art of so many of them is devoted to producing the illusion of almost directly evoked reality (*there* is the mystery perhaps) it is vilely easy to fall into a category mistake which would be unlikely to bother even the most naïve reader when presented with a sonnet, for example, or a highly structured play such as *Twelfth Night*. That part of *Sense and Sensibility* which patently explores the implications of the title offers – very like a Shakespeare comedy, in fact, though freer in some ways – a balanced pattern, the object of which is not primarily to simulate a running report on the fluctuating world, but to create and order imagined experiences into something lucid and comprehensible, which we can then take home and entertain.[1]

iii

In accord with this, and being an early work – not as yet perfectly sure in its flow – *Sense and Sensibility* can, like some of the over-emphasised parts of *Northanger Abbey* we have noticed – though in a different mode – be too overtly explanatory. Sometimes sister speaks to sister, though humorously, with academic deliberation:

> "I thought our judgements were given us merely to be subservient to those of our neighbours. This has always been your doctrine, I am sure."

"No, Marianne, never. My doctrine has never aimed at the sub-jection of the understanding. All I have ever attempted to influence has been the behaviour. You must not confound my meaning. I am guilty, I confess, of having often wished you to treat our acquaint-ance in general with greater attention; but when have I advised you to adopt their sentiments or conform to their judgement in serious matters?" (1, xvii, 94)

But the objection to this, if one is felt, should be that the reader is receiving redundant and rather over-generalised thematic directions – not that Jane Austen, elsewhere so inspired a recorder, is trying and failing to be realistic about the chat between nineteen and seventeen year olds. In later novels such material, completely *typical* in its comic seriousness, would be more naturally woven into the action and dramatised, subsumed. *Sense and Sensibility* differs from *Emma* or *Persuasion* (or from *Middlemarch* or *War and Peace* for that matter, both of which contain comparably weighty conversations) only in the degree of sometimes spare explicitness with which the debate is carried on.

These elementary points about the use of conventions in this genre granted, the reader will swiftly see from within that in spite of the prominence of the advertised primary opposition, the *context* in which it is worked out (and from which it is naturally inseparable) is at least as important as the contrast of qualities itself – it extends further than the moving vicissitudes experienced in the love stories of the two heroines. And the result of this interaction is the expansion of the two simple and perhaps quaint-seeming semi-philosophic categories into something far more permanently available and interesting than any simple titular apposition could imply. Through it sense and sensibility acquire new, delicate, experiential, meanings.

All the other completed Jane Austen novels are led by their heroines. The action evolves from them and through them. Here the exemplary dual theme, and its strict application, seems to dictate that the two remain at first relatively recessed, and relatively, so to speak, trans-parent – although I shall argue that Elinor later acquires more substance and depth as a centre of consciousness. To put it slightly differently: – compared with many eighteenth-century novels – those of Charlotte Smith, for example – the psychology of *Sense and Sensibility* is already rich and flexible: but it is not primary to the book. Rather the *emphasis* is felt to be on the boors, on whom, as often in life, the intelligent and sensitive have to rely for crucial information and whatever societal supports can be wrung out of them. At their mercy, Marianne and

Elinor do not have the full convincing energetic warmth and apparent freedom of speech and action possessed by other Jane Austen heroines (including the timid Catherine Morland). Perhaps this is also simply because there *are* two of them, explicitly sharing amiable qualities in different degrees of intensity, while we tend to admire and love individuals. (At any rate, Jane Austen never wrote of pairs of heroines with so equal an emphasis or sympathy again, even though this involves recessing Jane Bennet a little and sustaining a rather painful loyalty to Fanny Price at the expense of downgrading the enthusiastic Mary Crawford – a creation potentially not unlike Marianne.)

The opening two chapters together establish this balance with a force necessarily, and symptomatically, uneven. In them the nature of the life of the novel is exemplified.

The first chapter – incidentally the very first that Jane Austen published – is perhaps her least lively piece of writing. Its anonymous genealogies and stolid details of inheritance ("The late owner of this estate was a single man . . ." etc., 3) generate none of the brio belonging to the immediate introduction of someone's dauntingly banal views about the marital needs of rich young men of fortune, or to the brisk but subtle adumbration of the situation of a superior girl who has things a little too much her own way. That is to come. Instead an impersonal narrator dryly sets out, in the fashion of an older style of novel, the background to a family which has as yet no purchase on our interest, and then proceeds to make short character sketches. It is no wonder, partly in view of this and some similar later passages, and partly in view of Elinor's tendency to moralise her experience too frequently and too sternly (though it would be hard to over-emphasise the impact of openings on general impressions) that the book is, as I say, relatively unpopular, even with Jane Austen's admirers, and that descriptions can range down from "grey and cool" to "dark and disenchanted".[2] No wonder either, that here there is a little quarry for literary historians unafraid to assimilate genius to mediocrity by pointing out how similar Jane Austen can be to didactic writers of the 1790s – though the version we read was thoroughly revised before publication. No wonder even that it is said to have a relation to eighteenth-century 'conduct books' (a lowering thought).[3] Nevertheless, the diagram presented in this chapter is very firm – designed to stand the strains and complications to which it is afterwards subjected:

Elinor . . . possessed a strength of understanding, and coolness of judgement, which qualified her, though only nineteen, to be the counsellor of her mother, and enabled her frequently to counteract, to the advantage of them all, that eagerness of mind in Mrs. Dashwood which must generally have led to imprudence. She had an excellent heart; – her disposition was affectionate, and her feelings were strong; but she knew how to govern them: it was a knowledge which her mother had yet to learn, and which one of her sisters had resolved never to be taught.

Marianne's abilities were, in many respects, quite equal to Elinor's. She was sensible and clever; but eager in every thing; her sorrows, her joys, could have no moderation. She was generous, amiable, interesting; she was every thing but prudent. The resemblance between her and her mother was strikingly great.

Elinor saw, with concern, the excess of her sister's sensibility; but by Mrs. Dashwood it was valued and cherished . . . (6–7)

These descriptions, with their slightly dulling past tenses, interestingly resemble some inept critical accounts of the upshot of the whole book; but here, in its expository place, the matter-of-fact tone is adequate. The subject and its exemplars are explicit: Sense versus sensibility. Elinor and Marianne. What will become of them? And accordingly there enter soon two appropriate suitors for these disinherited girls: one all rational water and hesitant earth (Edward), one all air and elegant fire (Willoughby); each, it eventually transpires, with an amorous history that does them no credit; and each consequently obliged mysteriously to dissimulate and disappoint,[4] especially when the action moves to disagreeable and confusing London.

This system of balances is supported equally on each side of the question by subsidiary characters: by Mrs. Dashwood herself on the one hand and by good persistent Colonel Brandon – though he is as dramatically null as Marianne at first finds him to be personally – on the other. (It might also have been supported by the one completely superfluous figure in Jane Austen's novels, Margaret, about whose not so talented future we cannot feel the allied anxiety that was presumably the reason for her inclusion in the initial sketch (7) – as it is, she is left completely undeveloped and is, if anything, a miniscule embryo of Mary Bennet.) Such a plain structure means that no reader requires a guide to the detailed to-ings and fro-ings of these characters, and the qualities they embody, though one is often dutifully offered by critics. The actions are as straightforwardly illustrative and evident as they are in fact interesting. And it is equally true – if we look at a passage of representative detail – that no one needs to be informed by a commentator that Marianne's widely recognised romantic glamour, and the real charm of her spontaneous enthusiasm, are qualified dramatically by such drastic egocentric remarks as:

> "A woman of seven and twenty . . . can never hope to feel or inspire affection again, and if her home be uncomfortable, or her fortune small, I can suppose that she might bring herself to submit to the offices of a nurse, for the sake of the provision and security of a wife. In his [Col. Brandon's] marrying such a woman therefore there would be nothing unsuitable. It would be a compact of convenience, and the world would be satisfied. In my eyes it would be no marriage at all, but that would be nothing. To me it would seem only a commercial exchange, in which each wished to be benefited at the expense of the other." (1, viii, 38)

To do her justice, this, like her corresponding positive feelings, stops far short of the flamboyant Rousseau-style *sensibilité* that produced as its obverse the cruelty of the French Revolution; and her argument is actually not so extravagant as may first appear, given the difference in prevailing customs as to marriage – which is at root, I am sure, a difference determined by medical, especially gynaecological, advances in our case (notoriously one of the few certain areas of progress). It is even attractively brave on behalf of the imagined elderly female bargainer. Nevertheless, its ageist *excess* – just beautifully catching that perennial moralising complacency always adjunct to such over-rational speeches – is rebuked in the text and on the spot by Elinor's sensible mockery; rebuked on every reading by every reader; and even taken up in cool retributive justice by Marianne's destiny, already dimly perceived.

iv

So much then, for the moment, of the clarity of the primary interplay of heroines and ideas initiated in the title. But now for its context. The second chapter shifts perspective completely. In pointing to what she says is an extended structural use of a vivid new method of fictional creation, started as we have seen by Jane Austen in *Northanger Abbey*, Marilyn Butler claims that "*Sense and Sensibility* is the first sustained example of 'free indirect speech', for the entire action is refracted through Elinor's consciousness."[5] But this is a premature claim, an exaggeration that importantly omits a piece of bravura comedy – hardly surpassed anywhere in literature for its ruthlessness – and that is remembered by readers of good taste a long time after they have forgotten all the limpid and delicate pros and cons about prudence and feeling, reason and romanticism. Though it is nothing to do with Elinor's mind the conversation in chapter two between John and Fanny Dashwood is often recalled like some scene in Shakespeare or Dickens, or a James Cagney performance – a treat in itself, set off by its predecessor, but not thought to be strongly related to the main effect. Or if it is so related, then tenuously, in a general way, as a curious delicious preliminary negative definition of what, if overdone, being sensible may become. It is all this, but I think it is also placed with a clear provocative intent to initiate the second important thematic drive of the novel – which has as yet only a business relation, as it were, to the heroines, but which is eventually to dominate them. It unfolds in the vein of the comical/awful with a *logic* nearly identical to the following:

Lear	I can be patient; I can stay with Regan,
	I and my hundred knights.
Regan	Not altogether so;
	I look'd not for you yet, nor am provided
	For your fit welcome ...
Lear	Is this well spoken?
Regan	I dare avouch it, sir: what! fifty followers
	Is it not well? What should you need of more? ...
Goneril	Why might you not, my Lord, receive attendance
	From those she calls servants, or from mine?
Regan	Why not, my Lord? If then they chanc'd to slack ye
	We could control them. If you will come to me,
	For now I spy a danger, I entreat you
	To bring but five-and-twenty; to no more
	Will I give place or notice.
Lear	I gave you all –
Regan	And in good time you gave it.
Lear	... [*to Goneril*] I'll go with thee
	Thy fifty yet doth double five-and-twenty,
	And thou art twice her love.
Goneril	Hear me, my Lord
	What need you five-and-twenty, ten, or five,
	To follow in a house where twice so many
	Have a command to tend you?
Regan	What need one?

                                              (2. iv. 232–65)

With a similar lethal rationality John Dashwood, in collaboration with his Fanny, dismantles an intention to fulfil his dying parent's wish with the handsome, though not huge, gift of £3,000. The fascinating pair – really they convince the *reader* almost as well as themselves – go from £1,000 apiece for the sisters to £500 – in consideration of the possible future "numerous family" of the infant Harry (who is obviously a precursor, as soft pretext for the indulgence of the adult *will*, of "dear little Henry" in *Emma* and the "stout, forward" child Walter Musgrove in *Persuasion*); then they switch and descend to an annuity of £100 to Mrs. Dashwood – in consideration of possible fat marriages for the girls; then further to a "present of fifty pounds, now and then" – in consideration of her perhaps living to over fifty-five; and then, since:

> "They will live so cheap! Their housekeeping will be nothing at all. They will have no carriage, no horses, and hardly any servants. They will keep no company . . ." (12)

– Fanny is able to arrive at the pleasing conceit that they "will be much more able to give *you* something", and the couple pass to resentment about breakfast china and the resolution to limit John's largesse to "such kind of neighbourly acts as his own wife pointed out".[6]

The real charm of this slightly insane logic is that there is nothing really wicked about it. It resembles that of Lear's daughters in having its own internal consistency and reductive drive, but there is no provocation to respond at all tragically – as with "O! Reason not the need". Rather we enjoy John Dashwood because what distinguishes him, as Julia Kavanagh remarked in 1862, is "his lukewarm goodwill" and its repeated defeat so that he "stands before us for ever in all his respectable baseness".[7] He is a realistic, even familiar, figure, with no vestige of a metaphysical dimension. And the vein he initiates in chapter two is of mean, slightly timorous, pompous, self-deceiving self-serving – the depiction of which lies near the heart of the book. This wonderfully accomplished scene establishes the tone of much the greater part of the society we then go on to discover in following the progress of Elinor and Marianne. This is to say nothing very new[8] – but it does suggest a stress that counterbalances that of the title. We recognise over and around the axis of sense and sensibility another axis inextricably involved with the definition and operation of these powers. The poles of this are decency and a concern for others which – whether refined or not – can be satisfied with a very moderate style of existence, and, opposite, the idols of selfish, stupid materialism. All the sensibility and most of the sense in fact belong to the former, but the latter, the evocations of which are often subtle but always clearly marked, comes to bear a greater part of the weight.

Such an opposition between her favoured protagonists (whatever may be *their* internal flaws) and a surrounding compromised dullness is, of course, everywhere in Jane Austen: but I find the negative animus strongest of all in this early novel – which is another reason why, parallel to the occasional dryness, it is the least heart-warming and zestful of her works. Against the small core of the good-hearted constituted by our Dashwoods, Edward, Mrs. Jennings, Col. Brandon, Sir John Middleton and (eventually) the Palmers, not all of whom are intelligent, the other characters – with the exception of the more complicated and romantic Willoughby – are more or less ingenious variations on meanness of mind and spirit. They make up jointly a social disaster which is seen in a hard, bright light.

v

This is the general impression. Again I think it so likely to be assented to as obvious when stated, and so obviously commencing right from the second chapter, that a detailed evocation from (yet another) critic is not necessary. The reader is bound to notice things like the brilliant dramatisations of fatuity in, for example, the competitive comparison of children's heights as a social resource (1, xii), or admire the larger scale and more sinister fatuity involved in the terrible petulance and tyrannical inconsequence with which a mother disinherits her elder son – for reasons to do with flattery – in a work where practically every external event hinges on correct property inheritance (and which, curiously therefore, strikes some commentators as a demonstration of the evils of patriarchal ideology[9]). But the negative impetus – a harsher, blacker, thing really than what is often suggested by 'Jane Austen's satire' – produces some interesting effects which do require note and emphasis. One of these, which is useful to any definition of that satire, is that so stripped down and stark a version of the ghastliness of most people (especially when it comes to include even quite nice people such as Sir John Middleton) should make us firmly differentiate Jane Austen from another vein of English social comedy with which her work can be loosely identified.

For one of the positive aspects of the 'gentle Jane' image of Jane Austen, and a reason why I am less ready to be withering about it than are many modern commentators, is her natural association with the whole world of taste and feeling invoked by the mention of Mrs.

Gaskell's *Cranford* (1851–3). Mrs. Gaskell had a superb sensibility in literature. And *Cranford* was obviously influenced by Jane Austen. More importantly, it stands for a powerful sympathetic urge in English sentiment, and therefore in English fiction, in the nineteenth century and afterwards (one thinks of *East Lynne*, of Mrs. Oliphant's Carlingford novels, but also of some of Henry James's gentler accounts of provincial society, particularly in his short stories). This is the benign and creative side to that – on the whole irritating – impression of a genteel Jane Austen which I noted in chapter one as being both absorbed through, and resented by, James (see also chapter six, below). But insofar as it is genuinely related to Jane Austen it is only a pale and refracted impression of the real thing. One must distinguish – and the minor characters – the constituents of the world – in *Sense and Sensibility* offer an apt opportunity. By comparison with the *Cranford* tradition they resemble rather, in their greed and barely competent hypocrisy, characters in Balzac.

It is not that Mrs. Gaskell is unsatirical or unaware. Described from a distance, the idle and stupid Mrs. Jamieson in *Cranford*, the timid and slightly spiteful Miss Pole, Mrs. Fitz-Adam and Miss Betty Barker (heavily aspiring to a spurious gentility), the cruelly repressed and repressive Miss Jenkyns, the pathetically inept and unfulfilled Miss Matty, and above all the amused, intelligent, slightly detached narrator, might come straight from Jane Austen's minor work, or indeed from Fanny Burney. There are even passages strongly suggestive of Jane Austen's manner of humorous critique through pathetic cultural pretensions. In Mrs. Jamieson's drawing-room:

> There was a japanned table devoted to literature on which lay a Bible, a Peerage, and a Prayer-Book. There was another square Pembroke table dedicated to the Fine Arts, on which were a kaleidoscope, conversation-cards, puzzle-cards (tied together to an interminable length with faded pink satin ribbon), and a box painted in fond imitation of the drawings which decorated tea-chests. Carlo lay on the worsted-worked rug, and ungraciously barked at us as we entered. (Ch. 8, 'Your Ladyship')

But adjacent to and informing this is a vision entirely different from that of the earlier writer. Jane Austen frequently forgives the tedious and inept among her creations, especially on grounds of basic good nature (Mrs. Jennings, for example, or Miss Bates in *Emma*). But this has to be earned – people such as Mrs. Ferrars and Robert or Lucy Steele have no redeeming features, and there is no warm assumption about universal warmth and frailty. Whereas Mrs. Gaskell seems to raise the possibilities of genuine pain or really harsh consequences in her stratified little society only to step carefully away from them. Over the sharp concrete observation of petty lives there creeps a roseate glow which is perhaps *too* familiar to the British. Crucially, in the 'Friends in Need' episode in *Cranford* (ch. 14) when Miss Matty loses all her money (by the failure of what it is implied is a fraudulent bank, innocently but obstinately invested in by her late sister), this is not so that the reader should see her cast, Flaubert-wise, into real hardship, or that she and we should be invited to ponder the dark side of the genteel, idle, life which has been floated for her and her acquaintance by a naïve capitalism. On the contrary, it is so that her timid integrity can find expression in her paying a farmer real gold for his now worthless banknote (touchingly unmethodical), her servant show a moving and immovable self-sacrificial loyalty, and her friends, snobbish and foolish as they remain, supply their wonderfully tactful, ludicrous – but sterling – support. This vision has a deep fictive charm, and it would be crude to call it unthinkingly sentimental – one might note that the profounder satire of George Eliot is similarly qualified at times by the explicit desire for a warmth and ideality that she found wanting in Jane Austen.[10] But such Victorian consolations and elevations would blunt the bleak truths that stem from the harshness of *Sense and Sensibility*. I shall now look at aspects of two of these.

vi

The really amusing point about the unsympathetic world surrounding the sisters lies often in its banality, its commonplace lack of exciting evil, or exciting anything. We have observed this being established in the lambent chapter two. I shall expand on it shortly.

But before going on to explore its fuller implications, I want to suggest, as a preliminary, something which is portentous for Jane Austen's development: the interesting and even surprising results that occur from the dramatising of various forms of behaviour that come out of the banal *norm*, but veer away from it. For this will bring out again how relatively mild the creative charge behind the depiction of the heroines is, as compared with that behind that of their environment.

A lot has been written about the intensity of Marianne's suffering. In a way this is just. She is in outline a heroine of great dignity – a noble creature conceived almost in the Corneilleian mode compared with, say, Catherine Morland (Catherine is actually slightly 'older' than she is – an observation that underlines the different modes of the two novels).

She certainly impresses some readers. Marvin Mudrick, possibly dazzled by his own vigour, argues that, in effect, the depth of her conception defeats the author's own moral pattern; and Tony Tanner caps this with an account of her pain so enthusiastic that it overflows into the notion that the near fatal chill she catches is "psycho-somatic" – when really, according to the novel, it is the result of "sitting in her wet shoes and stockings" (3, vi, 306: though it is true that these are wet because only wild walks at Cleveland will satisfy her idea of her own romantic nature).[11] But at whatever level we see her, she is certainly conceived as a thoroughly superior girl whom it is a shame to offend – which is why the reader shares powerfully in the shock and anger at Willoughby's betrayal. Even the silly things she says confirm the impression of her fine direct honesty – as does her silence when faced with Lucy Steele's wheedling (1, xx, 122). Nevertheless, since the novel really is written mainly round the consciousness of Elinor, Marianne's sufferings tend to be things we are told about rather than feel dramatically. So that, for example, when on receipt of the coarse and dishonest letter supposedly from Willoughby she covers her face and "almost screamed with agony" (2, vii, 182), the effect is certainly powerful – is jarringly unpleasant in fact – but is still only the *idea* of intense suffering. The language is plain, merely descriptive: and it is that which jars because – like that of Catherine's first impressions at Northanger – it is too directly the vocabulary of sensation.

It is, therefore, in the sister's environment, in the parts of the book which surround the ostensible sense/sensibility subject, that there occur other, less obvious, kinds of extremity which strike and interest the thoughtful reader in a more solid and telling way. This is where Jane Austen's special perceptive talents seem to fizz. To start again in chapter two: what should one make of Fanny Dashwood's remark, embedded in the centre of an apparently rational meanness, that "if you observe, people always live for ever when there is any annuity to be paid them" (10)? Perhaps these are the exaggerations of an overreaching cupidity – and her imprecision the kind of verbal insensitivity she shares with Lady Middleton, who dislikes the satirical without being clear as to what it is (2, xiv, 246), and Sir John who comically persists in his coarse jovialities about "setting one's cap at a man" and "making a conquest" in the face of Marianne's unavailing scorn (1, ix, 45). But, as these other observations indicate, Jane Austen is usually very sharp about language, and Fanny's "always" and "for ever" are lunatic terms about something that cannot be observed – and seem more appropriate to teenage chatter *à la* Isabella Thorpe than to the scheming marital persuasions of this coldly correct woman. Are we to gather from

Fanny's language something about her emotional drives and spiritual impoverishment? Or is she just the vehicle for a sharp piece of wisdom which had to find its place somewhere – and not in the mouth of a sympathetic character? It is hard to tell. But the suggestion of a deeper observation cannot be dismissed, for later such oddities are re-produced and extended.

How powerful the Palmers are at first, yet how obvious. The frank unrestraint of their marriage – farcically at odds over everything – seems initially to stem from an older and broader comic tradition. "You and I, Sir John" says Mrs. Jennings in their presence "should not stand upon such ceremony" (as that of the genteel modern Lady Middleton who insists on tit-for-tat dinner invitations):

"Then you would be very ill-bred," cried Mr. Palmer.
"My love, you contradict every body," – said his wife with her usual laugh. "Do you know that you are quite rude?"
"I did not know I contradicted any body in calling your mother ill-bred."
"Aye, you may abuse me as you please," said the good-natured old lady, "you have taken Charlotte off my hands, and cannot give her back again. So there I have the whip hand of you."
Charlotte laughed heartily to think that her husband could not get rid of her; and exultingly said, she did not care how cross he was to her, as they must live together. It was impossible for any one to be more thoroughly good-natured, or more determined to be happy than Mrs. Palmer. The studied indifference, and the discontent of her husband gave her no pain: and when he scolded or abused her, she was highly diverted.
"Mr. Palmer is so droll!" said she in a whisper, to Elinor. "He is always out of humour." (1, xx, 111–12)

The quirks and unconscious self-betrayals of more or less gentrified 'Cits' are common joking matter for eighteenth-century novelists (mediated most directly to Jane Austen by Fanny Burney perhaps – probably especially through her Branghtons? – but stretching back at least as far as Dekker and Ben Jonson and early Shakespeare). Naturally Jane Austen is miles above any prissy snobbery common in such portrayals, and it is one of the triumphs of the book that Mrs. Jennings is beautifully characterised by the way that her good deeds and good nature shine through the excruciating commercial and mundane metaphors which she coins to encapsulate the finer operations of the spirit in other characters – "One shoulder of mutton, you know, drives another down" she comfortingly says of Col. Brandon's chances with Marianne after Willoughby has disappeared (2, viii, 197).

But Jane Austen's deployment of less amiable specimens of this type – like the Palmers at first – reveals even more of the *potentials* of her art. These personages usually start as kinds of walking, predictable, joke, reminiscent of the comic stage, and for which 'caricature' is nearly but not quite the right word. One is not invited to be at all inward with such secondary phenomena.[12] They do not penetrate into introspection, but bustle around the fringes and backgrounds of the stories in which the vibrant heroines and heroes enact their destinies. In fact, they can be found lurking within most of these fictional structures we are content to call realistic – and I suspect that this is consonant with how we take actual people we know only slightly (though we do not think we *should*). The corner chemist, the bus conductor and the Professor of Political Science all seem to act out their predictable little side roles in our dramas, and it is disconcerting (and usually quickly forgotten) if they show any raw individuality. Stars, no doubt, in their own stories, they are extras in ours. If we want to take them as substantially human we need to extend a more sensitive apprehension – for which it is hard to find the time or ability. As will be argued in relation to *Pride and Prejudice* and *Emma*, in literature such figures – the Mr. Cumming and Mr. Gowing of *The Diary of a Nobody* – are essential supports of the posited world, though in later Jane Austen they tend to be refined, integrated and made more substantial in such creations as Mr. John Knightley in *Emma* or Mrs. Clay in *Persuasion*. (They also have a relationship to another type obviously dear to her: the amiably insensitive older man such as Sir John Middleton in this novel and Admiral Croft in *Persuasion*.)

But to revert to the Palmers: the pervasive practice in *Sense and Sensibility* tends to be less comfortable than the above description suggests. It is more cutting, more like the hard side of Dickens in his creation of Uriah Heep or the lawyer-ghoul Vholes in *Bleak House*. In the passage above (as in their previous appearances) the brutal aggressiveness of Mr. Palmer and the apparent happy mindless invulnerability of his wife have an almost surreal effect. They seem to exist in a state where normal consequences are suspended. Nobody appears to notice properly the feelings of anybody else. Even benign Mrs. Jennings produces a typically robust metaphorical interpretation of familial power relations while seemingly unaware of its harsh implication. Perhaps they *have* no feelings and are really to be seen as George III 'humour' figures – Mrs. Folly, Mr. Surly and Mrs. Jolly? But no: Jane Austen invokes the drastic convention only to employ the reader's acceptance of it to go deeper into her subject. Elinor penetrates immediately to an interpretation of Mr. Palmer's behaviour that is not at all more cheerful, but very much more psychologically telling. *This* is why people behave like Punch and Judy:

> Elinor was not inclined, after a little observation, to give him credit for being so genuinely and unaffectedly ill-natured or ill-bred as he wished to appear. His temper might perhaps be a little soured by finding, like many others of his sex, that through some unaccountable bias in favour of beauty, he was the husband of a very silly woman, – but she knew that this kind of blunder was too common for any sensible man to be lastingly hurt by it. – *It was rather the wish of distinction she believed, which produced his contemptuous treatment of every body, and his general abuse of every thing before him. It was the desire of appearing superior to other people.* The motive was too common to be wondered at; but the means, however they might succeed by establishing his superiority in ill-breeding, were not likely to attach any one to him except his wife. (1, xx, 112, my italics)

Elinor is far from infallible, and this has a slight note of the catty which some readers – often with the pleasure of a superiority they rashly assume to be shared – confuse with that of the author: but it is very likely, very lifelike and very much like that movement of focus onto the substantiality of others that I have argued is difficult to make in ordinary, fleeting experience. Moreover, it arms the reader with a key or method for reading further. The full realisation, through the fastidious Marianne, of the coarsely kind virtue of Mrs. Jennings is the obvious case in point (though it seems probable that, as she wrote or revised deeper into novel writing, Jane Austen softened the presentation of this character, as of subsequently the Palmers, away from the harmful obtrusiveness in her first conception). But we are also led to see something similar about Mrs. Palmer, initially without the mediation of Elinor (who has rested at her judgement of a "very silly woman") or Marianne, when the sisters arrive at Cleveland in 3, vi:

> ... the rest of the morning was easily whiled away, in lounging round the kitchen garden, examining the bloom upon its walls, and listening to the gardener's lamentations upon blights, – in dawdling through the green-house, where the loss of her favourite plants, unwarily exposed, and nipped by the lingering frost, raised the laughter of Charlotte, – and in visiting her poultry-yard, where, in the disappointed hopes of her dairy-maid, by hens forsaking their nests, or being stolen by a fox, or in the rapid decrease of a promising young brood, she found fresh sources of merriment. (303)

Here the laughter is so obviously that of hopes dashed that we are led to reflect that a similar process might determine her reactions to her husband's brusqueries – at first sight so mechanical. It seems the response of nervous hurt as well as of silliness – and for a moment the characterisation deepens towards the interestingly painful. Elinor's attitude now seems merely fair, whereas it is usually *more* generous than the reader is inclined to be:

> The openness and heartiness of her manner, more than atoned for that want of recollection and elegance, which made her often deficient in the forms of politeness; her kindness, recommended by so pretty a face, was engaging; her folly, though evident, was not disgusting, because it was not conceited; and Elinor could have forgiven every thing but her laugh. (304)

The hard mean world is sometimes just about tolerable.

Reading in this way may even lead to a limited compassion for another at first grotesque figure. Anne Steele's maddening vulgar chirpiness, her clearly rather *passé* slang about beaux etc. has a freedom from the educated that shames the canny Lucy:

> "Norland is a prodigious beautiful place, is not it?" added Miss Steele.
> "We have heard Sir John admire it excessively," said Lucy, who seemed to think some apology necessary for the freedom of her sister. (1, xxi, 123)

The apology is presumably pointed at the diction as well as the over-familiar question. But Anne – Nancy to friends – is undeterred, with her "Nay" and "an't", "vast many", "as lief be" and "dress smart and behave civil" chattering fluently off. She is much less in control of her language than Fanny Dashwood in chapter two. Later in Kensington Gardens she reports unstoppably on the banishment of the Steeles from the Dashwood's house, and on Edward's honouring of his engagement to Lucy:

> "I am monstrous glad of it. Good gracious! I have had such a time of it! I never saw Lucy in such a rage in my life. She vowed at first she would never trim me up a new bonnet, nor do any thing else for me again; but now she is quite come to, and we are as good friends as ever. Look, she made me this bow to my hat, and put in the feather last night. There now, *you* are going to laugh at me too. But why should not I wear pink ribbons? I do not care if it *is* the Doctor's favourite colour . . ." etc. (3, ii, 272)

And she continues in this vein until she comes to some consolation for her disaster:

> "... to be sure they did send us home in their own chariot, which was more than I looked for. And for my part, I was all in a fright for fear your sister should ask us for the huswifes she had gave us a day or two before; but however, nothing was said about them, and I took care to keep mine out of sight." (275)

This thin pathos – she has gone on for four pages – together possibly with the fact that we already intuit what Jane Austen drastically confirmed outside the novel, that "she never succeeded in catching the Doctor" (quoted in the *Memoir of Jane Austen*) may incline to pity as well as to social despair. As in the case of Mrs. Palmer, the inconsequence of a comic character can be taken to imply suffering. Occasionally Jane Austen shows for her mean-minded creations the same kind of flickering magnanimity (though not, of course, on the same scale) as does Wagner for Beckmesser in *Die Meistersinger*. Anne is nearly thirty; ignorant and stupid; chanceless and never likely to live properly – and, unlike her sister, not particularly malicious. The painfulness of her situation is not dwelt upon or further explored – or enveloped in any *Cranford*-style warmth. But the negative prospects of a spinster trapped in this society are firmly indicated – to be taken up in a fuller and more moving way in Miss Bates.

These are some of the ideas generated by Jane Austen's hard look at trivia. The fine little dramatisations teeter on the edge between farce and pathos and they imply the *same* keen observation as other, quite different, insights which are scattered throughout the book. The remark about the pleasures to be derived from pain in Marianne's career of suffering, for instance: "In such moments of precious, of invaluable misery, she rejoiced in tears of agony to be at Cleveland" (3, vii, 303) is a moment of high realistic penetration, though not unique to Jane Austen. So is Willoughby's refutation of the commonplace account of the classic figure of a maiden betrayed when he justly protests to Elinor, during his confession about the younger Eliza, that it would be false to suppose that "because she was injured she was irreproachable, and because *I* was a libertine, *she* must be a saint" (3, viii, 322). This has a whiff of La Rochefoucauld, a whiff of the writer of *Lady Susan*; it at once lifts us out of identification with Elinor's point of view, and at the same time enhances our respect for her ability to cope with such truths.

However, to insist too much on this side of things would be to falsify the main drift of this novel. Behaviour in its bleak *milieu* may have edges that invite or imply a more compassionate, George Eliot-like glance, but my second suggestion about the banal norm which surrounds the sympathetic little cluster of people at the centre must be to emphasise how brilliantly, comically and nastily banal it after all is. For example: immediately after we are invited to enter into the Palmer's marriage in the more understanding manner indicated above, our nascent sympathies are amusingly dried up. Mr. Palmer, after all:

> ... was nice in his eating, uncertain in his hours; fond of his child, though affecting to slight it; and idled away the mornings at billiards, which ought to have been devoted to business. (3, vi, 304–5)

For the well-judging Elinor even the sex of the offspring of such parents – "it" – with their "Epicurism ... selfishness ... and ... conceit" (305) is a matter of indifference. And in view of what they say and do we feel that she is likely to be right. Our incipient interest in them as offering interesting psychological cases is deflated. The *forte* of this part of the novel – as opposed to the equally hard-seeing but deeper dramatisations through their heroines in *Mansfield Park*, *Emma* and *Persuasion* – is in the unrelenting scorn of its observation, the glittering series of harsh comical negatives initiated in the second chapter. The consequent relative denial of complexity of course makes *Sense and Sensibility* a lesser work – it is, after all, in conception earlier than *Northanger Abbey*, and the manifesations of a pure "regulated hatred" tend to be in the early work. But it also allows a certain comic freedom to enforce and reinforce points which a more rounded and humane character-isation might blur: it is the art of Ben Jonson rather than Shakespeare, of the polemic rather than the fully balanced statement.

To return to John Dashwood for another example in comic form: we know that for him an attractive and marriageable woman is a large piece of capital, or an estate, plus, if required, "those little attentions which ladies can so easily give" (2, xi, 223); and that he "had just compunction enough for having done nothing for his sisters himself, to be exceedingly anxious that everybody else should do a great deal" (228). So far not unreasonable, and certainly not unfamiliar, attitudes – though, of course, crass in their effects. But what is so reassuring about the book, what gives such a feeling of complete *integration*, is the certainty with which these touchingly predictable views will be held up and scored off whenever he appears. There is no room in Jane Austen –

and this in its full rigour is probably new to the novel with her – for a neutral passage of narration, for getting on with the action in a purely functional way. This uncomplicated type of a figure is there to be pilloried again and again, be it ever so unobtrusively. When the sisters are about to leave London, for example:

> One other short call in Harley-street, in which Elinor received her brother's congratulations on their travelling so far towards Barton without any expense, and on Colonel Brandon's being to follow them to Cleveland in a day or two, completed the intercourse of the brother and sisters in town; – a faint invitation from Fanny to come to Norland whenever it should happen to be in their way, which of all things was the most unlikely to occur, with a more warm, though less public, assurance, from John to Elinor, of the promptitude with which he should come to see her at Delaford, was all that foretold any meeting in the country. (3, vii, 301)

Read neutrally this does just retail facts and get on with the story, with a slight glance at Fanny (which in a later work would not need the underlining it receives). Read in the context of John's humours it is redolent of his rich man's meanness (the expenses) and his self-exculpating deluded hopes about Elinor catching Col. Brandon (directly, and in the "more warm" hint about Delaford). We also deduce – once more – from the relative privacy of his warmth, that he is afraid to be too nice to his sister in front of his formidable wife and mother-in-law. A base immortal indeed.

viii

So much for this created world: in its own manner just as cruel, obtuse and asking to be despised by the reader as that of any of the Reeds, Ingrams or Brocklehursts in *Jane Eyre*, though not denounced with the same passionate *naïveté*. It is a panorama of the quarrelsome, bitchy and money-proud – all lacking in self-knowledge. Again the clarity with which it is created and exposed renders more extended exposition critically unnecessary. There is, however, a result at which we should glance again: that the full apprehension of this context naturally and continually redefines and qualifies our appreciation of sense and sensibility.

The chief thing it leads us to see is that these are qualities, although no doubt naturally present, which are to be deployed as *defences* in a largely hostile environment. It is a commonplace about the novel that both Elinor and Marianne exhibit both sense and sensibility. Indeed, as Mudrick perceptively argues,[13] Marianne's use of her idealist sensibility as a mode of judgement – though hardly ironical – is initially potentially accurate, as well as extremely attractive. Her championship of intuitive valuation, for example, is articulate and compelling:

> "You are mistaken, Elinor," said she warmly, "in supposing I know very little of Willoughby. I have not known him long indeed, but I am much better acquainted with him, than I am with any living creature in the world, except yourself and mama. It is not time or opportunity that is to detemine intimacy; – it is disposition alone. Seven years would be insufficient to make some people acquainted with each other, and seven days are more than enough for others." (1, xii, 58–9)

That the specific action of the novel shows her (and Elinor) to be wrong about Willoughby does not mean that we are to be contemptuous or dismissive of such generous principles. She is, after all, completely right by instinct about the John Dashwoods, Lady Middleton, Mrs. Ferrars, Lucy Steele and so on; she comes to value Mrs. Jennings (admittedly after a longer acquaintance); and eventually we learn that she is not so very mistaken in Willoughby after all. The trouble is that she is so dashing as to leave her sister to do the day-to-day protective work demanded for tranquillity. She is fine in defence of Elinor's screens from Mrs. Ferrars ("it is Elinor of whom *we* think and speak", 2, xii, 235 – fine like Mary Crawford on a similar fiery occasion) – but this is a special and dramatic moment. Usually she has to be shielded. Notably:

> ...upon Elinor...the whole task of telling lies when politeness required it, always fell. (1, xxi, 122)

Everybody quotes this remark; I suppose because everybody who has ever had a haughty and sensitive friend or relative must have felt its truth, and things have not changed.[14] But we should also remember that it is the very nature of the environment envisioned and created in *Sense and Sensibility* that makes such prudence a bread-and-butter necessity as opposed to a temperamental or theoretical preference. In a maze of Ferrarses and Steeles etc., one would not survive in the least comfort without it. (Marianne only just does survive – it being one of Jane Austen's plays on novel convention, though not in the joking manner of *Northanger Abbey*, that a rebuffed heroine *can* live through a fever.)

Correspondingly, the inner picture of Elinor's coping with aggressive vacuity is not solely, or really, an illustration of the fairly dry idea that a person of sense will develop the willingness and ability to descend to social manoeuvring. Her response to the challenges posed in her world is not so simple as that – for it is only in *relative* terms that this heroine is transparent.

Melancholy from fairly early on about Edward's unsatisfactory withdrawals and his lack of any apparent drive either for an occupation or a wife, she finds Boethian comfort in a thought here phrased in a staple late eighteenth-century manner, but which spans the ages. Achieving internal solitude:

> Her mind was inevitably at liberty; her thoughts could not be chained elsewhere; and the past and the future, on a subject so interesting, must be before her, must force her attention, and engross her memory, her reflection, and her fancy. (1, xix, 105)

Despite such philosophical resource, however, much of the book shows her actively grappling with the dreary social world – shows it so dramatically and from moment to moment that what is often thought of as a somewhat forbidding and schematised sketch becomes in this respect the portrait of a very sympathetic young woman. I suspect that the main difficulty really felt with Elinor is the result of the tepidity of her relation to Edward – he being hard to see in any relation at all because he is such a nonentity, even at times disagreeable, and not giving off even a hint of glamour either in conception or realisation. Otherwise, while she may be less completely lovable than other Jane Austen heroines – and, of course, lacks the inimitable *élan* of Elizabeth Bennet or Emma (or Lady Susan) – it is precisely her beautiful thoughtfulness and moderation in the face of galling tedium and provocation that can, with a little patience, endear us. She is the prototype of Anne Elliot while being perfectly herself. When the reader feels outrage at Willoughby for his treatment of Marianne at the "insufferably hot" and meaninglessly splendid party in 2, vi, then relief must follow from these reflections on it:

> Her indignation would have been still stronger than it was, had she not witnessed that embarrassment which seemed to speak a consciousness of his own misconduct, and prevented her from believing him so unprincipled as to have been sporting with the affections of her sister from the first ... Absence might have weakened his regard ... that such a regard had formerly existed she could not bring herself to doubt.
>
> As for Marianne, on the pangs which so unhappy a meeting must already have given her, and on those still more severe which might

await her in its probable consequence, she could not reflect without the deepest concern. Her own situation gained in the comparison . . . (178–9)

Such candid reactions are almost as natural in Elinor as meanness is to her step-brother, though not at all easy or mechanical. And it is this feeling rationality that gradually defines the positive side of 'sense'. It is manifest throughout, but perhaps the force of the concept or code is most fully felt, at least retrospectively, when it is most under challenge. The challenge is from inside. But it is a response to the development of the most dramatic and troubling – though, because of Willoughby's relative superiority, not precisely banal – transgression to issue from the conventional society in the novel. There is something peculiarly fraught and *nerveuse* in Elinor's response to his exciting scene of repentance in 3, viii. This is itself a fine piece of work, even though it resembles in its sudden block of revelation a reversion to an earlier, less developed, kind of novel than the fully integrated drama Jane Austen was evolving. One particularly admires the artistic decision to have him play it before Elinor rather than his victim, for her response is of the highest thematic and human interest. In spite of being greatly "softened" by what he says, she is able at first to offer herself a completely fair *moralisation*, an epitome of sense about the society we have observed through and about her:

> Her thoughts were silently fixed on the irreparable injury which too early an independence and its consequent habits of idleness, dis-sipation, and luxury, had made in the mind, the character, the happiness, of a man who, to every advantage of person and talents, united a disposition naturally open and honest, and a feeling, affec-tionate temper. The world had made him extravagant and vain – Extravagance and vanity had made him cold-hearted and selfish. Vanity, while seeking its own guilty triumph at the expense of another, had involved him in a real attachment, which extravagance, or at least its offspring, necessity, had required to be sacrificed. (331)

And she continues in this strong, somewhat Johnson-like, vein. She has responded with what Marilyn Butler terms the "objective morality" of the Christian heroine of the period.[15] The moral and psychological vocabulary is one we still naturally use – although we may sometimes be unable to feel all of its firm confidence of definition when we do so. However, there follows a little series of modifying actions, often commented on but rarely satisfactorily resolved. On Willoughby's departure Elinor begins to manifest some of the charm commonly inherent in relenting against reason. She thinks of him "with a tenderness, a regret" unworthily caused (according to the Christian moralist) by his good looks and openness (3, ix, 333) – by his wonderful style, in short, which we have experienced earlier and might even like to see expanded further. Sleepless and exhausted that night she thinks of him as "poor Willoughby" and has the most unChristian wish "for a moment" that he might be freed by the death of his wife to marry Marianne and thus be kept in the family – which is itself corrected not by the application of a general religious or moral scruple, but only by remembering the desserts of poor Col. Brandon (3, ix, 334–5). In short, she is much more moved than her perfectly upright mind should allow. And the feeling is not just a reaction produced by the shock of the visit, the joy of Marianne's simultaneous recovery, and general overstrain: some time afterward (it is uncharacteristically not clear whether this is a few days – 335 – or the next day – 336), when Mrs. Dashwood makes a typically enthusiastic attempt to elevate Col. Brandon's stock in comparison, Elinor silently "could not quite agree" (338) and though wishing success to "her friend" the Colonel continues naggingly to feel her really unjustifiable "pang for Willoughby" (339). Clearly for her his glamour is never going to be assailable.

The point of this sequence is a matter for disagreement.[16] I think that Elinor's feeling response, its *lack* of rigid objectivity – although that objectivity has been attained and is afterwards reverted to – is entirely favourable to the way we see her. It makes her human in an obvious way within the interplay of the given ideologies. In retrospect it seems a clue to the way in which Jane Austen's genius was to develop, into the presentation in novels of a real, fallible consciousness. The abstract of 'sense' is given extra life and interest and substance when, at the moment it is most needed, we see it to be most faltering. Furthermore, casting the mind back over the action, this episode is likely to give an even stronger weight to the *emotional* constituent in Elinor's typically fair and balanced response to events. This, added to Marianne's nearly tragic stature, further highlights the sisters *contra* their unfeeling, unintelligent world. And if that makes them appear vulnerable – almost victims – so the more will we value in its turn Elinor's protective sense.

ix

So what of the happy end of the book with all its obvious counter-romantic ironies, prudent settlements, vindications of second attachments, acceptance of flannel waistcoats, and so on? Like some other

Jane Austen heroines Elinor is not given a proposal scene, and it is clear that few readers are keen to make the considerable effort and investment in thinking coolly about what constitutes a virtuous man and a good husband which alone could produce *pleasure* in Marianne's toned down marriage – though of course we accept it all. Everything is correct, but everything is reduced. Every virtuous character is happy, but our share of the happiness is insipid. It feels a little like the ending of *Rasselas* (and that book's strange mirror in *Candide*) in its turning away from a world that has been shown to be of little comfort or cheer, to a kind of worthy reclusiveness – though here presumably the wishes of the characters have been "obtained". The muting is highly deliberate, even to giving Willoughby the compromised peace of *l'homme moyen sensuel* (3, xiv, 379). But somewhere the energy is lost in the appropriateness. The main disappointment to sentiment ought not to be Marianne's marriage, which has been so heavily determined by the structure; but rather the impression that it is indeed a dull world in which the interesting and sensitive, if sensible, Elinor can be left in a happy love marriage wishing mainly for "rather better pasturage for their cows" (3, xiv, 375) – upon which we leave her.

This effect is the appropriate outcome of what have become the novel's central drives, and is necessary to their completion. A formal ending has in any case its own requirements. But it makes entire sense overall that the liveliest piece of writing in the final chapter is not about the heroines and possibly sympathetic people, but a sharply sarcastic attack on the world they live in – or just out of. It is a serious version of the piquant mock moral-drawing at the end of *Northanger Abbey* ("I leave it to be settled by whomsoever it may concern . . ." etc.):

> The whole of Lucy's behaviour in the affair, and the prosperity which crowned it, therefore, may be held forth as a most encouraging instance of what an earnest, an unceasing attention to self-interest, however its progress may be apparently obstructed, will do in securing every advantage of fortune, with no other sacrifice than that of time and conscience . . . (3, xiv, 376)

(One just wishes dimly that Anne is made fairly comfortable – though, of course, Lucy is not really happy.) Such unillusioned truths, free from bitterness because of the unresentful clarity in which they appear, are the main truths to be taken from the book. They are also its most comfortable entertainment – for the striving after duty and self-discipline that is embodied in Elinor is something most of us spend our lives (sheltered perhaps by the external pressures of making a living) trying to avoid. We like to feel free to pursue what we happen to desire, vaguely in hope that our desires will turn out in some way to be virtuous, or at least consonant with virtue. The hard world of *Sense and Sensibility*, like that of the much more complex *Emma* later, does not, for all its glittering humour, much encourage such hopes. There could hardly be a greater proleptic contrast in tone than that with its brilliant successor, *Pride and Prejudice*.

Chapter Five

Questions about
Pride and Prejudice

I shall try to pay tribute to the ease of Jane Austen's most popular novel, and her favourite, by a variation in critical form.

In view of the argument in this work that the novels do not require, though they may on occasion benefit from, a fully armed and authority-laden academic approach, it seems to me apt to *represent* this conviction – as well as further asserting it – by casting this chapter in a more colloquial mode, with a minimum of references and footnotes,[1] and in the shape of a dialogue. The idea is of a lightly dramatised talk about books – or, literally, 'book-chat' (Gore Vidal's generic name for literary criticism).

I want also to create an opportunity to test and stabilise my high claims for Jane Austen by availing myself initially of a minor *advocatus diaboli*. I think there is a place and a use for a voice that can be sceptical of those simple assumptions of significance and *importance* that we tend to bring automatically to classic novels; and that has even the liberty to be philistine – though not uneducated. Such a voice is, naturally, rarely present in books on Jane Austen. But it is heard often enough in the world; and it can phrase, in face of the first undoubted masterpiece, a few of the larger-scale general objections that might be made to the scope of her art (some of these have been touched on in chapter one, and are to be considered further in chapter seven). Naturally there must also be a voice which answers. For convenience both are allowed to quote with unnaturistic accuracy, and at large: the questioner is called Alec, and the answerer, or defender, Henry. And this being to some extent a conversion narrative, the former will be heard mostly at first, and later mostly the latter.

The possible advantages are – not to mention the lack of clutter – a flexibility, suggestiveness and capaciousness made available, even enforced, by the form.[2]

The dialogue starts in the middle, with an answer.

Questions *about* Pride and Prejudice

i

Henry Jane Austen's popularity? You doubt whether so bright and easily available a comedy can be really great Art – art even in the same class as Shakespeare and Homer and Dante and Goethe and so on? World-historical art? Well, I won't insult you with the obvious arguments that intelligence and memorability and depth clearly don't require grandeur or breadth of subject – the latter in fact often go with stupid and superficial work. Breadth of *appeal* in both time and space is a different matter, and here impressions and gossip suggest part of an answer – I'm told, for instance, that in Bulgaria in the mid-1980s the State publishing house's issue of a translation of *Pride and Prejudice* vanished within a week or two – 100,000 copies and only so relatively few because they hadn't paper to print more. Apparently these Bulgars liked the story. It makes one think.... But the more serious and substantial answers to your objections are to be got only by looking closely at what Jane Austen's comedy is *for* – at the ends encompassed by what you think merely a light amusement. I find that in its peculiarly vivid way this book shows, among other things, that the qualifications requisite for satisfactory marital relations, and thus for the maintenance of the health of the society to which they are central, are as much, if not more than, intellectual and spiritual as they are physical. A not unimportant matter surely? Observe in the first chapter ...

Alec How pompous this is! Of course such ideas are made clear as day by your novelist. One of her great virtues, so obvious that nobody seems to mention it, is the absence of blurred focus or double and contradictory meanings – ambiguity and all that. But does this encourage a profound vision or a vision relevant to us now? I fear that your Bulgarians wanted to escape into a fresher fantasy world, as remote as possible from shortages and politics and the twentieth century! As to what is 'said': – If I wanted to be entertained by little English moral commonplaces *naked*, as it were, I'd go to a philosopher or an essayist – even a sociologist. I'd find them too, I admit, in many modern writers on Austen who seem unable to distinguish between the truisms she's supposed to have got out of eighteenth-century moralists' platitudes and her structural use of them – I assume it's only *Mary* Bennet who could stand Mr. Collins reading from the sermonising Fordyce. I'd even pay attention to life in the Home Counties – then and now. But where I wouldn't look is in this very expert and cosy comic art. Moral sentiments just happen to be part of the raw material for clever novels of that period.

Henry   What matters is the force and quality of the moral ideas.

Alec   Isn't that just the trouble? – they're simply impeccable – and therefore easy, comfortable and unexciting. Nobody *could* disagree with, let alone be disconcerted or challenged by, all this sensible decorous correct stuff about the desirable relations between the sexes. You want to take Austen as a didactic writer – or if not consciously that, someone from whom one may learn lessons. Well, they're rather boring lessons unless you really want to know what the undiscriminating 'they' of that particular past undiscriminatingly thought. You're talking as though Austen was representative of the conditions and the commonplaces of her age – as schoolmasters or politicians or second-rate daily papers would be. It's like looking at Shakespeare through Roger Ascham or Gabriel Harvey – boring, even when followed, as it sometimes is, by vague talk of the artist in question 'transcending' these local conditions in the direction of universals – though others say we mustn't universalise anything more than ten years old in case we hurt their timid relativism. Boring too, to people like me who care about the real world, because . . .

Henry   The real world, hum. Well . . .

Alec   Because you could derive the same ideas, *precisely* the same mark you, from lesser figures – from Elizabeth Hamilton or Fanny Burney and Mrs. Inchbald. No doubt you could deduce them from people now totally forgotten, reputations buried by the propriety of Time. Like taking in our own terms the current *bien pensant* platitudes as much from Ian MacEwan or David Hare as from . . . whoever is any good these days. However, my problem is why Austen lends herself so easily to such treatment? It can't be just critics' stupidity . . . I've noticed that even distinguished readers, professors at ancient universities, find themselves – when talking about Austen's ideas – or the 'ideology' they deduce from the novels – coming in a rush of frankness near to admitting that she is not, after all, so very great an artist! Obviously not in advance of her age, like Wollstonecraft; obviously not innovative in subject matter, like Scott. So where? Just snugly sitting there at the centre, writing highly skilled little comedies . . . ? Well it might after all be as well to settle for that. There'd still be a grateful public. But "the book shows" you say, and it's the kind of thing everybody says. I could sum up some of my general doubts by recording the nagging feeling that *Pride and Prejudice* encourages one too much to say it, in a rather complacent way. Too often. Too easily . . .

Questions *about* Pride and Prejudice

Consider the central illusion of supposedly realistic fiction – that it's a reflection of, and on, everyday life, like Stendhal's travelling mirror. Life organised and pointed up perhaps, but none the less the kind of thing that prompts a traditionalist like you to prose on about virtuous marriages, or a feminist – who is the obverse of the same moralising coin actually – to claim that she learns about Regency patriarchy or phallocracy and the female subject – and even about Austen's attitude to her own marital prospects. You both take too much for granted. In this book life is so conventionalised and so patly put as to have no relation, no exploratory relation at any rate, to any conceivable real.

Henry It's difficult to counter such sweeping assertion, as you know. But I'll try. Look at the terms in which the novel is praised. It's wonderfully comic – and entertains the Bulgarians. Very well. But it's possible to be too much delighted with that, and miss the true, unique, distinction. This begins with the observation that the structure of *Pride and Prejudice* is so clearly articulated and cleverly played against *conventional* expectations about love stories that at least two strange and original effects are taken in by any reader without the least difficulty: first, the dynamic of love is based on initial disconcertment, dislike and embarrassment instead of the commonplace melting moods, so that obstacles are psychological and internal, not a matter of external bars – bars, by the way, which are later parodied in the ineffectuality of the would-be tyranny of Lady Catherine de Bourgh. In this way Jane Austen dramatises a deep insight *vis-à-vis* the genesis of passion by showing it as an emotional disturbance or a nagging disquiet which can first of all be interpreted by its subject as prickling hostility. I think we are likely to infer that Elizabeth probably loves Mr. Darcy, so suitable really, from the start. Second, the relatively simple question of who loves whom is settled almost exactly two-thirds of the way through so that the rest can be devoted to a comical dramatic analysis of notions of proper dignity; and a demonstration that the *justification* of rank may be through decent conduct – both of which are much more amusing and interesting.

I'd add that for this Jane Austen further develops her use of free indirect speech – though not so far as in *Mansfield Park* or *Emma* – as well as the scintillating dramatic dialogue for which the book is famous. And what is not so often noticed as that brave comedy is, is the habitual vivid energy and economy of phrase like that when, invited to Brighton "Lydia flew about the house in restless ecstacy". Notice the open vowel sounds, as one might say of Lord Tennyson.

Alec   Very true. No one denies that it's a brilliantly written comedy. But so much of what you've said is about *art* – words, technique and the necessarily generalised and metaphorical notion of structure. I grant all this – but I still want to be convinced that this is a novel about serious issues. The conventions that you say Austen is so innovative about and with are predominantly the conventions of novel writing – polite female novel writing at that. The insight about falling in love might occur in any number of romantic stories.

Henry   Ah, yes, it's interesting that people who attack Jane Austen almost always merely dogmatise, usually, to do feminists justice, from a snottily male point of view – like H.W. Garrod and Sir Kingsley Amis – though there's always Charlotte Brontë with her tactless high Romantic scorn and demands for blood and passion. Yet it's exactly the modern female point of view that might interest you. It's true that you hear some feminists nowadays saying that it's our, or their, first duty as responsible readers to be alert to the primacy of pleasure – the *jouissance* inherent in the play of signifiers. But they also argue that a lot of the interest of Jane Austen's work lies in what it says – or rather in what it can yield when its basic assumptions are called into question – examined – about early-ish capitalist power structures. Thus you can argue that Elizabeth seems to be able to win against her father and against Darcy only by manoeuvering within a system – a discourse – that inevitably privileges the male – who is, well, the controller of the means of production and exchange, isn't he? Accordingly, who could fail to notice the prominence accorded, in the revaluation of Darcy within the novel, to his character as a good patriarch? – a wonderful landlord and a hero to his housekeeper as well as to the conventionally over-submissive Georgiana – who could at least have been *freer* with Wickham – and an authoritarian figure in the neighbourhood. This seems much more important than the fact, which we discover rather late, that he's tall and handsome. And who, by contrast, could fail to notice that much of the irresponsibility of Mr. Bennet himself is comprised in his failure (like that of Austen's own father it is sometimes hazarded, though unfairly and anachronistically) to supply the wherewithal for a marriage in that society – a large dowry? Obviously Mrs. Bennet's instinct is absolutely *right*, although, being a pathetic victim of the same system, her expression of it is fuddled. The entail on the estate, directed away from women and toward the, well, the really creepy Collins, stands as a symbol and the reality of male oppression: a masculine heir by irrational blood *has* to inherit the money, and therefore the power, absolutely irrespective of merit and of the human feelings that the institution of the patriarchal Family pretends to protect. The only problem with this is that the more extreme feminists seem unsure as to whether Jane Austen herself was sufficiently conscious of this, which I'm confident she was. But otherwise it's an argument that seems to me both true and powerful. Is that serious enough for you?

Alec The last point is the most interesting. How can we tell how conscious the comic moralist is of what can be inferred from her works, when we dethrone intention and treat them as *documents*? But I'm so far convinced by what you say, or report, as to want to imitate Jane Bennet's candour and to "take the good of every" critic's "character and make it still better, and say nothing of the bad" – though I suppose the book shows that it's unlikely to work unless accompanied by luck and a clever sister. . . . But there you have it, that catching uncritical critical habit: "the book shows" again, but this time from me! My real point is that most of your argument, like most of what you said earlier, may well be true but, as the terms used to describe it suggest, it doesn't require a *novel* to say it in. In fact, the charm and success of the dramatisation may get in the way, may distract and blur and sugar such cutting analyses. To be candid, it's a point that ought to be made about a lot of novels, not just *Pride and Prejudice*. They are entertainments *primarily* – as you seemed to hint but very much didn't explain. The pleasures to be derived from them are artistic affects which, of course, use experience but don't really add to it except in the obvious and ordinary, circular, sense which logical positivists used to call 'analytic' – didn't they? This is why I'm alarmed by critics who by way of commentary – enthusiastically co-operating with the author as they seem to think – trundle out more or less severe or indulgent moral-isations at the expense of the characters. The materials, and the morals, are commonplace – though Austen is never less than intelligent. What is distinct and fun is the way she is handles things . . .

Henry I'm amazed how confusing this really somewhat elementary subject can become. Is it beneath you to descend into the specific? – people make such a virtue of the high abstract these days.

Alec I'd be glad to. Let's sample the texture of the novel.
In *Sense and Sensibility*, as even you might agree, there's at least the danger of a rather pi moral framework clamping down on the spon-taneous fun and leaving the sisters to survive – a bit drearily – on the periphery of a mean world. But here there's supposed to be a difference . . .

Henry   Ah, yes! It's "light . . ."

Alec   Please don't say "and bright, and sparkling". Like all of Austen's surviving remarks – I suppose because there are so few of them – that one's done to death. Besides she prefaces it with "rather too" as I remember. But it brings me to the point: – the action around the central consciousness – Elizabeth – is typically a matter of stock responses which are evinced with that kind of predictability that tells us very little indeed new about the human soul – but a lot about comic effects. The figures whose moral and spiritual welfare – and even social and political implications – you profess to learn from or about are stereotypes who delight us by reacting regularly – even oppressively so – to a flat pattern. And 'flat' precisely in the sense meant by E.M. Forster – the general inert overuse of whose terminology proves, I suppose, its usefulness in describing so common a novelistic effect. Consider a typical situation near the beginning, in chapter seven – Jane has received a letter and Mrs. Bennet says "Well, Jane, who is it from? what is it about? what does he say? Well, Jane make haste and tell us . . ." and so on. – By the way that quiet assumption of "he" should fuel your kind of admiration: it's an example of remorseless, subtle, routine authorial devastation which reminds me of Flaubert's equally pitiless application of the formal "Madame Bovary, jeune" to Charles's scraggy first wife. – Anyway, the letter turns out to be from Miss Bingley asking Jane to dine because – this is the point – her brother won't be there, and "the gentlemen are to dine with the officers". Hark what discord follows:

"With the officers!" cried Lydia. "I wonder my aunt did not tell us of *that*."

"Dining out," said Mrs. Bennet, "that is very unlucky."

"Can I have the carriage?" said Jane.

"No, my dear, you had better go on horseback, because it seems likely to rain; then you must stay all night."

"That would be a good scheme," said Elizabeth, "if you were sure they would not offer to send her home."

"Oh! but the gentlemen will have Mr. Bingley's chaise to go to Meryton; and the Hursts have no horses to theirs."

"I had much rather go in the coach."

"But, my dear, your father cannot spare the horses, I am sure, They are wanted in the farm, Mr. Bennet, are not they?

"They are wanted in the farm much oftener than I can get them."

"But if you have got them to day," said Elizabeth, "my mother's purpose will be answered."

She did at last extort from her father an acknowledgement that the horses were engaged. Jane was therefore obliged to go on horseback, and her mother attended her to the door with many cheerful prognostics of a bad day. (1, vii, 30–1)

Terrific. This isn't a highlight or a great set piece as it might be in a lesser author: it's part of the ordinary stuff of the book. But it'd be just puttery and bad faith – and an offence against decorum and the law of kinds – to claim to see in it great psychological insight. "People are trapped in their characteristics. They act parts." says the extra-modern Nicholas Mosley – "If you see that, then part of you has a certain degree of freedom." But freedom isn't the aim for a comic novelist. Writers are said to be capable of killing for a joke, and I believe it.

Henry   But the jokes are brilliant serious jokes – about moral qualities or their absence. I don't see what you're claiming here.

Alec   I'm claiming to be faithful to what Austen really offers as opposed to what you want her to offer. In this passage, as, incidentally in the best Fanny Burney, or in Charlotte Lennox, we're not far away from the old comedy of humours. I remember the catty remark of Horace Walpole's about Fanny Burney writing *Cecilia*, that she's so frightened of making her characters speak out of character "that she never lets them say a syllable but what is to mark" it – which he – the author of *Otranto*! – considered "unnatural". What distinguishes Austen is her speed coupled with what I expect some of your marxising feminists would call the essential conservatism of a practice through which entirely predictable effects about entirely predictable moral attitudes are secured and enjoyed. The *point* is the predictability. We don't want to learn anything new. So: Lydia catches at any mention of officers; Jane doesn't want to presume on staying the night and getting a chance of seeing Bingley; Mrs. Bennet wants the weather and *no* carriage, to make sure that she does; Elizabeth is amused and wants to expose these subterranean meanings; Mr. Bennet embraces a chance to be sardonic about his family. There's an extension just over the page, when Jane falls ill. Lizzy doughtily proposes to walk to see her – the subsequent reactions of propriety to *that* really should appeal to feminists – and, before, Lydia and Catherine offer to accompany her part of the way on the offchance of a glimpse of Captain Carter, Mary is put on display. "I admire the activity of your benevolence", she lumbers out in the style of the most hackneyed eighteenth-century essayist, "but every impulse of feeling should be guided by reason; and, in my opinion, exertion should always be in proportion to what is required." Awful girl! – but it's a kind of principle with these novelists that all their figures inevitably *speak up* consistently. It's just as bare as *Sense and Sensibility* here – like a mechanism, a chiming clock – and so far from the lively untidiness of real existence as to rule out any but the charming, light, effects of Art. The implied author, and her collaborator, the reader, are always too right, according to their little code, to allow in the breath of life. I know that you'll trot out in reply *your* – the professional critic's – commonplaces to the effect, endlessly reiterated, that good comedy is always serious. You may even mention Mozart, I fear. But in this book the morality is too pat, almost complacent. And, really, it's the morality of a past age and a limited society. So tiny and insular that I'm amused at the antics; touched by the consummately judged little love story – but for any breadth and passion I go elsewhere! The effect is charming – but it's an airless perfection. Though I can't admire his manners, I feel that D.H. Lawrence hit the nail on the head in writing about "knowing in apartness" and Jane Austen's being "English in the bad, mean, snobbish sense of the word". Do you truly never feel how *provincial* the English novel is?

Henry All I feel is that you agree that Jane Austen is writing in a convention. What does your demand for passion or grandeur amount to? Must one be always meditating Michaelangelo on the Capitol? Perhaps you're one of those readers who only recognises seriousness when it appears in conscious and semi-clerical dress. But in my opinion you appreciate no art at all if you appreciate *all* art in a solemn or grandiose sort of way. As to "provincial", everything is rooted somewhere, and life is as real in Hampshire and Surrey as it ever was is St. Petersburg or Elsinore. But let me emulate your candour and approach the question indirectly and gently by the consideration of what is done through Jane Austen's handling of characters within the convention. Let us juxtapose, for a change, creations who are very *different* from the heroine and very different from each other in fictional kind. Darcy and Collins ...

ii

... As a glamorous aristocratic hero, universally felt to be spendidly manly, Mr. Darcy is not always popular these days. I've even read the accusation that, when he wittily tries to chill off Sir William Lucas with "Every savage can dance" (1, vi, 25) he is being "contemptuous of the indigenous populations that England's colonial ventures were just beginning to exploit."

Alec   Gruesomely tendentious and inaccurate, of course. Nevertheless, I must say that Darcy's a bit of a stick, a bit of a lay figure of the kind I've described – to hang the comedy around – and not nearly as fully imagined as the later heroes are. Though I didn't when I first encountered him at the age of thirteen. I thought he was *marvellous* ...!

Henry   Never mind the stick-like nature for a moment – or, rather, mind exactly how Jane Austen makes him grow through and *out* of it. After his initial offensiveness – and surely, in retrospect anyway, a lot of that's shyness, isn't it? – the novel gets busy with placing and dramatising him as a Grandison figure: a re-writing by Jane Austen, that is to say, of the perfect hero, perfect lover and perfect landlord of eighteenth-century fiction. A lot of women's writing at this time, scholars tell us, is concerned with siting the male 'lover-mentor' as a solution to the heroine's faults *and* ills – this scholarhip being perhaps not often enough as aware as Jane Austen is of the essentially patronising, *de haut en bas* conception of such a person, and possibly also ignoring the extent to which the figure is a psychological given irrespective of sex and period.

Alec   Yes: Knightley is obviously Austen's major creation here, but it starts with Henry Tilney, whom I find really irritating sometimes, I must say.

Henry   If you do, you have at least one area of agreement with some of the feminists I've been referring to. But let's not fall into the common trap of treating Jane Austen's *œuvre* as if it were one world with an interchangeable cast. Have you noticed the subtle manner, in *this* work of art, in which the initially traditional hero – traditional even down to his celebrated pride and stiff preconceptions–is made a convincingly good man? – quite apart from his obvious fine and hero-like behaviour over the mess and embarrassment of Lydia, and so on? He's a sincere Christian, for example. His letter to Elizabeth after the first proposal is real – meant – a letter such as a person might write after having blundered so badly, and *not* simply an unassimilated hangover from the epistolary style of novel: and he ends it "God bless you". This might seem *just* conventional if Elizabeth didn't recall it with such affectionate power on their lover's walk after his successful proposal, when they touchingly review past errors: "The adieu is charity itself" she says (3, xvi, 368) – which tells it all.

Alec "Tells it all"?

Henry Yes – a very acceptable phrase, you'll find. Elizabeth thinks that Jane's and Bingley's faces "would have told it all" after the episode of *their* proposal just before.

Alec I admit that you're a close reader. But don't you rather overdo it? Such a small detail . . .

Henry I don't see that I do. If you really pay attention to the finely controlled emphases as well as to the comic set pieces you'll see that the same point is ever so gently edged into Darcy's letter itself when he says of Wickham's attempted seduction of Georgiana that "no obligation less than the present" should induce him to unfold it "to any human being" (2, xii, 201). He's such a careful, rather latinate, speaker that he must mean that it *can* be unfolded to God. And this part of his nature goes with that natural *gravitas*, shading into pomposity, that traditionally makes the traditional Englishman so formidable a figure – and so attractive perhaps.

Alec But isn't it the point in *Pride and Prejudice* that Elizabeth can't take all this grandeur quite neat, so to speak? That the, er, Patriarchy has to be qualified by some kind of flexibility?

Henry Precisely. Jane Austen's brilliant achievement is to make the Grandisonian hero so really grand in order that he can then be sent up by a woman who isn't impressed by all that social and financial power. It's admittedly wonderful to have the great *Mister* Darcy teased! What a transgression! What joyful and orderly subversion! He likes it, and so have generations of readers. Happiness at Pemberley, and ponies round the park! And, of course, the teasing and good humour and candour are seen as moral forces – not just the 'fun' you seemed to see – as generations of critics have pointed out.

Alec Yes. I see. So you don't think Darcy's relatively conventional ontological status should worry us much?

Henry No. But what it does serve to emphasise is how much more devastating Jane Austen's critique can be allowed to be when it plays round a different kind of conventional figure, an avowedly comic butt, Mr. Collins. Did you know that there's a recent critical book named after him? – he has almost the status of Falstaff or Hamlet or Don

Quixote – as a person who is somehow perceived as having a life independent of the work of art that contains him. And he's such a famous, quasi-proverbial figure, as to have spawned a noun – a 'collins' is, or was, upper-crust slang for a pompous letter of thanks – a glutinous bread-and-butter letter. But within the novel his very realistic but conventional grotesqueness, the fact that he's to be despised and dismissed traditionally as a servile flattering careerist, allows Jane Austen to examine the assumptions of her society – of patriarchy, I suppose – in a way that even she doesn't allow herself with her conventional heroes – or even with charming villains like Wickham. The comedy is a fine non-abrasive device for introducing radical criticism of an establishment in which women can be openly bought – obtained or, some might say, prostituted – as wives in a society which otherwise offers only the drudgery of spinsterhood at home – and we're talking about the 'better class of people' remember – or a horrible job as a governess or something of that kind. After all, Darcy's original scepticism about Elizabeth's attractions is obviously so important to her – though youth and liveliness may deny it – precisely because it might compromise her negotiable value – it reminds her of her real vulnerability in the marriage market. It should make your blood boil.

Alec   Well, I suppose it would help if it had made Austen's blood boil too. You make her sound like Dickens. What about the comedy?

Henry   Yes. Of course I go too far. Blood boiling indeed! – that's what comes from abstracting and triangulating from the real texture of feeling in a literary work. I apologise. Nevertheless, your reference to Dickens is welcome here. In English fiction only Uriah Heep can really vie with Collins for sheer physical repulsiveness – and Homais in *Madame Bovary*, wonderful as he is, is a comparatively laboured creation. Collins, you see, starts off exactly like Mrs. Bennet – the way you describe most of the characters as *always* being – as the incarnation of specific human qualities and foibles. *Sense and Sensibility* starts like that too, and even *Northanger Abbey* in its mischievous, undermining mode. We are told that the eighteenth century felt that something real and substantial in Nature was being invoked by the use of such general psychological and moral terms as 'Pride', 'Understanding', 'Temper' and the like. Jane Austen's method at the beginning of *Pride and Prejudice* is to have a dramatic scene or scenes which introduce the characters and show how they speak, and then to come in unashamedly – though briefly – with a quite un-Henry Jamesian summation and extension of what we've experienced, in precisely such language. That this is so clear is, incidentally, evidence, I suppose, that in some ways she's still learning at this stage in the book to write her particular innovative kind of novel. The passage about Mrs. Bennet's mean understanding and uncertain temper at the end of the hilarious first chapter is famous, and it's very much the same after Collins's introductory letter, and his first evening at Longbourn. We have the entail... the humble abode... Lady Catherine de Bourgh...little attentions...then:

> Mr. Collins was not a sensible man, and the deficiency of nature had been but little assisted by education or society; the greatest part of his life having been spent under the guidance of an illiterate and miserly father... (1, xv, 70)

See how, exactly as in the case of Uriah Heep, the novelist is not at all concerned to *excuse*, as opposed to noticing, the results of childhood deprivation. And:

> The subjection in which his father had brought him up, had given him originally great humility of manner, but it was a good deal now counteracted by the self-conceit of a weak head, living in retirement, and the consequential feelings of early and unexpected prosperity ... and the respect which he felt for her [Lady Catherine's] high rank, and his veneration for her as his patroness, mingling with a very good opinion of himself, of his authority as a clergyman, and his rights as a rector, made him altogether a mixture of pride and obsequiousness, self-importance and humility. (*ibid.*).

You wouldn't think a character could survive, dramatically, after that, would you? He's been authoritatively damned. In a later, Victorian, novel – by George Eliot, say, or even Mrs. Gaskell – such a figure might become the object of compassion, as Bulstrode does in *Middlemarch*. But here he remains as he is – gets worse actually – but survives wonderfully for the reader precisely because he's such a received comic figure. In fact he's *just* the kind of person you pointed to; he reacts with clockwork precision, exactly and always in character, and is extremely funny. But he's certainly not solely a provision for the light comedy you want to read into the whole text. He's also gruesome because he's a sexual threat and a lively *embodiment* of a system. Perhaps the more so as he's a perfectly respectable minor character. Did I say how physically repellent I find him?

Alec Yes – with Uriah Heep. And I felt that to be odd at the time, since, as usual with Austen, there's little or no physical description. But

I agree that we do get a sense of – how shall I say? – a sweaty presence there. Perhaps it's connected to the fact that both Heep and Collins are explicitly after our – er, the people in the book's – womenfolk. Like the Hun and so forth, you know.

Henry   Well, I'd put it a bit differently. I'm arguing that he's as much a part of the normal marriage subject as are Darcy and Bingley. He *is* respectable. There's nothing overtly wrong, let alone villainous, in his behaviour. He starts off as a purely comic figure, verging on caricature. Yet the proposal to Elizabeth is an exposure of the contradictions inevitable to her situation – and the situations of any girl of like status – which is energetic enough to match the second chapter of *Sense and Sensibility*! Note that it's explicitly marked out by the narratrix as a set piece, as in the theatre:

> The next day opened a new scene at Longbourn. Mr. Collins made his declaration in form. Having resolved to do it without loss of time, as his leave of absence extended only to the following Saturday, and having no feelings of diffidence to make it distressing to himself even at the moment, he set about it in a very orderly manner, with all the observances which he supposed a regular part of the business. (1, xix, 104)

How beautifully evocative that awkward, flat, professional vocabulary is! – "observances which he supposed a regular part of the business"!

What follows must be one of the most central and influential scenes in English literature. I once thought of comparing *Pride and Prejudice* to *Much Ado About Nothing*. But I let it go because there isn't much more than a general resemblance given by the pairing of a bland couple and a sharp couple in each case, the temporary defection of the bland male owing to misinformation from the outside, and, of course, wit contests as a courtship model. All this is quite common.[3] Actually, Jane Austen's comedy strikes me as often more interesting. But it's a different matter when we consider subsequent literature. The *Pride and Prejudice* scene reappears, with the obtusely self-important and clumsy male, his inability to take no for an answer and his version of "elegant females" – insisted on *five* times by Collins – which actually insults them as brainless, uneducated flirts in a supposedly complimentary prelude to a lifetime in their husband's service . . . – This scene reappears in count-less novels – functions as a kind of repeated device or figure for the subject.

Alec   Ah, but wouldn't you also want to say that the marriage situation isn't present in literature alone – but a product of the fact that men did indeed in the vast majority of cases wield economic power produced *and* justified under a half religious, half politico-moral ethic? They often still do. Perhaps women only survive and flourish because they usually have much stronger wills – or value a different kind of inner life. But *I* agree, now you remind me of it, that in dealings with any girl with the least bit of spirit any male reader of *Pride and Prejudice* secretly and intimately suspects himself of being a Collins. It's unnerving. I suppose even Darcy's first proposal is a grander version of the same structure.

Henry Yes, as I'd hoped to suggest by talking about Darcy first, these novels develop in an almost musical way – taking themes and motifs and varying and expanding them. But what I had in mind just now is the persistence of the basic structure of the Collins scene in some traditionalist twentieth-century women's writing. In a violent, quirkily tragic, mode it's surely taken up and adapted in Elizabeth von Arnim's creation of Everard Wemyss's cap-à-pie complacent self-centredness when he takes over without question the life of Lucy in *Vera*, published in 1921 – though, to admit your argument just now about its not being solely a siuation in literature, this is said to be an acid rendition of the author's husband, Lord Russell. More obviously and more generally recognised is the way in which this particular scene, its highly charged comedy and even its language, recurs in Barbara Pym, who, visiting Chawton in 1969, felt the dust on Jane Austen's desk and remarked "Oh that some of her genius might rub off on me!" Barbara Pym was completely decorous about this – she felt the reviewer's predictable puffery comparing her with Jane Austen to be "mildly blasphemous", according to her friend Hazel Holt. But, being sharp like Jane Austen, she saw through and presented masculine pretence in a way clearly facilitated by *Pride and Prejudice*. In her first novel, *Some Tame Gazelle* of 1950, the polite spinster heroine Belinda has to refuse a surprise off-the-peg proposal from the fatuous Bishop Grote, who then goes off and marries a weaker Charlotte Lucas in the person of a Miss Aspinall re-encountered by chance in the Army & Navy Stores! It's extremely funny, but also slightly desperate. And then there's *Crampton Hodnet*, another early novel, published posthumously in 1985. The curate and lodger in North Oxford suddenly asks Miss Morrow, the lady's companion, to marry him, even though he thinks her name is Janie when it's Jessie. It's really a re-writing of Jane Austen, using the same vocabulary but in a convincing modern way:

"Well, I am certainly flattered that you should have wanted – or thought you wanted – to marry me," said Miss Morrow calmly, "but I'm afraid my answer must be no." She paused and went on in a solicitous tone, "I don't think you're quite yourself this evening. Perhaps you're overtired. I'll ask Florence to make you some Ovaltine, shall I?"

"You might at least give me the credit of knowing my own mind!" said Mr. Latimer angrily. "I respect and esteem you very much," he went on in the same angry tone. "I think we might be very happy together."

"But do you *love* me?" asked Miss Morrow quietly.

"Love you?" he said indignantly. "But of course I do. Haven't I just told you so?"

"You have told me that you respect and esteem me very much," said Miss Morrow without elaboration . . . (Ch. 10)

Here we see only the sunnier side of the Collins syndrome, but Barbara Pym shares with Jane Austen the ability to make one delight in the internal dramas of characters who live in English worlds which, on inspection, are pretty dull and cramping – though, of course, she doesn't see round her characters nearly as fully.

Alec Respect and esteem. . . . Well, like the Gratitude in Richardson which Austen joked about but treats as a serious feature in Elizabeth's later appraisal of Darcy, there are less substantial things, in my view. I'm thinking about it in relation to *Mansfield Park* . . .

Henry They're seen as very important, if finally insufficient qualities for marriage. Surely the reason, incidentally, why Jane Austen's final brief proposals are so moving is that they typically involve recognition and *respect* for past emotions – and the vindication of the other person's conduct in that stuffy and contingent world. But to revert to Collins himself: his comicality is the precipitant for a penetrating analysis of value exactly because Jane Austen doesn't rest content with the episodes of this proposal and Charlotte's subsequent, resignedly realistic, bargain with him. The latter goes out deliberately to meet "so much love and eloquence" – which is almost a savage phrase in context – in the lane; and all readers are compelled to admit, even if reluctantly like the more glamorous Elizabeth, that her reason – "I am not romantic you know . . . I ask only a comfortable home" (1, xxii, 125) is a sound one – even if it's terribly sad. One is reminded of Johnson's remark that the Lord Chancellor may as well make marriages for all the happiness that personal predilection achieves! But after that it was open to Jane Austen to leave the Collinses be as an established term in the debate. She doesn't. Immediately there are the catalogued comic reactions to the engagement of the kind *you* noticed, Alec. The next chapter, twenty-three, has a series of paragraphs starting in form: "Elizabeth, feeling. . . . Mrs. Bennet . . . too much overpowered . . . Mr. Bennet . . . much more tranquil. . . . Jane . . . a little surprised. . . . Lady Lucas . . . not insensible of triumph" and so on; but *then* the point is really continued and enforced by having Elizabeth go on the visit to Hunsford. This visit has multiple functions naturally – some are ostensibly more important ones because of Darcy's reappearance – but what I get the strongest feeling of is the terrible domesticity at the Parsonage. Phew! The circumstantiality of it and its garden! Apparently it's both "comfortable" and "neat", which are praise words for Jane Austen, and not so cramped as to prevent Elizabeth's having a private room – Collins is not at all dishonest about what he has to offer: but it reads as, well, claustrophobic. I think the great telling detail comes after Elizabeth has been there a week when she notices that the sitting-room is of inferior size and aspect but has been chosen by Charlotte because it doesn't, unlike Collins's book-room, front the road, and therefore doesn't open on to a possible view of Miss de Bourgh's phaeton:

> . . . she soon saw that her friend had an excellent reason for what she did, for Mr. Collins would undoubtedly have been much less in his own apartment, had they sat in one equally lively . . . (2, vii, 168)

Clever of Charlotte. But the question arises therefore: *can she avoid him in the bedroom?*

Alec   Steady on. . . . Do you really think we're meant to think that far, and in what would have been such an un-ladylike way?

Henry   I think you underestimate Regency ladies. Surely you agree that Jane Austen is a moral realist, even if you have thought her superficial? Perhaps you haven't read her letters recently?

Alec   Yes – I suppose that one does give way to historical stereotypes. I wasn't thinking. . . . So much is a matter of working out the implications – even though they're clear when you do. Charlotte is expecting an "olive-branch" near the end – I expect that she will have at least ten little Collinses.

Henry   And I hope that Wickham will get killed two years after the novel at Waterloo – like George Osborne in *Vanity Fair*. But are these strictly *literary* responses ... ? Whether or not, they're certainly common responses to literature and they're entertaining – and actually show how the comic mode involves one through pleasure. You'll remember the traditions about how Jane Austen herself indulged such little fancies within her family?[4] Nevertheless, *Pride and Prejudice* does unremittingly emphasise the moral squalor of a marriage contracted on those terms. Recall how callous Collins is about the Bennets' feelings over Lydia's elopement, and how self-importantly creepy about Lady Catherine's wrath over Elizabeth and Darcy – there's nothing to distance Charlotte from this, rather the opposite: – "Mrs. Collins and myself". And earlier, near the end of the Hunsford visit, Jane Austen has transferred specially into her point of view to find her thinking "it admitted not of a doubt" that Elizabeth would snap up Darcy if she "could suppose him to be in her power" (2, ix, 181) – she's always on the *qui vive* for advancement. It's a great credit to Elizabeth's feelings of female solidarity that they can remain true friends.

Alec You're not the only one to sense an implied sexual exploitation, I now recall. I grant you the remarkable ability of Austen's novels to make even very sophisticated literary people go on about her figments as though they were real people who in some sense might produce new behaviour, have unmentioned attributes and so forth. Actually, it's 'the world of Jane Austen' over, and ever, again and really a great tribute to her. Recently I was privileged to hear a conversation between a woman author of a book on George Eliot, a serious West End playwright, and a distinguished retired female Professor of English, all about how lecherous Collins must have been, how very insistent on the marital rights and duties upon which he no doubt divagated at length and with due gratitude. Sweaty, as I think I said ...

iii

Henry It might be *painfully* sweaty – menacing and even disgusting – except that in *Pride and Prejudice* the comedy steers away from pain. Mr. Bennet, to take another instance, has all the makings, deeply conceived, of a tragically destructive and self-destructive figure, but, once we realise the stifled nature of his feeling, and our and Elizabeth's distance from him, he almost qualifies for the Austenian *élite* because he's sensitive and hostile to the same banalities as are the other 'good' characters – and, of course, so cogently witty about them. Also, I suppose that by the end he's learnt something from female wisdom – and from Darcy about how a man might act.

113

Alec   Austenian *élite*?

Henry   Yes – the word doesn't mean undemocratic and all that nonsense thrust upon the world by modern would-be politicians, but that you can elevate yourself in morals and taste, given the effort, the serendipity – or the moral luck. Where I think you go badly and obviously wrong – when you describe Jane Austen as merely prosecuting the predictable follies of her cast and providing amusement by a series of scenes or *tableaux* based on variations of convention – is in not seeing that the work is a creative critique of the very commonplaces that amuse you. That amuse you and Mr. Bennet and, initially, Elizabeth – and even Darcy in his disdainful way. Out of this critique emerge the few who are genuinely superior. I've already indicated how we are led, through the comedy, to feel something serious about Mr. Collins. I see the whole book as being like that, from the word go.

Alec   The word "go"?

Henry   Really the famous first paragraph "It is a truth universally acknowledged, that a single man in possession of a good fortune, must be in want of a wife." (1, i, 3) We know from then on that we're to encounter and explore a minefield of subversible *cliché* in both the art of this novel *and* the life of its characters. The question is, how much damage can such practical banalities do?

Alec   Before you tell me that let me add the point – and this does indeed get us far from the Home Counties, whatever one thinks of them – that the situation of the opening was internationally observed. Compare *Eugene Onegin*, the first and greatest verse novel, completed seventeen years after the publication of *Pride and Prejudice*. When Pushkin moves Vladimir Lensky down close to Onegin in the country:

> Meanwhile another new landowner
> came driving to his country seat
> and, in the district, this *persona*
> drew scrutiny no less complete...

Then:

> Vladimir, wealthy and good-looking
> was asked around as quite a catch –
> such is the usual country cooking;
> and all the neighbours planned a match

between their girls and this *half-Russian*.
As soon as he appears, discussion
touches obliquely, but with speed,
on the dull life that bachelors lead . . . [5]

– I always think it a disappointment that Pushkin didn't actually meet
Lord Byron. – But in both instances the idea that such men "must be in
want of a wife" is natural enough – and justified. To broaden and
intensify parallels on the subject: influence can't plausibly be thought of
in Pushkin's case – though it would fit with our looser contemporary
talk of 'intertextuality'. But the real connection between Austen and
George Eliot is plain and evident when Grandcourt arrives at Diplow
in chapter nine of *Daniel Deronda*. Here likewise there is the consciousness both of a literary context and of the situation being one of
the quotidian pleasures for the observer of life. Eliot is very deliberately
an ironist:

> Some readers of this history will doubtless regard it as incredible that
> people should construct matrimonial prospects on the mere report
> that a bachelor of good fortune and possibilities was coming within
> reach, and will reject the statement as a mere outflow of gall: they
> will aver that neither they nor their first cousins have minds so
> unbridled; and that in fact this is not human nature, which would
> know that such speculations might turn out to be fallacious, and
> would therefore not entertain them. But, let it be observed, nothing is
> here narrated of human nature generally . . .

Henry   Does it go on?

Alec   Rather. But it becomes more specific, and funnier.

Henry   Yes, it's ridiculousy easy to underrate George Eliot's fine social
comedy. Even so that's rather *thorough* as a rewriting, I must say.

Alec   I think that it illustrates very well what I said earlier about
Austen's deftness and lightness of touch – the opening chapters of *Pride
and Prejudice* must be unrivalled for speed and concision. I expect
everyone notices that they get longer as the book progresses, even to the
extent of having sub-divisions marked by little lines across the page?
How very important the *look* of a text is! Anyway *she* can, as you said,
rely on her readers apprehending and supplying meanings for the key
words in a way that was obviously impossible in 1876. I suppose it's an
argument for the continuities of culture – or the slowness of real change

underneath the surface scurry – that *we* still feel capable enough of supplying them when they're offered with such confidence.

Henry   It's also because sympathetic readers – obviously this class may soon include you? – become, however temporarily, members of the Austenian *élite*. But, to continue on the cue of that first sentence: it's the beginning of a series of commonplaces that are caught up and examined in the course of the book. They are examined by the drama, by the fall of events, and – largely – by their sifting in the mind of Elizabeth Bennet, even when she's making her obvious mistakes. This is rather nicely reflected upon near the end, when Bingley reoccupies Netherfield, and amidst rewakened hope and plans for Jane she thinks:

> . . . it is hard . . . that this poor man cannot come to a house, which he has legally hired, without raising all this speculation! I *will* leave him to himself. (3, xi, 332)

Nevertheless, it must be amusing that such self-correction – so typical, incidentally, of an Austenian heroine in its rightness and honesty of intent and its imperfectness of realisation – I think of Emma – is decisively capped two chapters later, when Bingley has proposed, by one's not being able to deny the superficial justice of Mrs. Bennet's terrible rejoicing to Jane that:

> "I was sure you could not be so beautiful for nothing! I remember, as soon as ever I saw him, when he first came into Hertfordshire last year, I though how likely it was that you should come together. Oh! . . ." (3, xiii, 348)

What she doesn't realise, in common with some critics, is that it's not the expectation that's incorrect, but the way in which it manifests itself in behaviour – just as elsewhere Elizabeth is shocked to hear Lydia phrase what had been her own sentiments about Wickham's mercenary pursuit of Miss King. Mrs. Bennet's behaviour has almost cost both her older daughters their future husbands – and, by extension, got for the too willing Lydia a callous, if charming, rake. Such comedy is aimed at the refining out of folly, Alec, not its airless parade: and note that it operates effectively far outside the range of Collins – we feel just as laughingly frustrated here as with him.

All this is obvious enough to the attentive reader. As obvious, say, as the style in which Collins's horrid discordant *clichés* about naming the day and – *ad nauseam* – being "the happiest of men", are made alive and true to the experience dramatised in the text – all *clichés* are potentially accurate – when Elizabeth writes to Mrs. Gardiner in the penultimate chapter that "I am the happiest creature in the world". By then the commonplace has been given substance – and she really can be so described, so far as anyone ever can. But the largest-scale instance in this novel of the use of the comically loathsome to define by negatives the values of the Austenian *élite* is in the whole complex of excruciating effects to do with the limitations of Meryton society – in effect, the representative limitations of English society in the upper and middle levels. These do indeed occur with the delightful predictability described by you, but my point is that they aren't just presented for what you rather unsophisticatedly seemed to conceive of as a kind of free-floating aesthetic amusement. They cohere with, when they don't actually constitute, the careers of the main characters. By this I mean nothing so confusing, and, frankly, so merely speculative and un-exemplified, as to say, with some modern marxists, that in Jane Austen the self-determining *bourgeois* 'subject' – created in accord with the ideology of free-production capitalism – offers a structural homology with our conception of her work as somehow autonomous, and having unexamined claims to permanence. Nothing so impressive I'm afraid, nor so difficult to establish. Only that you, like a number of Jane Austen's professed admirers, were failing to register – explicitly at any rate – the true nature of a comedy which *depends* for its effect on perceiving the serious consequences of what is going on for the people in whom we're interested, centrally Elizabeth. The comedy and the serious feeling aren't simply adjunctive. One doesn't start when the other leaves off in the manner of the inferior contemporary art of, say, Mary Brunton or Charlotte Smith – or of some of Richardson. The effects – and affects – are simultaneous. If we care about what happens to Elizabeth, then ludicrous events take on a kind of concurrent gravity. Bear in mind that this is a world in which sensitive minds have a duty to repress even so radical a disturbance as that caused by Darcy's letter in order not to be "unfit for conversation" with such people as the Collinses and Maria Lucas! And then consider that, in detail, what is immediately devastating about Darcy's letter are the "terms of such mortifying, yet merited reproach" (2, xiii, 209) he uses about Elizabeth's family – and there's the nub. She can deal with the corresponding absurdities of Lady Catherine and Rosings with amused contempt. But home strikes home. I, like Elizabeth at that point, think particularly of the Netherfield ball. That appalling extra quarter of an hour obtained by Mrs. Bennet's manoeuvre at the end "which gave them time to see how heartily they were wished away"! (1, xviii, 102) The whole of chapter eighteen contains acute embarrassment for our heroine. The awkward silences of her dances with Darcy. The chill engendered by her sprightly but temerarious references to Wickham, followed by Miss Bingley's snobbish rebuke. These could be tolerable, even in the face of Jane's report that Bingley thinks Darcy must be right about Wickham, if only Elizabeth's rather precariously proud with-drawal could be supported and given some colour by those that belong to her. But no: – excruciatingly no. Her cousin Mr. Collins, insisting on his superior "understanding", solemnly intrudes his servility upon Darcy; then the "audible whisper" of her mother conveys to the latter the confidence that Jane will soon entrap his rich friend as well as her contempt for himself – Elizabeth, though she still thinks she doesn't care, finds herself constantly consulting a face that "changed gradually from indignant contempt to a composed and steady gravity". Then comes her sister Mary's long, affected and talentless vocal exhibition, which is stopped only by a rebuke from her father which is in itself unpleasantly sarcastic and therefore unseemly. Collins makes another insufferable and very comic speech. In short:

> To Elizabeth if appeared, that had her family made an agreement to expose themselves as much as they could during the evening, it would have been impossible for them to play their parts with more spirit, or finer success ... (1, xviii, 101)

The sense of frustration puts me in mind of the oppressions of the picnic at Box Hill in *Emma*. But note that in the earlier work Jane Austen sums up the dramatic action in the same way that she sums up the characters of Collins and Mrs. Bennet after *their* first mani-festations. It's a method the explicitness of which she tended to fine down in subsequent novels. But here it seems utterly appropriate in confirming the fact that this grotesquerie, this really bad behaviour, is not simply a comic parade but a damage and a humiliation to the central consciousness and heroine – how very material a damage we don't, of course, quite realise until Darcy's letter begins the process of changing Elizabeth's feelings for him from anger, and an increasingly puzzled rejection, into desire.

Alec   Yes, I see – and by the way, wouldn't it be for you another facet of Austen's originality not to have the young *woman* fall, *à la* Jane, in love first? – I seem to remember there's quite a point about that in *Northanger Abbey*.

Henry   It's certainly a popular erotic debating point – but mustn't it always have been one? In any case the passage I've quoted is a prelude to that awful final quarter of an hour in which yawns and withdrawn silences and spurts of chatter over "the long speeches of Mr. Collins" lead only to Lydia's ill-bred adolescent exclamations of "Lord, how tired I am!" One can almost see the smoke from the snuffed candles and the soiled tablecloths! And the shame of it.

Alec I expect it is this sort of thing that prevents the reader from dismissing Darcy's later proud "Could you expect me to rejoice in the inferiority of your connections?" – in the first proposal scene – as merely proud or prejudiced – hard though it seems.

Henry It *is* hard – as Elizabeth says of the speculations and expectations surrounding Bingley. We can go along with her so far in coping with aristocratic pretension by being able to equate it with, for example, the humanly futile, embarrassing, stupid power represented and displayed in the amount that the glazing at Rosings "had originally cost Sir Lewis de Bourgh" – I suppose modern grandeur tended to be expressed in large windows? But when it comes to feelings and behaviour . . . ! The failure to maintain civilised values on the part of her nearest connections inevitably leads her to the famous and justified rebuke to her father during the minor climax of Lydia's elopement, strategically placed near the end of volume two. And his response "What, has she frightened away some of your lovers? Poor little Lizzy!" (2, xviii, 231) is even more inept than she finds it.

Alec You speak with some heat. I suppose all this *is* really there – in, er, Jane Austen?

Henry Good. It is obvious if you let yourself respond with the appropriate ease. *Feeling* – frustration and sheer joy – is what finally marks *Pride and Prejudice* off from the kind of comedy you described. It is what makes the book so often read and re-read – read often in times of crisis, in times of grief. Mere bright jokes wouldn't do that. And, of course, out of such confusion springs the truly beautiful character of Elizabeth, defined in resistance to it. Nothing could be more warm and natural than that, over Darcy's part in Lydia's deliverance, the virtuous correctness of her resolve to be satisfied with "ignorance" is succeeded *immediately* by:

> "Not that I *shall* though," she added to herself, as she finished the letter; "and my dear aunt, if you do not tell me in an honourable manner, I shall certainly be reduced to tricks and stratagems to find it out." (3, ix, 320)

And nothing could be more fiery and inspiriting than the full repertoire of educated disapproval that she can bring counter to Lady Catherine's articulate and very weighty assertion of the values of the marriage market, as conventionally conceived. It will, I think, help finally to get rid of your sense of this being a mere light comedy, deploying only predictable and disposable pawns, if you consider with what unconscious ease and enthusiasm, in the fire of the drama, the reader takes equally as perfectly natural – from a young girl – an authority and phrasing truly worthy of Dr. Johnson:

> "Allow me to say, Lady Catherine, that the arguments with which you have supported this extraordinary application, have been as frivolous as the application was ill-judged. You have widely mistaken my character, if you think I can be worked on by such persuasions as these . . . (3, xv, 357)

Persuasions against a marriage founded on compatibility and love – that's literally another story. But I don't need to labour my point further. Elizabeth is one of the finest products – strong and intelligent yet bewitching in a completely traditional feminine way – of our civilisation.

Alec   I suppose so. But I wonder now what one should make of Fanny Price . . . ?

Chapter Six

Mansfield Park, Fanny Price, Flaubert, and the Modern Novel

Although Jane Austen's quintessential quality is very clearly manifest to the reader, it is extremely difficult to define, or fix. Let us look again at some of the salient features of established response to her.

First there is the lingering impression, always popular, and in a simple but undamaging sense true – as we have seen – that she is a limited writer, confined to a small group of the gentry and their domestic affairs. This might be called the 'no French Revolution' point and be taken for granted.[1]

Then there is an equally lingering temptation, for every kind of reader, from the most naïve to the most sophisticated, to treat of her novels unusually freely as though they were only casually separate manifestations of *one event*. Formulations such as "A Louisa Musgrove is not to be compared with a Maria Bertram; but . . ."; or "Anne, unlike Catherine or Emma, has no illusions about her place in society . . ." etc. occur with great frequency. Of course, such talk is liable to surround any author who has a distinct manner and distinct subject matter. We are equally prepared to hear with complacency that "Milly Theale, unlike Isabel Archer or Fleda Vetch, has no fear of the Kingdoms of the World . . ." etc., or even that "What distinguishes Emma [Bovary] from Frédéric [Moreau] is an appetite for experience . . .". But these tend to be part of grand summaries, not the usual casual currency. With Jane Austen they are so much the usual currency as to form the unsurprising basis for what is in other ways the least impressionistic of enterprises: J.F. Burrows's putting her "common words" through computer analyses in his vividly modernising *Computation into Criticism*. Here remarks such as "Fanny speaks 6117 words and, on my reckoning, 'thinks' 15,418. For Anne it is 4336 as against 5667. But, for Emma it is 21,501 as against 19,730 . . .",[2] do not, unlike warmer or blinder comment, at all naïvely imply that Jane Austen's people are real figures abstractable from their fictional contexts. But the assumption is, nevertheless, that of a single solid world, the inhabitants of which can be compared without apology or ado. The separate nature of each novel is slightly obscured in what is usually a real delight in 'the world of Jane Austen' – a common phrase even amongst the most self-conscious commentators.[3] The Revd. Ivor Morris, for example, in his agreeable chat *Mr. Collins Considered*,[4] is unusual only in being explicit when he says, "it has seemed appropriate to treat the novels together in determining the groundwork of social assumption and convention".

What these two types of response have in common is their tribute to the solidity and integrity of the illusions created in the novels. And this is related in turn to the introduction of the third, grander – and mainly unexamined – term, which haunts the critical lexicon. I have found myself using it once or twice already. Now I want to introduce it as a way in to Jane Austen's great transitional work, *Mansfield Park*.

When critics speak, as they often do, of Jane Austen as 'the first *modern* novelist', at least part of what they have in mind – consciously or not – is likely to be the modest but easy, confident, air of self-contained substantiality that breathes from the books. As we have seen, these novels tend to seem free, to depend only on the goodwill of their contract with the reader. 'Modern' may at first seem to be only a literary-historical adjective. But apropos of Jane Austen it becomes a praise word which not only places her creation after Fielding and before James Joyce but also suggests a new timeless perfectness of achievement. It translates as 'fully grown and equipped' as well as 'only 180 years ago, and at the beginning of our era'.

Nevertheless, the idea remains nebulous. One obvious way to render it more precise is to make comparisons with other novelists before and after – an agreeable process to be continued later in this chapter. But a related project, which I shall try now as well, is to ask a series of questions which may seem a little impolite in literary criticism. Direct questions such as: 'Do we ever feel that this writer is patronising the reader?' 'Are these books addressed to the grown-up person?' 'Do we have to make allowances for an outdated code, the prejudices of a particular reading public, the need to spare the blushes of the young, the need to uphold the current political and religious *status quo*?' 'Are those "bad habits which belong to the childhood of art and to the moral style made fashionable by Richardson", upon which Stendhal animadverts in his notes to *Lucien Leuwen*, left quite behind?' In short: Do we ever have to defend this favourite reading with 'Oh, it is only a novel!' before turning back to it? Such challenges seem crude. But – to mention only a few instances from the higher reaches of art – what honest reader has not felt patronised by George Eliot's insistence on the simple virtue of Adam Bede, or most of Balzac's explanatory politics; felt addressed below an acceptable intellectual level by Goldsmith's sly pieties or the apostrophes to Youth made by Conrad's or John Buchan's narrators; marked spiritual time while reading Sir Charles Grandison's speeches on masquerades and duelling or David Copperfield's identification of Agnes with stained glass? The subject is enormous, if ungrateful, for, as in human relations, we tolerate more than we would like to admit to a third party, no doubt in the interest of being tolerated ourselves. At any rate, part of Jane Austen's 'modernity', or perhaps just her fully formedness, may be demonstrated by asking such questions about this most complex novel – poised as it is between her earlier bright conquests in the tradition she had inherited, and her subsequent, fullest, achievement in *Emma*.

I   FANNY

i

Thus: *Mansfield Park* is the first of the 'Chawton' novels, the first of Jane Austen's three late great works, and according to Q.D. Leavis, "the first modern novel in England".[5] But it is also a problem novel. It resolutely disturbs the usual gratifying decorum by which good manners, good appearance, good taste in the arts, intelligence, and liveliness and charm accompany, while not being identical with, good people. The Crawfords have all these, but are spiritually inferior; Fanny Price possesses them, but only in limited and secondary ways – and is the centre of the novel. She is the leading edge of Jane Austen's ambitious enterprise. But she provokes feelings in critics that range from constrained and dutiful pity and admiration to positive repulsion. The former are the most sympathetic, rising occasionally to enthusiasm as in V. Nabokov's praise of "her delicate grace and subdued loveliness"; the latter, the most striking, from Reginald Farrer's "cast-iron self righteousness and steely rigidity of prejudice" to Sir Kingsley Amis's "odious" and "morally detestable" (in an essay that puts the untenable adverse point of view with admirable economy and point). The common word is "priggish". And many readers would agree with Lionel Trilling that "there is scarcely one of our modern pieties" that the novel "does not offend" – something from which he, oddly, determines the profundity of the work.[6] It is therefore clearly *the* – vulnerable – book about which rude questions may be asked and most tellingly answered. Does *Mansfield Park* really require the reader to accept allegedly traditional – out of date? – values of passive suffering in the cause of allegedly traditional Principle? Or even to take the theme of Anglican 'ordination', mentioned in passing by the author in a letter to Cassandra,[7] as an apt subject for modern fiction? Only, I shall argue, in a sense so qualified by a highly wrought art as to nullify the need for grudging response or embarrassed apology.

The disconcerting, brilliant, episode of the rehearsals for *Lovers' Vows* at the end of the first volume indicates the kind of answer required. At the end of the chapter in which the slightly absurd play is proposed, half cast, and thoroughly squabbled over, Fanny is left alone with a copy:

> Her curiosity was all awake, and she ran through it with an eagerness which was suspended only by intervals of astonishment, that it could be proposed and accepted in a private Theatre! Agatha and Amelia appeared to her in their very different ways so totally improper for home representation – the situation of one, and the language of the other, so unfit to be expressed by any woman of modesty, that she could hardly suppose her cousins to be aware of what they were engaging in and longed to have them roused as soon as possible by the remonstrance which Edmund would certainly make. (1, xiv, 137)

This is typical of Fanny. Her idioms of alarm and trepidation, coupled with a troubled conventionality, are by this stage in the book familiar. It is part of a sequence of such responses which may disquiet many modern readers, just as they seem to have comforted some of Jane Austen's contemporaries ("the pure morality with which it abounds" – Lady Rob: Kerr). It is therefore of particular importance to read it with care, and in context. How authoritative – i.e. near to the author – is Fanny's reaction? How far should it be ours if, like the historical author, we normally find theatricals innocent and yet want to go along with the book? We naturally expect to concur with the prejudices of a heroine. Are we asked to here? I think it obvious that only a half assent is called for, and deliberately so – a subtlety that would escape readers who feel obliged doggedly to follow Fanny all the way. For these are the thoughts of a timid and repressed young woman "born to struggle and endure", with whose girlhood, unlighted by close affection and endorsement from anyone but Edmund, we have been led tenderly to sympathise.[8] Most of them – "a private Theatre! ... the situation of one and the language of the other ... the remonstrance which Edmund would certainly make" – are close to the mode of *style indirect libre* or free indirect speech (related terms for something we have met before, especially in discussing *Northanger Abbey* – which critics make a lot of nowadays – and which is indeed an important feature of the developed, modern, novel[9]). The implied slur on professional actresses we soon find to be shared momentarily with Edmund – who nevertheless admires them as being "hardened" – but the gentle, mistaken, attribution of unconsciousness to Maria and Julia, and the faith in the efficacy of Edmund's disapproval are all Fanny's. Therefore if we think the morality over-scrupulous we should attribute this to her, in her position at that particular time, not to the author. And, of course, Edmund's swift capitulation to the scheme under the lure of Mary and the threat of a possible outsider at Mansfield shows precisely *how* fragile Fanny's real position is, how much her response only a harassed wish for the thoroughly proper.

Even so, is not Fanny generally right? I have argued in the cases of *Northanger Abbey* and *Sense and Sensibility* that it is a characteristic of accomplished works of art to contain all that is needed for their understanding – it is through them that we understand their literary and historical contexts rather than *vice versa*. And here I do not really think it even especially desirable for every reader to go through Chapman's handy reprint of Mrs. Inchbald's version of *Lovers' Vows* in the 'Oxford' Jane Austen – nor to consider the Rousseauist implications discovered by scholars in Kotzebue's play. Given that we know from the *novel* that in *Lovers' Vows* Agatha is wronged and Amelia amorous, and given the characters of the sisters and, as it turns out, Mary, Fanny's fears are justified. Nor is there is a need to invoke Plato's distrust of representation (as Tony Tanner follows Trilling in doing[10]) to see that even pleasantly exhibitionist people will be fired by a chance to show off in disguise, as it were. Anyone who has played at charades will know this. And the situation with the charming but cruelly flirtatious Henry, stupid Rushworth and vulnerable Edmund is clearly dangerous. As the psychiatrist Robert Jay Lifton says, "moral judgements inevitably include psychological assumptions"; and Fanny's only error is in being too hopeful and nice about her cousins.

I stress this fairly obvious point because readers seem to be thrown by Fanny's confusions and initially dim views of life, whereas they are quite at home with, for example, the over-confidence of Emma in *Emma*. There is perhaps something awesome or at least respectable in timidity – while we are glad to laugh complacently at the mistakes of the dynamic or complacent. Certainly readers are likely to be more excitedly alert to characters – in art – who set out to be illimitably wicked than to those who are unrestrainedly virtuous. At any rate, Fanny's struggle with her unloving environment is so evident that attention to it should prevent an overall identification of her point of view with that of the novel. The palpitations in the East room which come soon afterwards confirm this. It is worth looking closely at these, and their context near the climax of the first volume, as an example of the strong, close subtlety by now natural to Jane Austen's writing. Fanny's state is close to self-pity, that least appetising of emotions:

> ... though there had been sometimes much of suffering to her – though her motives had been often misunderstood, her feelings disregarded, and her comprehension under-valued; though she had known the pains of tyranny, of ridicule, and neglect, yet almost every recurrence of either had led to something consolatory ... (1, xvi, 152)

Out of context this seems to belong to another kind of fiction. Tyranny? The reader may be inclined to respond with an impatient or uneasy version of Henry Tilney's remarks to Catherine Morland – "Remember the country and the age in which we live ...". Indeed, there is often an awkward literary woodenness (what Kenneth Moler calls her "bookish" voice) in Fanny's necessarily sheltered emotional vocabulary. In a different context her earlier disappointment that the chapel at Sotherton fails to call up Sir Walter Scott – "no aisles, no arches, no inscriptions, no banners. No banners, cousin ..." – receives a Tilney-like affectionate damper from Edmund: "You forget, Fanny, how lately all this has been built ..." (1, ix, 86). And this interesting pattern is repeated on a larger scale when she admires the landscape of the August night from within the drawing-room at Mansfield:

> "Here's harmony!" said she, "Here's repose! Here's what may leave all painting and all music behind, and what poetry only can attempt to describe. Here's what may tranquillize every care, and lift the heart to rapture! When I look out on such a night as this, I feel as if there could be neither wickedness nor sorrow in the world; and there certainly would be less of both if the sublimity of Nature were more attended to, and people were carried more out of themselves by contemplating such a scene ... (1, xi, 113)

"... In such a night as this/When the sweet wind did gently kiss the trees" – Lorenzo and Jessica call up Troilus and Cressida, Thisbe and Pyramus, Dido and Aeneas, Medea and Jason, and Portia talks of a good deed in a naughty world. But nearer home the good Edmund only remarks that "I like to hear your enthusiasm, Fanny" and is soon beguiled from star gazing by Mary's glee at the piano, while Fanny is scolded away from the window by Mrs. Norris.

From scenes like these it would be absurd to think of Fanny as other than – in Mary Lascelles's phrase – "youth sympathetically observed".[11] It would be vulgar to talk of her, as Tony Tanner does, in quasi-religious terms, as though she were someone out of a version of late Henry James – "She suffers in her stillness. For Righteousness' sake." Or even, I think, to follow at all John Hardy's over-solicitous admiration of this harmonious night-time speech, and of her later odd little sub-Ramblerian disquisitions on Memory and the Evergreen to Mary (2, iii, 208–10 – these latter evoke shades of the sententious Mary Bennet: – even Fanny says, self-consciously, "You will think me rhapsodizing").[12] Nevertheless, the little piece of near hysteria in the East room seems to me to have a touching truth to nature which only those who have never ever indulged their feelings can afford to find "priggish" etc. Mary Lascelles even underrates the spread and depth of such feelings when she adds that this is "not youth re-lived". Such feelings surely derive from something felt very inwardly, if only in the imagination? For in the drama the setting of this potentially reader-repellent outburst is the morning after one of Fanny's cruellest trials during the period of the theatricals. Just previous she is being urged to act – almost bullied in public – by Tom and the others. Edmund tries to shield her but Mrs. Norris intervenes with her peculiar knack of dressing the spiteful and domineering in the garb of conventional virtue:

> "I shall think her a very obstinate, ungrateful girl, if she does not do what her aunt and cousins wish her – very ungrateful indeed considering who and what she is." (1, xv, 147)

Ingratitude to benefactors – amongst the lowest of the vices for Shakespeare – is very important in this novel, as in Jane Austen generally (of which more later). But one does not need to reflect on that to feel something strictly inappropriate to art, like rage, at this galling humiliation. It is also a misrepresentation, for Lady Bertram (if as is likely it is she who is being invoked), is clearly indifferent, and part of Fanny's motive for declining derives from her sense of what is due to the real master of the house, Sir Thomas. But the worst is to follow. She is used to such treatment from Mrs. Norris, and perhaps inured: but on this occasion she is defended, and admirably – the reader's enthusiasm wells up – by Mary Crawford. "I do not like my situation; this *place* is too hot for me", says she, "with astonished eyes" at Mrs. Norris, and moves over to comfort Edmund's cousin. The narrator remarks, what Fanny may feel, that this act of spirited charity "and the really good feelings by which she was almost purely governed, were rapidly restoring her to all the little she had lost in Edmund's favour". (Note the exceedingly fine detail in the "almost".) Fanny is rightly bound to feel "obliged" by this kindness, especially when Mary consummately embarks on flattering talk of William and his naval career. She thus becomes the victim of a situation in which to respond negatively would be genuine ingratitude. Hence the fervour of her reflections next morning.

It is further characteristic of Jane Austen's compressed art, packed with implication under the straightforward clarity, that these dire reflections have a little internal material frame which also helps in assessing their proper place. The comforts of the East room are enjoyed only on Mrs. Norris's conditions of its having no fire and being spoken of as an undeserved indulgence. In it "Her plants, her books . . . her works of charity and ingenuity" are gathered, just as such maidenly things are later gathered by a succession of poor but honest – sweet but secretly powerful – heroines of Victorian fiction who incline us to doubt of the grown-up reality of what we are reading.[13] But here the note of coyness is sounded only for a moment. Feelings of the "pains of tyranny" and so on are followed immediately by consolatory thoughts which, by a tilt of the frame as it were, are infected by a slight, affectionate air of the ludicrous. "Transparencies" in which "Tintern Abbey held its station between a cave in Italy, and a moonlight lake in Cumberland" are completed by William's sketch of HMS *Antwerp* with "letters as tall as the main-mast". Fanny is seen as poised between the school-room and the world, trying if "by giving air to her geraniums she might inhale a breeze of mental strength herself". Earlier Mary has asked "Pray, is she out, or is she not?" (1, v, 48) – suggesting a problem that Henry James three-quarters of a century later was to see as the starting point for a novel (*The Awkward Age*). This passage contains a better answer than Edmund then gave. She does have "the age and sense of a woman" but is still more than commonly vulnerable, still the girl who, going to encounter her uncle on his return shortly afterwards, seeks "a courage which the outside of no door had ever supplied to her" (2, i, 177).

It would be positively hard boiled therefore to feel repelled into mere tolerance ("only a novel") by this stage. Indeed, throughout the book there is a subtle system of apologetics for Fanny's case – until the end, when, presumably, she no longer has need of them.

> . . . She would be an easy victim of scientific criticism if she were not intended to awaken on the reader's part an impulse more tender and more perfectly expectant . . .

– says the comparatively brash and blunt Henry James of his vulnerable young Isabel Archer in *The Portrait of a Lady*. Jane Austen is less overtly directive, but we can catch her at the same process, as it were, in the odd organising turn of phrase in passages such as the following. A few pages after the episode I have been discussing Edmund has agreed to play Anhalt to Mary's Amelia:

> Her heart and her judgement were equally against Edmund's decision; she could not acquit his unsteadiness; and his happiness under it made her wretched. She was full of jealousy and agitation. Miss Crawford came in with looks of gaiety which seemed an insult.... Every body around her was gay and busy.... She alone was sad and insignificant; she had no share in any thing; she might go or stay... without being missed... Mrs. Grant was of consequence; *her* good nature had honourable mention... and Fanny was at first in some danger of envying her the character she had accepted. But reflection brought better feelings... (1, xvii, 159–60)

At first sight a (freely indirect) report of what is going forward; but on closer inspection patterned by signals from the author to see Fanny from an appropriate distance. It is her "jealousy" that makes Mary's looks seem an insult; loneliness and lack of attention that put her in "danger of envying" Mrs. Grant. The feelings are named for what they are; but they are part of a context which is real, and really troubling. Typically they are motions to be conquered by reflection. But again, a reader who feels obliged to identify as opposed to sympathise with Fanny's situation is not reading attentively.

In a less gloomy mood, when the threat of acting has been replaced by the threat of Henry Crawford's initially light-minded wooing, the narrator makes a rare personal appearance:

> ... although there doubtless are such unconquerable young ladies of eighteen (or one should not read about them) as are never to be persuaded into love against their judgement by all that talent, manner, attention and flattery can do, I have no inclination to believe Fanny one of them, or to think that with so much tenderness of disposition, and so much taste as belonged to her, she could have escaped heart-whole from the courtship (though the courtship of only a fortnight) of such a man as Crawford... (2, vi, 231)

What is particularly interesting about this (apart from a characteristic side-swipe at the kind of incredibly virtuous fiction that this is not) is the slight unease of rhythm, the uncharacteristic choppy length of the sentence with all its qualifications. I do not think that it is *quite* what the reader would feel if he were not told to do so. There is a sense of delicate patching up and realigning – the reason, as we soon learn, being that from now on Henry, for the deep purposes of the book, must appear more amiable. It is perhaps significant that much later this direct narrative "I" reappears (there seems to be a general erroneous impression that it is reserved for the final, winding-up, chapter) when he is at his most convincing, in the relatively relaxed though noisy and embarrassed scenes in Portsmouth. He deals admirably with her family:

> ...and I believe, there is scarcely a young lady in the united kingdoms, who would not rather put up with the misfortune of being sought by a clever, agreeable man, than to have him driven away by the vulgarity of her nearest relations. (3, x, 402)

Note that here Henry has advanced from being a talented flatterer to being genuinely "clever" and "agreeable".

But, granted Jane Austen's care to explain her heroine, to normalise and put into understandable and compassionable context those reactions that may appear negative or too consciously virtuous to be real – the kinds of thing that make the *hasty* reader mutter with Richard III "So wise so young, they say, do never live long" – we are still stuck with the obstinate fact of Fanny's lack of glamour. The likely expert Nabokov offering no comment here, I find it impossible to agree with Margaret Kirkham's clever idea that "her apparent saintliness is closely connected with her ability to excite sexual passion".[14] It may have been possible in the bad old days to think of "religiosity in pretty young women" in "a salacious way". I expect that salacious thoughts are always possible. We all know what an irritant as well as an obstacle Lovelace finds Clarissa's virtue, and of the nature of the feelings analysed so acutely by Diderot in *La Religieuse*, or so thunderously by Lewis in *The Monk* (for that matter, it may have been Penelope's seemly weaving that drove the suitors mad). But Fanny is not 'religiose', only religious. Jane Austen's heroines are never seen on their knees in church or out of it. Nor – this is what is important – is Fanny saintly. As Mary observes, it is "her not caring about you" that initially tickles Henry's resolve (2, vi, 230), rather than any villain's urge to defile. We do not need the banal profundities of the Marquis de Sade to read Jane Austen, and must be content with the ordinary sense exemplified by Tony Tanner when he speaks of Fanny's as "perhaps the most nearly asexual marriage among the marriages achieved by Jane Austen's heroines". For me the "perhaps" is unnecessary.

Neither saintly nor sexy then, Fanny is evidently a beautifully seen case of timidity in adversity. And since the word 'case' can have semi-medical connotations, I think it only moderately daring to hazard an analogy drawn from modern life. Margaret Kirkham could find indirect support for some of her arguments in the contemporary, advertisement reinforced, cult of eggshell feminine fragility which has as one of of its nastier probable consequences the plague of *anorexia nervosa*. A good deal of work is being done on the putative history of feminine neuroses.[15] And it is not entirely irrelevant to Fanny, or she to it. Of course, Fanny has no problem with food, nor is she neurotic. But one point of my argument about her is that Jane Austen is carefully plotting a pattern manifest in grosser and much more lamentable form in the modern affliction. I do not want to speculate about the results of the inadequacies of Lieutenant and Mrs. Price, Sir Thomas and Lady Bertram as parents. These are obvious and will occur to any reader, not just the modern one. Rather it is a question of Fanny's superlative moral rectitude – the core of the matter for her personal admirers and detractors alike ("She is never, ever, wrong" – Tanner; "a monster of complacency ... under a cloak of cringing self-abasement" – Amis). One of the mechanisms of anorexia is the control of disturbing circumstances, inside or outside the person, by abstention. The refusal of intake is strangely akin to the abuse of intake by a heavy drinker (an observation that is sometimes recognised clinically nowadays by both afflictions being treated under one roof). It is an attempt at chemical control of the world. In particular, perhaps, a control of the stirrings of sexuality. In the analogue offered by Fanny's case, it is her tendency to withdraw into conventional negativities when the Crawfords appear that strikes one first. Then one recalls her insistence, so useful to those who use her, on personal order, neatness, and related virtues. It is Fanny, not Henry (who admittedly has his reasons), who is so very shocked and disapproving and bowled over by the noise and mess of Portsmouth. She is right about this, just as she is right morally most of the time: but she is right in something the same way as a self-starving girl is right in washing, ironing, tidying and preparing food for her mother. The particular virtue is substantial in itself but is overdone, done in the service of something other than itself.

For Fanny's are not exhibitions of priggishness for its own sake. In this novel everyone, excepting Lady Bertram, is, as in life, full of their own judgement – Sir Thomas and Mary making an odd leading pair in their positiveness. Mrs. Norris particularly is characterised by her obsession with economy and arrangement and wastefully making do. But Fanny's judgements (those that have a hint of the mean minded or mealy mouthed) and her excessive decorum, are typically responses to threats to her precariously held calm. This is obvious in the disturbance caused by *Lovers' Vows*. But almost as soon as Mary begins to attract Edmund the defences are alerted. He wants to talk about Mary and dangles for reassurance:

> "It is her countenance that is so attractive. She has a wonderful play of feature! But was there nothing in her conversation that struck you Fanny, as not quite right?"

Of course there was:

> "Oh! yes, she ought not to have spoken of her uncle as she did. I was quite astonished. An uncle with whom she has been living so many years . . ." etc.

And on the moralising goes, even up to Fanny's offering to extend its scope: "Do not you think . . . that this impropriety is a reflection itself upon Mrs. Crawford . . . ?" But this is a mistake, because here Edmund is able to find the excuse he wants – "Yes, we must suppose the faults of the niece to have been those of the aunt; and it makes one more sensible of the disadvantages she has been under" (1, vii, 63–4). The reader may think that it does not make Edmund immediately sensible of the disadvantages Fanny has been under with Lady Bertram and Mrs. Norris – but by this time the unpleasant sententious tone has done its damage. They are a picky couple. The obvious difference between them is that Edmund wants to allow himself to fall for Mary, to expand, while Fanny uses moral notions – sincerely, no doubt – in order to conduct a losing defence of the proper, which is also a defence of her own emotional position. Her *need* to be right, given her capacity for being so, is very different from Mrs. Norris's almost equally evident need for bustling censoriousness, which is less deeply analysed though brilliantly indicated. It is the very opposite to the complacent confidence of Tom, the impervious rectitude of Sir Thomas, or the neutral-to-negative unimpeachability of Lady Bertram who "thinks justly on all important points". They all recognise the same code – from whom else but Edmund has Fanny internalised it? – but she requires it as a prop for existence in a way that none of them could do. When Sir Thomas wonderfully erupts into the theatricals:

> Her agitation and alarm exceeded all that was endured by the rest, by the right of a disposition which not even innocence could keep from suffering. She was nearly fainting . . . (2, i, 176)

This is not Fanny's thought, free indirect style. It is a narratorial statement which claims for her a right to suffer. Which would be curious if we did not already see her as having need of a special and tender attention.

ii

The reader is reminded of this disposition with growing force at the point when, after Sir Thomas's return and partly as a consequence of his increasing estimate of her value, she is indeed 'coming out' socially. Henry begins his initially frivolous wooing; Mary becomes more and more her friend with Edmund's approval; she is asked out to dinner (actually for the second time); and the sequence finds its local, if not universally agreeable, climax in the ball at Mansfield – its larger one in Henry's proposal. These are, roughly, the contents of the second volume (the brilliant and decisive use of volume divisions is a minor literary pleasure in itself) which Jane Austen described as having "a larger proportion of narrative" than the other two and therefore, presumably, a larger proportion of narrator's directive prose (this is something towards which J.F. Burrows might direct part of his future analyses).[16] It is easy to notice a packed series of more or less direct alerts about Fanny's progress in the larger world, starting from the point when "Mrs. Grant, with sudden recollection, turned to her and asked for the pleasure of her company too" (2, iv, 215). We may, if attentive, recollect the hidden reason for this recollection – but Fanny, though Edmund himself is delighted, manages to find an obstacle in Lady Bertram's putative needs. She "would not venture, even on his encouragement, to such a flight of audacious independence . . ." Three pages later, having approached Lady Bertram with a "self-denying" tone, Fanny feels "anxious . . . more anxious than she ought to be" and slips out of the room rather than hear Sir Thomas discuss this mighty question. Then, its having been resolved in favour of her going, we learn that "Simple as such an engagement might appear in other's eyes", it is a strange enjoyment for her (219). Mrs. Norris brutally reinforces this timidity: "Remember, wherever you are, you must be the lowest and last" (one cannot always see, incidentally, why this completely lifelike woman is known as a comic creation) – and, brusquely observing how likely it is to rain, denies her the use of the carriage. Fanny's reaction is not of resentment or even disappointment: "Her niece thought it perfectly reasonable. She rated her own claims to comfort as low even as Mrs. Norris could"; and she is struck literally speechless when Sir Thomas, casually for him, offers the carriage as a matter, now, of course (221).

But in spite of this official encouragement, the signs of Henry's unforeseen arrival at the parsonage, the prospect of being observed by him "was a great increase of the trepidation with which she performed the very aweful ceremony of walking into the drawing-room" (223). Of course, there is an element of mock grandiosity in the vivid language of this last sentence – shades, perhaps, of eighteenth-century domestic satirical verse, such as Gray's *Ode* on the death of his favourite cat. Nevertheless, we get – here in a short space – an extremely powerful sense of what a nervous minefield the life of one "incumbered by refinement and self-distrust" is, and has been up until this point in her development. Misery, conveyed by these unobtrusive hints and touches, to live in such a way. And scarcely the portrait of the confident "christian heroine" and moralist descried by some critics (Marilyn Butler, for example) – the torch bearer for the traditional order and dignity of (of all places) Sir Thomas Bertram's worldly Mansfield Park. To adapt the picture of another outsider, Pope's Pamela:

> A meek, unquiet, quailing, wretched Thing!
> Prim Proper calm but paints her outward Part
> She sighs, and is no *Miss Price* at her Heart.

iii

Shortly afterwards comes the episode of the necklace which provides a wonderfully subtle, telling and nervous dramatisation of the state of Fanny's soul; and which, often mentioned, has never so far as I know been understood in print (though I assume it is understood by the majority of ordinary readers). The common commentatorial response to it is exemplified by Tony Tanner (who elsewhere, however, commends "a minute attention to local detail") – "Henry slyly forces a fancy chain on her".[17] This is just wrong. Mary is the agent, there is no forcing, and the Crawford object is decidedly a necklace not a chain. However, these pedantic objections are nothing compared to that to the missing of the real, clear, implications of the scene. Critics, flattering themselves on their temporary adoption of a rigorous propriety supposed to prevail in the past, tend to be so busy exclaiming with impeccable morality over the shallowness and mere speciousness etc. of the Crawfords' harmless (to me entirely amiable) little ploy that they miss the point about Fanny, which is the main point:

The gift was too valuable. But, Miss Crawford persevered, and argued the case with so much affectionate earnestness ... as to be finally successful. Fanny found herself obliged to yield that she might not be accused of pride or indifference, or some other littleness. . . . She looked and looked, longing to know which might be the least valuable; and was determined in her choice at last by fancying there was one necklace more frequently placed before her eyes than the rest. It was of gold prettily worked; and though Fanny would have preferred a longer and a plainer chain as more adapted for her purpose, she hoped in fixing on this, to be chusing what Miss Crawford least wished to keep. Miss Crawford smiled her perfect approbation . . . (2, viii, 258)

Then it is teasingly revealed that it was Henry's "choice in the first place", which may mislead careless critics (for all I know). But Fanny blushingly denies a suspicion that what Mary is "now doing is with his knowledge and at his desire" – a "confederacy" (259). And although Nabokov thought the necklace "bought for Fanny by Henry Crawford"[18] we have, like Fanny, only Mary's evidence to go on – that it was "purchased three years ago, before he knew there was such a throat in the world" – when both throat and owner were fifteen, in fact, and the East room still the school-room. It should not be possible to escape the substantial, poignant drift of all this: that Fanny, tremulously preoccupied as usual with defending her equilibrium against the disturbance of Mary and Henry – it is hard to tell which is the chief threat, the siren or the lover – and primarily afraid lest she be "accused of pride or indifference, or some other littleness" – fears hard to justify objectively in this friendly context – does really achieve littleness. One must ask oneself what kind of person it is who faced with a generous and considerate act of giving longs to know which alternative is the "least valuable" and then – worse – what the giver "least wished to keep". She may be jealous of Mary, frightened of her, but it is unpleasantly mean to think of her as trying to give away the cheapest and least wanted article. It is also a mistake about Mary's action (incorrect especially should we want to disapprove of the Crawford plot which would be to foist upon her the greatest possible obligation). We cannot imagine Fanny thinking herself capable of the behaviour and motives she *automatically* attributes to Mary. Actually she is judging Mary as morally inferior in the midst of a genuine pleasure and recognition of "kindness".

The scene is therefore full of ammunition for those who find Fanny repellent, whether its implications are fully realised or not. But its close is often cited as confirming an anti-Crawford line. Fanny thinks Henry "wanted . . . to cheat her of her tranquillity as he had cheated them" –

Maria and Julia – by his attentions, and is still suspicious about the necklace despite her protests to the contrary, because she judges (on what evidence?) that "Miss Crawford, complaisant as sister, was careless as a woman and a friend" (260). So, given a handsome and needed present which she does not actually know to be prompted by Henry at all until a hundred pages later (362) she makes her fraught way home full of distrust and disapproval with "a change rather than a diminution of cares since her treading that path before". Oh dear. This is precisely why Jane Austen has been at such pains up until now, and especially just prior to this, to make us understand the science, genesis and aetiology of Fanny's moral fastidiousness – how her negativities are functions of her real suffering.

But the moralising tone is too catching. This is an episode (*pace* Sir Kingsley) from Jane Austen nearing the height of her powers, and not one of the gloomier parts of Richardson, Flaubert or Ouida. The next chapter brings the gift of Edmund's chain, and a lighter or even satirical tone. Fanny having "all the heroism of principle" but "also many of the feelings of youth and nature" (many, not all) behaves with a beautiful absurdity about Edmund's scrap of an unfinished note which prefigures the episode of Harriet's "Most precious treasures" in *Emma*, and anyway recalls the life of sensitive eighteen-year-olds at any time:

> This specimen, written in haste as it was, had not a fault; and there was a felicity in the flow of the first four words, in the arrangement of "My very dear Fanny", which she could have looked at for ever. (2, ix, 265)

A literary critic, then. The effect of this is not to belittle the emotions and vulnerabilities just previous to it, but to humorise and therefore humanise them. A frame is, as so often, provided by the context. The change is not final, of course, nor even particularly lasting. The ordeal of the ball is still to be faced. But by now we are fully aware of the extra-delicate structure of shrinking feeling emanating from Fanny, and its effects on her judgement.

iv

But there is more to it than that. There are lots of novels about nervous girls; the nervous girl is one of the most familiar figures in fiction from *Clarissa* to, say, *A Dream Came True* by Betty Neels (1982). Fanny's half-misleading reputation for a moral rigour equal, or in excess of, that of her creator, would not exist if the over-sensitive and tender nature, the fearfulness and so on, were not part of the very same character which ultimately impresses both the other people in the novel and the reader with a feeling of *respect*. Fanny has the courage which is often the direct result of weakness acknowledged – in a different sphere she confirms the military commonplace that the brave man is not he who feels no fear. As her physical apearance and health, her "bloom" and carriage, improve, so do her mental and spiritual charms. Up and down her progress goes, but as the novel advances, up begins to predominate. The ease with which this is felt is one of the reasons why she is totally solid to the reader. She may sometimes act as a tax on our tolerance, but never a tax on the sense of the book being about the real world and not "only a novel". Progress is, of course, manifest from the beginning: but the really significant positive movement starts to prevail as a result of Henry Crawford's wooing. At the Grants' dinner party he starts – superbly cavalier – to chat about the fun of the theatricals, and even achieves the flirtatious conspiratorial about Sir Thomas's return. If *we* "had had the disposal of events . . . I think, Miss Price, we would have indulged ourselves with a week's calm in the Atlantic at that season". But he has not – yet – had the opportunity to study Fanny at all intelligently and receives a reply that amazes all parties, including the reader:

> . . . Fanny, averting her face, said with a firmer tone than usual, "As far as I am concerned, sir, I would not have delayed his return for a day. My uncle disapproved it all so entirely when he did arrive, that in my opinion, every thing had gone quite far enough."
>
> She had never spoken so much at once to him in her life before, and never so angrily to any one; and when her speech was over, she trembled and blushed at her own daring. (2, v, 225–6)

Typically this admirably positive self-assertion is couched in terms of disapproval, and is flanked by the authority of Sir Thomas. But it *is* courageous, and therefore attractive. It is the key to what follows: Henry's falling in love.

> He was surprized; but after a few moments silent consideration of her he replied in a calmer, graver tone, and as if the candid result of conviction, "I believe you are right. It was more pleasant than prudent. We were getting too noisy".

After this she becomes too shy for further conversation. But in spite of the small reservation given in the "as if . . . candid", the interchange improves both of them for us. From then on they flower for the reader in a way so evident and so well discussed elsewhere – his real sensitivity and love – her more and more controlled responses in which he can (mis)interpret her modest shyness as encouragement enough – the Shakespeare reading later on – that further blow-by-blow comment here is superfluous.

The proposal is, as I have said, the climax though by no means the end. It is the grandest statement and amplification of the pattern I have traced so far. Henry's courtship has become so gracious and above all sincere: "Had you seen her this morning, Mary ... attending with such ineffable sweetness and patience, to all the demands of her aunt's stupidity ... her colour beautifully heightened" (2, xii, 296) – that nearly every reader likes *her* better and wishes for *his* success. Unlike the luckier Frank Churchill in *Emma*, he percipiently sees the spiritual qualities of his beloved as being part of her physical ones. Henry Austen thought that he conducts himself "properly, as a clever pleasant man"; and even Cassandra is said to have warmly argued that her sister "alter the end ... and let Mr. Crawford marry Fanny Price".[19] On the contrary, Fanny's reaction far exceeds a mere refusal, or even an extreme version of the virginal modesty appropriate to an eighteen-year-old ward and *jeune fille de la maison* of that period. She does not believe that he can possibly be serious. In spite of the evidence he means "only to deceive her for the hour", and she is hurt and angry – "She could hardly stand" (2, xiii, 301). Even admitting how right she is to feel warned and impressed by his light dalliance with Julia and grievous flirtation with Maria, this particular form of response is special to Fanny – Disbelief which turns into a flutter of withdrawal and judgement:

> Every thing natural, probable, reasonable was against it. ... How could *she* have excited serious attachment in a man who had seen so many, and been admired by so many, and flirted with so many, infinitely her superiors – who seemed so little open to serious impressions ... who thought so slightly, so carelessly, so unfeelingly on all such points ... (306)

The point of such a turmoil is obvious in the light of the foregoing analysis and needs no further stress here. But what might be expected to follow such panic in *her* breast? Exactly what does: a courageous and successful defence of a moral and prudential principle subscribed to by everyone at Mansfield but mocked at by Mary, and in the test of practice denied by Mrs. Rushworth's approved marriage. The principle – central to Jane Austen's work – that, at the very least, mutual respect is essential to a good marriage.

It is tempting to elide this into a loftier, vaguer idea concerning Love.

But to do that is to enter a realm of ideal contention and a thousand happy endings where "Oh, it is only a novel" becomes a more and more cogent response. The great novelists are very rarely able to endorse purely love matches at the expense of more modestly compatible unions which may, of course, include love but are not solely defined and justified by it. Here Fanny is defending in her own delicate young person the initially minimal position that she "cannot like" Henry and "thinks ill" of his principles. The wonderful interview with Sir Thomas that opens the third volume focusses on her all the weight of a complex and mainly respectable – this is the point – tradition of Paternal Authority, reinforced by the obligations due to a patron. Just as Henry's interested but real kindness to William confuses her response to his proposal, so Sir Thomas's belated kindness about a fire in the East room makes it more difficult to resist his incredulous disapproval of her refusal. His arguments evoke all the terrors of a Patriarch demanding obedience, duty, respect, consideration for the family, prudence for herself, and gratitude. He speaks like Cicero and emerges almost like the Commendatore's statue. If Mr. Harlowe in *Clarissa* rules by sheer attributed power, Sir Thomas complicates his by a lofty benevolence. Fanny cannot defend herself by admitting a love for Edmund, nor her real evidence against Henry. But her trembling evasion remains firm. She cannot hope for "delicacy" from the father of Maria, but defends herself simply by being unable to give in; "embarrassed to a degree that made either speaking or looking up impossible" before his attack, she can only stick to being "very sorry indeed" after it. The question of gratitude is the most awful of all: "Heaven defend me from being ungrateful" she thinks to herself, and we may be put in mind of this author's apparent approval of "gratitude and esteem" as "good foundations for affection" in the process of Elizabeth Bennet's change of heart towards Darcy, or of Edmund's later appeal to Fanny to "prove yourself grateful and tender-hearted" (3, iv, 347).[20] But heaven does defend her because she is not ungrateful, far from it, and is only giving life to the principle she has learnt and is now able to fall back on.

It is, however, her capacity for gratitude and esteem that is to be tried throughout most of the rest of the book. The key points are obvious. The *Henry VIII* reading puts the whole business of Henry's acting a part, even including the momentary impulse to act at being a sailor ("The wish was rather eager than lasting", 2, vi, 236) and the current one, confessedly dilettante, to have a go at being a preacher, in a much pleasanter light. Especially since in the latter case he has estimably "thought before, and thought with constancy" (3, iii, 340) on Church matters and even extorts "half a smile" from grave and badgered Fanny – which qualifies her often quoted questioning of the consistency of his self-knowledge (343). Then Sir Thomas's statesmanlike "medicinal project" of sending Fanny to Portsmouth can only raise by contrast the gratitude she really owes to Mansfield. And Henry's behaviour at Portsmouth speaks for itself. Perhaps most weighty of all is the influence exerted by Edmund's approval of Henry, the obscurely painful concomitant of an equally potent probable loss of him to Mary. None the less, under all this pressure – the pressure of virtually everything significant in her world besides – Fanny not only maintains her position, but by an extension of it clears herself from the last suspicion of mere pale negative obstinacy. While her love for Edmund – credible though it is as an only slightly developed *donnée* (he is not the "cipher" he is often described as being, but grows on one through his decency) is simply reinforced – the as it were theoretical position from which Fanny acts is extended, strengthened and articulated. We know from J.F. Burrows that she has quite a small speaking part for a heroine. So the grand speech that is provoked by Edmund's reports of the amazement of Mrs. Grant and Mary at her refusal of their brother has a rarity and a cogency very different from her earlier defensive retreats into ordinary morals, yet is most convincingly derived from her character and experience:

> I *should* have thought . . . that every woman must have felt the possi-
> bility of a man's not being approved, not being loved by one of her
> sex, at least, let him be ever so generally agreeable. Let him have all
> the perfections in the world, I think it ought not to be set down as
> certain, that a man must be acceptable to every woman he may
> happen to like himself. . . . How was I to have an attachment at his
> service, as soon as it was asked for? (3, iv, 353)

This is unanswerable. In a way it is an argument to counteract the emphasis on gratitude as a motive for love, or the idea that the wish to marry follows on from esteem. It is not a specifically feminist assertion in the sense of being limited to women in its application. – We may reflect that Henry's later elopement with Maria entails his – somewhat incredible – failure to act on the same principle. There a woman apparently compels a man she happens to like to find her disastrously acceptable. Fanny's speech is, rather, an energetically rational account of the logical consequences of holding that people are free to choose. Edmund recognises it as a "truth" even if he does still, heartily, go on to predict Fanny's eventual capitulation – in accord with wishes natural to him and to the novel reader.

v

It is from this position that the resolution of *Mansfield Park* derives. The reason for that dissatisfaction with the ending which is generally rightly felt, but often rationalised away in criticism, is not that it is, as Reginald Farrer puts it, "a dishonest bit of sheer bad art",[21] but that the honesty modifies the art. Or, more accurately: if the point of the bulk of the novel centred in Fanny is to be sustained, a gratifying end (marriages to the Crawfords) as opposed to a formally happy and correct one (which happens) is felt to be impossible. The art does falter, but this is because the *important* subject is the emergence and survival of the tender and vulnerable Fanny. In a way the gratifying would be banal beside this. An alternative obvious ease would have been gained by continuing throughout to render Henry as as flighty as he first is, and as much less pleasant than his sister. Indeed, there is a hasty undramatic, offstage, return to this. Or resort could have been had to plot devices such as misunderstandings etc. – But Fanny is too serious a theme for this kind of novelising. It is essential that she be subjected to the full force of Henry's peculiarly Austenian charm and to survive it by a finger, for if she were not so exposed the point residing in her integrity would be destroyed. Unfortunately this leaves no room for the cosy. Having achieved the courage to say it, she must be seen to mean "Never". And the result is that if Jane Austen is not to embark on another novel on a different subject at once, she has to destroy Henry and Mary by an arbitrary exercise of authorial power which involves a regression to earlier and inferior ways of writing. In other words, the achievement of the conception and creation of Fanny and what she represents involves the sacrifice of some of the more attractive things that surround her. Not so much bad art as art limited by its ambitious success.

I do not mean to be paradoxical. *Mansfield Park* is lopsided. But as I have said, it goes further and deeper than *Pride and Prejudice* and perhaps deeper even than the masterpiece *Emma*, which many of its creative practices foreshadow. Especially it shows how the fully defined and self-sufficient modern novel is being evolved from existing materials. To give only the more obvious instances: the removal to Portsmouth is a brilliant stroke of Sir Thomas's evolving out of the situation at Mansfield. It is a brilliant stroke also for an author wishing to set her heroine in a different and even more sympathetic light, to focus on her and to distance the reader from the other important characters – except Henry, the struggle against whom is her final important trial. It is in itself a superb episode: Jane Austen's most celebrated excursion into the materially necessitous life beneath that of the landed gentry, and a fit subject for Admiral Foote's surprise "that I had the power of drawing the Portsmouth-Scenes so well". But it nevertheless involves also a calculated partial harking back to the old epistolary mode with some of its virtues but also its most important inherent drawback: the lack of an as it were impartial dramatisation, and thus the withdrawal of that check on feasibility which direct presentation supplies. (Q.D. Leavis's celebrated argument that the work originally derived from the epistolary *Lady Susan* has great force – although the strange delights of that wonderful little *novella* seem, as I have argued above in chapter two, to indicate a sceptical and disciplined refinement of Richardson on lines similar to those of Laclos, rather than a preparation for the tender subject of *Mansfield Park*.) The cost of the liberties thus earned – for the presentation of others than Fanny – is particularly felt in the sudden coarse coyness of Mary's speculations about the benefits accruing if Tom should die, followed presumably by Sir Thomas:

> Fanny, Fanny, I see you smile, and look cunning, but upon my honour, I never bribed a physician in my life. Poor young man! – If he is to die, there will be *two* poor young men less in the world. . . . I put it to your conscience, whether "Sir Edmund" would not do more good with all the Bertram property, than any other possible "Sir". (3, xiv, 434)

It is a consolation to the many admirers of Mary (Reginald Farrer seems to have wanted to marry her in preference to any other figure in Jane Austen) that this gross flippancy is not a revelation of the true nature of a real character but the skilled expedient of a novelist disposing of her artefacts in the interests of a major theme. Most obviously the 'real' Mary has been, at the very least, far too clever to offer such cynical fare to little Fanny. She is a frank exponent of *laissez-faire* practice in the matter or marital conquest and treaty: "It is every body's duty to do as well for themselves as they can" (2, xii, 289 – notice "duty"); but this is a simplification running into mere fiction.

Similarly, the narrator's voice, so subtly present previously, develops an arbitrary note. At the end we are *told*, fairly drily, if amusingly enough, of things that before have been the subjects of delicate presentation and dramatisation. The manner is one of abstraction in both senses; of the settlement of issues in a way that is consonant with the main action but very much less interesting. Not only are the characters' fates disposed of in a series of summarising paragraphs of the sort familiar and not entirely unwelcome to the novel reader (everybody wants to know what happens in a story be it ever so cursorily stated), but what have been questions of palpitating interest and engagement are frozen into a relatively pallid permanency. How sincere is Henry? Answer: he "had rationally, as well as passionately loved" Fanny (3, xvii, 469). Would she have had him at last? Answer: "Fanny must have been his reward" (467) The whole of the final chapter is a very superior version indeed of the "distribution at the last of prizes, pensions, husbands, wives, babies, millions, appended paragraphs, and cheerful remarks". Its superiority is attested by the local brilliancy and lack of false cheer in these remarks – the "mutual punishment" of Mrs. Norris and Maria, and Sir Thomas's recognition that the former had been "a part of himself", now purged *à la* Shakespeare and Middleton (465), being only famous examples. But the even more celebrated opening paragraph, often ineptly taken as a general characterisation of Jane Austen's art by herself, is actually an illusion-stripping device telling the reader not only that the novel is ending but that the register is changing into a more obvious, distant and merely fictional mode:

> Let other pens dwell on guilt and misery. I quit such odious subjects as soon as I can, impatient to restore every body, not greatly in fault themselves, to tolerable comfort, and to have done with all the rest. (461)

This is 'auto-critical' or 'meta-fictional' talk (of a kind elsewhere often rather strangely welcome to modern critics as representing a sophisticated progressive tendency in fiction). It implies having explored a convention of lively realism which is now being temporarily abandoned. Here the best word *is* "impatient" rather than the "weary" often used by critics (e.g. Nabokov, Fleishman). Nevertheless, such defensive deliberateness does not, I think, save us from a justifiable dissatisfaction about the Crawfords. Henry's elopement is frequently piously explained away as though we were dealing with an unfortunate piece of history. But:

> When he returned from Richmond, he would have been glad to see Mrs. Rushworth no more. – All that followed was the result of her imprudence; and he went off with her at last, because he could not help it, regretting Fanny, even at the moment . . . (468)

This does not have even a plausible internal logic – say what one will about Henry's vanity and bad upbringing. Bolting with someone else's wife is doubtless a "dreadful crime" as Fanny thinks. But we know far too little about it that is internal. As Reginald Farrer, eloquently testy, says, "Henry was no mere boy, to be rushed by any married woman into a scandal . . . one utterly declines to believe he ever did so". The fact is that most readers love the Crawfords, which is why some critics have to work with such nit-picking assiduity to find, or even create, retrospective faults in them.[22] In a novel which had not so vital a conflicting theme to establish and vindicate, brother and sister might have passed admirably. What is important is not to let the essentially small local failure with them at the end obscure the brilliant, serious success of the whole – which is centered in Fanny.

II FLAUBERT AND JANE AUSTEN

vi

To look at this success in another way – and to return to the general question of the modern novel. The creation of realistic fiction depends on the reader's being only momentarily and fleetingly conscious of the artifices and conventions that sustain the illusion. Of course, there are exceptions to this from Fielding to Martin Amis. It is regular practice for the 'author' to intrude even if this person turns out not to be the Author at all but one of her or his chosen narrative voices. Some kind of tale teller is present. But units such as soliloquy, anecdote, lyrical description, set dialogue, literary allusion, *sententiae* etc. are de-stressed as units and dissolved and melded into a general flow which is misleadingly but purposefully like our own general flow of written or spoken conversation. This is obvious – immediately sensed by any reader if not articulated; and one is surprised at the surprise of critics who find such observations excitingly new. Thus M.M. Bakhtin, writing in the 1930s but a name to conjure with nowadays, is only stating a commonplace well when he remarks that to look for discrete, set "traditional" stylistic forms in the novel is to "transpose a symphonic (orchestrated) theme on to the piano keyboard".[23] But the metaphor of the symphony – frequently used by Flaubert in his letters – is apt. The Novel is a dynamic construction which more and more conceals its formal components and origins, a complex fluid organisation of recurring themes, or "musical complex of associations" as Thomas Mann very deliberately put it.

It is no surprise, therefore, that what people naturally have to say about Jane Austen's novels is set up not in terms of components but of characters and their destinies. We rightly surrender to the idea of the real and the solid, and are momentarily dispirited to learn concordance facts such as that Emma has a "speaking-part of 21,501 words".[24] Surely Emma is illimitable, eternally there? Could yet speak another word? Might even speak to us – and so on. Nevertheless, she is, like the equally vivid Hamlet, an artefact, a series of well-disposed words.

With this in mind I want to look again in brief and summary form at the description of Jane Austen as "modern" by invoking at some little distance the shade of Flaubert. Flaubert mainly because while she is often called modern, he virtually *always* is. My limited intention is not to provide new light on him (a very rash enterprise for the English critic) but to allow some of his enormous status – as the ultimate or near ultimate in the highly developed modern novelist – to reflect justly back on her.

They are both early grand exponents of a form which, like the symphony, was emerging as the dominant growing point of the art. And though there is no simple theory of progress relevant to art, there is local development and mastery. A few creators take what has gone before and cast it into a new mould – though not necessarily with the calculated fuss and clash often associated with twentieth-century experimentalist propaganda. The precise dates of Jane Austen and Flaubert do not matter, influence being in any case out of the question: nor does precise valuation – that she is the greater artist is not here to the point. I am really invoking reputation, and in doing so trying to qualify again the merely English 'Janeite' ethos – which yet retains, as I have said, some real *charm* in relation to recent reactions against it.

Flaubert has very occasionally been mentioned in relation to Jane Austen, but – with the odd exception such as that of W.L. Phelps of Yale: "fully as conscientious an artist and fully as courageous and firm in her realism as was Flaubert"[25] – the comparison is either absent, nugatory[26] or derogatory. As Phelps probably knew, the most persuasive voice here, though his views were widely shared, is that of Henry James, whose remarks in "The Lesson of Balzac" about the "unconsciousness" of her grace – quoted at the start of this book – are not the less damaging because of the clearness of the artistic debt he owed her in those of his early works which he was shortly to omit from his own collected "New York" edition. But the most villainous remark is in his 1902 introduction to *Madame Bovary*:

> Jane Austen was instinctive and charming...however.... For signal
> examples of what composition, distribution, arrangement can do, of

how they intensify the life of a work of art, we have to go elsewhere; and the value of Flaubert for us is that he admirably points the moral.[27]

It is impossible to know how many readers have been swayed, perhaps indirectly, by this "warbling her native Wood-notes wilde" line. It was only after some decades that James became widely revered as a critic, but its reverberations of charming innocence are very generally evident – one is unlikely ever to encounter a book affectionately called *M. Homais Considered*. And though Nabokov included *Mansfield Park* in his course of Great Books (on the suggestion of Edmund Wilson), he can still say that "Novels like *Madame Bovary* or *Anna Karenin* are delightful explosions admirably controlled. *Mansfield Park* on the other hand, is the work of a lady and the game of a child".[28] A mysterious remark but unfortunately well within a tradition.

So where is further comparison possible or useful? Certainly the *images* of the authors are very different. The great bear-like anti-bourgeois bourgeois Norman with his fairly gross appetites, his whores and buggery and syphilis in Egypt, his lavish romantic theological strain, his mistresses, and his much talked over martyrdom to ART (his wonderful *Lettres* can, I think, mislead); and the busy English gentle-woman with her brothers and sisters and nephews and nieces, her domestic cares, her Anglicanism, creaking door and limited travelling (the surviving *Letters* are virtually void of intellectual content except by implication): where can these near stereotypes meet? Actually, tem-peramentally, in surprisingly many ways. They are both severe and even unrelenting moralists. They both create limited realistic detailed everyday worlds close to or in their own time and habitat (I am thinking, of course, only of the great Flaubert of *Madame Bovary*, *L'Éducation Sentimentale*, *Bouvard et Pécuchet* and "Un Coeur Simple", not of the other Flaubert who is scarcely a novelist at all). These worlds tend to be cramping to the spirit and largely inhabited by fools, good or bad. In both of them the great events and ideas of the time, even in *L'Éducation Sentimentale* – perhaps most pointedly in that work – do exist but only at the fringes and by implication, as in life. They both have very mixed feelings about Romanticism, as about progressive politics, and prefer to go back to the past for literary models and inspiration in spite of being in the very front of their time (they have Shakespeare in common). They are sceptical about human nature. And so on.

Nevertheless there is something un-English about Flaubert. It would be exotic to press the comparison of spirits too closely. Much more interesting and pertinent are the resemblances between their creative methods – that area in which James could find no examples, he says, in Jane Austen.

First an obvious contrast. Probably the most famous single passage in Flaubert is that when Frédéric, having witnessed, typically by chance, the cutting down of Dussardier by Sénécal during the coup of December 1851 – the cutting down, that is, of one of the exceedingly few sympathetic characters in Flaubert by the ambitious revolutionist turned bourgeois policeman – tries, in definitive disgust, a geographical cure for his soul:

> Il voyagea.
>
> Il connut la mélancolie des paquebots, les froids réveils sous la tente, l'étourdissement des paysages et des ruines, l'amertume des sympathies interrompues.
>
> Il revint.
>
> Il fréquenta le monde, et il eut d'autres amours encore. Mais le souvenir continuel du premier les lui rendait insipides; et puis la véhémence du désir, la fleur même de la sensation était perdue. Ses ambitions d'esprit avaient également diminué. Des années passèrent; et il supportait le désoeuvrement de son intelligence et l'inertie de son coeur. (*L'Éducation Sentimentale*, 3, vi)

To this wonderful rhetoric – of which an intelligent second-year undergraduate in English pertinently hazarded, "Is it Baudelaire?" – there is no equivalent in Jane Austen. Neither is there one to so extended, even over-extended, a set piece of the symphonic as in the 'comices agricoles' in *Madame Bovary*.[29] But the voyaging passage stands out because, save in one respect, it is untypical of Flaubert too. Unlike the shabby or pathetic lyricism he gives to his characters, which is qualified because it is their's, it signals a release from the tautly stretched fabric of the mundane into the glamour of a bitter but resonant nostalgia, and begins the coda of the novel. And unlike "Let other pens..." etc. in every other way, it yet resembles it in being a conscious shift of gear. Nevertheless, the respect in which it *is* typical of Flaubert's methods in his realistic prose indicates a much less one-off difference. Proust, in 'A Propos du "Style" de Flaubert' (1920) – the essay in which he perhaps infuriatingly claims that Flaubert's use of certain tenses, pronouns and prepositions reorders our vision of things almost as much as do the major works of Kant[30] – was probably the first to remark how the shift from the Perfect to the Imperfect at "rendait" brings us back to the quotidian world of the novel, which has been temporarily annihilated by the gloomy poetics of "paquebots". 'L'imparfait' with its potential for suggesting boring repetition, and only clumsily rendered into English by 'She used to . . . she would . . . she used to . . .' is perhaps the most vastly discussed feature of Flaubert's manner; and I expect Roy Pascal is quite right in saying that it is a device "hardly available in other languages".[31] Certainly there is nothing in Jane Austen that calls for a similar, tense, resource. The frustrations of every day in her novels are the result of definite, contained acts and speeches. When her Emma frets it is for a specific number of hours or days. The hovering between definite events and the dreary impression of never-ending routine which is so wonderfully captured from early on in Mme. Bovary's "Elle allait jusqu'à la hêtrée. . . . Elle commençait par regarder tout alentour. . . . Elle retrouvait aux mêmes places les digitales et ravenelles . . . " etc. (1, vii) is alien to what Jane Austen presents in, as opposed to what may be inferred from, her books. He artfully creates pointlessness. She equally artfully gives point even to the listless routine of Lady Bertram. Perhaps this is to say no more than that their subjects are different.

This contrast acknowledged, it is possible to recognise the more significant similarities. I shall attempt only a brief list, but one indicating, at least, a very large part of the novelist's art.

The first shared area is connected with what has just been said. In the rendering of the action through the consciousness of their characters both novelists are great innovators. Discussions of Flaubert's Imperfect almost inevitably merge with discussions of his supposed *creation* and virtuoso exploitation of the *style indirect libre* – which was still an "invention", a "major discovery" for Mario Vargas Llosa in a book published as late as 1986. Indeed, the passage from Merimée's *Colomba* which earlier this century became the *locus classicus* of debates about this style hinges on a change from the Perfect to the Imperfect.[32] "Nor does it seem to me impossible to give psychological analysis the swiftness, clarity, and impetus of a purely dramatic narrative", Flaubert wrote to Louise Colet in July 1852. But one of the reasons why we can assume that he had not read Jane Austen is that he continues, "This has never been attempted, and it would be beautiful". A less pardonable inadvertence is that of Roy Pascal when he argues of free indirect speech that "until Flaubert no writer seems to have used it with a clear consciousness of its stylistic identity and meaning" and yet can say a few lines later that in Goethe "and Jane Austen, it is already used with the greatest skill and propriety".[33] But the *non sequitur* is of little importance. The fact is that Jane Austen is one of the first novelists, if not *the* first, to work through a self-accomplished command of a way of perceiving and presenting which is extremely important in modern prose literature, and incidentally now probably unduly prestigious with critics. As we have seen before this chapter, and well before

Mansfield Park, Jane Austen is an exponent of the style *without* the resources lent by the particular resonant French tenses. Philip Roth's description of what he was up to with his characters in *When She Was Good* reads completely naturally nowadays, seems obvious. It was:

> ... their own conventional and upright style of speech that I chose as my means of narration – or, rather, a slightly heightened, somewhat more flexible version of their language, but one that drew freely upon their habitual clichés, locutions, and banalities. ... their way of saying things, their way of seeing things and judging them. (1969)

But it should not be Flaubert alone whose shade we detect in the background of this development.[34]

So much had free indirect speech become a part of Jane Austen's creation that page after page of *Mansfield Park* dips dramatically in and out of it (and related, less indirect, modes) – to the extent that it expands as a method, and almost becomes what Nabokov calls with conscious daring a "stream of consciousness".[35] So that Fanny's large progress into unconstrained confidence is made fully evident in the direct vehemence of her reaction to Edmund's late-continuing favour for the Crawfords (and her being stuck in Portsmouth until after Easter): the following, for instance, gives the air of almost unmediated thought:

> "I never will – no, certainly I never will wish for a letter again" was Fanny's secret declaration ... "What do they bring but disappointment and sorrow. ... There is no good in this delay," said she. ... "He is blinded, and nothing will open his eyes, nothing can. ... He will marry her and be poor and miserable. God grant that her influence do not make him cease to be respectable!" – she looked over the letter again. "'So very fond of me!' 'tis nonsense all. She loves nobody but herself and her brother. Her friends leading her astray for years! She is quite as likely to have led *them* astray ..." (3, xiii, 424)

This combines the directness of a letter with the swift moving, far-seeing comprehensiveness of third-person narration: and, very far from conveying any defensive closet morality, is a fine internal drama and a large extension of the presentation of Fanny from within.

vii

The second great area shared by the two novelists lies in the realms, which I have touched on before in Jane Austen's case, of exclusion.

Every critic knows, or at least used to know, that to point out that every seemingly circumstantial detail in a novel is relevant to its main themes is to praise that novel. The ambitious analogy is with lyric poetry. Indeed, it can be carried far too far and wish away the kinds of fine exuberance found in Dickens or Dostoevsky – or even in Flaubert's introduction, late in *L'Éducation Sentimentale*, of Mlle. Vatnaz's past, and a non-personage specifically called Hortense Baslin[36] – an equivalent, in her way, of the non-apparent Skinners and William Coxes and Dr. Shirleys in Jane Austen. The idea of totally pervasive, immanent meaning or set of meanings in a work of art (in common with the idea of *totally* almost anything, in my opinion) is very attractive, but it can wish away also the irreducible, to itself, unportentous, non-transitive nature of some of the (as it were uncontrolled) particulars in works of art – especially novels; it can tidy out and forget uniqueness and distinction and even inconsequence in favour of an insistence on the seemingly grander, and at any rate more communicable, possibilities offered by the detection and elaboration of inter-connected significances – which can then be applied to the world. So when reading critics, one often wants in reaction to stop and say "wait – this is just *this* and not other, this is Mary, this is the East room . . ." and so on.

Nevertheless, it is possible – necessary – to hold two perspectives at the same time, and a commentator must leave the particular to assert itself – as it will – and deal in what can be generally agreed upon and what is discussable as opposed to what is simply there – however glowing its *haeccitas*. Informed generalisation is valuable as an aid to thought – and therefore I shall continue to insist on the development of artistic discipline and take for granted that readers will have noticed the dominance of a fine *economy* in both Flaubert and Jane Austen. It goes with their eye for (often damning) behavioural tics and give-aways; with the superb parade of pipes and watches and statuettes and gruel and sprigged muslin; with the way in which characters nearly always respond in character, and in which platitudes are brandished to characterise and condemn without authorial comment. But a less explicit trait also unites them as writers for the grown-up. It is perhaps too obvious to be mentioned often enough outside the broadest of literary surveys. But it is vital. If we look around we notice the near total absence of much of the content of most previous and contemporary fiction: There is a duel in *L'Éducation Sentimentale*, but even for the characters it is a conscious literary farce. And there is the bloodless offstage meeting of Willoughby and Col. Brandon in *Sense and Sensibility*. Otherwise not only is there no real Gothick or Supernatural: there are no abductions (as in Richardson, Fanny Burney etc.) no rapes, no chases, no moonlight escapades by flood and field, no deserts, no burglaries, no secret murders, no battles – nothing of the sort save as the subject of satirical allusion or the illusion of a character. Accordingly, there are no gratuitous scenes, no intellectual flights such as the history and theory of architecture that Flaubert so admired in *Notre-Dame de Paris*, no descriptions of nature for their or its own sake, no interpolated narratives outside the relative crudity of Willoughby's and Brandon's respective explanations in *Sense and Sensibility* and the tired intrusion of Mrs. Smith in *Persuasion*, no retrospective anecdotes or flashbacks, no set pieces with a life of their own, no sub-plots. What Jane Austen found risible about some of her contemporaries can be gathered from her reaction to Mary Brunton's *Self-Control* (of which a recent reprinter, Sara Maitland, falsely says she was a "great admirer"): "I declare I do not know whether Laura's passage down the American River, is not the most natural, possible, everyday thing she does".[37] And part of Flaubert's famous self-scourging discipline was to channel his wilder impulses into *La Tentation de Saint Antoine* and *Salammbô*, or into his account of Emma Bovary's destructive reading – itself a much graver and more grandiose version of Catherine Morland's.

Such massive exclusions of the overtly exciting are not, of course, necessarily in themselves admirable. The stranger paths of the psyche find symbols and expression in other kinds of fiction. But the exclusions certainly get rid of a lot of rubbishy mechanism, and reaffirm our sense of the real, the adult.[38] It is perhaps superfluous to add that they are a great deal of what Henry James spent much of his life as a critic advocating for the modern novel. In view of the example of Jane Austen (and of course others after her) it was late for him to be making a point in his 1907 preface to *The Portrait of a Lady* (written in 1880) that *his* modern girl should enjoy "independence of flood and field, of the moving accident, of battle and murder and sudden death – her adventures are to be mild". Fanny's are even milder.

viii

Related to this, a third area of similarity lies in the use of physical environments or accessories in both authors. Again this only needs to be indicated. The spiritual axis in *Madame Bovary* between Yonville and Rouen is much noticed and insisted on. But so is the contrast between London and Bath and the country in Jane Austen. Much psychological power is added, for instance, by Flaubert's selective notation of material correlatives: the interiors of the Bovary houses, of the gradually disintegrating plaster priest, the contents of Rodolphe's den, or those of the hotel room in Rouen. But these are like the fire in the East room, or the disturbed bookcase in Sir Thomas's study. Appurtenances are *usually* relevant in these highly developed fictions. They tend to aspire to be – to return to that point – not simply realistic furniture, but agents of meaning or confirmations of it: the works of 'art' at 'L'Art Industriel' in *L'Éducation Sentimentale*, or the chaos of the Prices' Portsmouth, with the silver knife singled out as a sort of contrast to it, spring to mind. Whole actions are involved: in Jane Austen the dances are almost always psychological dramas, as is the ball at Vaubyessard in *Madame Bovary*. And so on. As in life, the distinction between real and symbolic qualities is hard to fix. And some sequences are even more charged and urgent with meaning. The quasi-symbolic significance of the garden, wilderness, gate and Park at Sotherton and the actions and interractions of the characters therein are a staple of many excellent commentaries on *Mansfield Park* – "Shakespearian", says Q.D. Leavis meaning something more detailed than what Lord Macaulay meant by *his* grand and famous early tribute.[39] Emma Bovary's desperate recourse for spiritual help to the entirely banal Abbé Bournisien, with his food-stained cassock set in a wilderness of ecclesiastical junk and mutinous choirboys, advertises an even clearer significance. The point here is that Jane Austen creates at least equivalent means to those of Flaubert – in a slightly different way we could compare the expressive uses to which Mme. Bovary's greyhound and Lady Bertram's pug are variously put.

ix

A fourth large area of similarity between Flaubert and Jane Austen is in their modification of the 'Omniscient' – or at least the heavy-handed – authorial commentator – for which they are, again separately, famous. This is also a large subject discussed over and over again, like free indirect speech and its cognates. I want only to comment that Flaubert's late-night suggestion to Louise Colet in 1852 that "An author ... must be like God in the universe, everywhere present and visible nowhere" – an idea later translated and propagated with fruitful vigour by Henry James – has been taken far too literally, or even metaphysically, by twentieth-century critics and theorists. He is protesting against overt preaching by a novelist, specifically Harriet Beecher Stowe: "Does one have to make observations about slavery? Depict it: that is enough. . . . Look at *The Merchant of Venice* and see whether anyone declaims against usury". This fine outburst does not really want anything so radical (and meaningless?) as the "death" (or elimination from critical consideration) of the author. In fact Flaubert himself is quite prepared to deal swipes literally right and left in his narrations. Of socialist ideas in the mid-nineteenth century we read, for example, that:

> . . . elles épouvantèrent les bourgeois . . . et on fut indigné, en vertu de cette haine que provoque l'avènement de toute idée parce que c'est une idée, exécration dont elle tire plus tard sa gloire, et qui fait que ses ennemis sont toujours au-dessous d'elle, si médiocre qu'elle puisse être. (*L'Éducation Sentimentale*, 3, i)

God interviews his universe with considerable – if even-handed – severity here. Equally, there is no reason for surprise at the introduction of Rodolphe in *Madame Bovary* as "de tempérament brutal et d'intelligence perspicace". Jane Austen, while never feeling moved to such expanded contempt as in the first passage, frequently includes a judgement of people with mean Understandings and so forth. What they have in common is that their creations stand independent of such overt comment – which is usually subsequent to dramatisation of what is at issue – and certainly do not exist in order to facilitate it – as *Uncle Tom's Cabin* (for Dickens also "scarcely a work of art)" perhaps does.

* * *

I hope I have indicated the proper standing of Jane Austen in the creation of the modern novel. If she and Flaubert had lived in a period about which we knew less I am sure there would be talk of an 'influence'. It may be objected that James in specifying "composition, distribution, arrangement" had in mind the mysteries of 'Form'. But this cannot be held as an objection for an instant if we recognise the way in which every episode in Jane Austen unfolds interrelatedly from a previous episode, or how rigorously she abjures sudden shifts, or the introduction of new characters who do not bear on the main meaning. All is order and disciplined purpose. Her novels even approach something like the neo-Classic 'Unities' in the singleness of their action, time and place(s). In fact, for what it is worth – which is not a vast amount in view of the legitimate variety of forms in the novel – she is a stricter author than Flaubert. *L'Éducation Sentimentale* obviously has a looser, more extended, *bildung*-like shape than any of her novels; and there is no such nonce-person as the schoolfellow of Charbovari who starts as the presenting voice of *Madame Bovary* with his famous

"Nous étions à l'étude . . ." but disappears for ever within eight pages or so. This in itself does not matter. But one still wonders what James can have had in mind – and wonders even more when going on to read *Emma*.

Chapter Seven

Emma's Choices

The ease afforded by Jane Austen to her readers is nowhere so evident as in contemplating the formidable intellectual structure that underpins the bright and lucid comedy of *Emma*. The novel is a structure of the utmost complexity and delicacy. Everything in it depends on everything else and on its context within the fiction. Since this texture *is* so dense it is easy to represent by brief analyses of suggestive examples. So – as a beginning to this chapter – I shall take two of these: the opening, and a passage near the end. Then, having, I hope, built up an impression of the compressed economy immanent in the work, I shall go on to look once again at some of the characteristics of Jane Austen's unique kind of realism – which should illuminate both characteristics and this novel, inter-actively. Finally, I shall offer some reflections on the significance of the heroine's trajectory through the book and into the future.

i

The opening of *Mansfield Park* is one of the great bravura expositions in fiction. It is a massively improved and enhanced re-writing of the first chapter of *Sense and Sensibility*, in that it summarises, though with a wonderful characterising dramatic touch, the *past* of a situation:

> About thirty years ago, Miss Maria Ward, of Huntingdon, with only seven thousand pounds, had the good luck to captivate Sir Thomas Bertram...

The whole moral *ambience* into which the heroine is to be cast becomes present, and succeeding pages, chapters, sustain the impetus. The opening of *Emma* matches and even surpasses this, but with a focus on the immediate subject, Emma, (almost *in medias res*) and brilliantly entertaining from the first paragraph:

> Emma Woodhouse, handsome, clever, and rich, with a comfortable home and happy disposition, seemed to unite some of the best blessings of existence; and had lived nearly twenty-one years in the world with very little to distress or vex her. (5)

This, of course, is so famous as almost to blind the reader with familiarity. But consider it. It invites quick and easy reading partly because it is a single sentence. It promises a happy and attractive theme. Nobody could take it for the opening of a tragedy. There is no tedious indirection or scene-setting to allow the mind to wander, or to wonder when the real story is going to start. It is not self-conscious, or learned or allusive – and so on. Yet all this happy plainness is qualified by the first verb – at first unobtrusively charged – which is to be crucial to the action: "seemed".[1] Emma's advantages only potentially confer the best blessings of existence – as is obvious if we think about the question.

The second paragraph extends the effect. It is similarly crisp, informative and subtle. In the major key, as it were, we learn of Emma's "affectionate" father, her being mistress of the house so young, and of her excellent and loving governess. In the minor, that her father is over-"indulgent", her mother, long dead, and her governess, however admirable, "short" of a mother.

These subtle qualifications extend into the third paragraph. Miss Taylor's love and kindness had resulted in her having only a nominal authority; she has been able to impose hardly any restraint, and Emma does what she likes. It comes as no surprise, therefore, when the fourth paragraph starts by taking up the "seemed" with: "The real evils indeed of Emma's situation were the power of having rather too much her own way, and a disposition to think a little too well of herself". Real evils? Are we then, contrary to the expectations excited by the light and happy opening, to be faced with a story solemnly moralising about how dangerous it is to be handsome, clever and rich? Fortunately not, for the subtle qualifications have now gone over to the other side: "rather too much", "a little too well". Happiness begins to reassert itself.

In very few words Jane Austen has not only stated her subject, but also alerted us as to how to read about it. In the rest of the first chapter the idea of an only apparent happiness remains subdued, but is in fact crucial. Emma lives in a desperately dull society: and it is in this context that we are asked to see her impetuous and high-handed actions. "Highbury ... afforded her no equals" (7): this states a satisfying social eminence, but it also suggests the possibility of a demoralising tedium. (We later learn that although Emma has been to London she has never seen the sea – a poetically suggestive limitation, which also differentiates her further from the heroines just before and after.) The very first *action*, accordingly, in this powerful blend of retrospect, dialogue and action, is of Mr. Woodhouse composing himself for his "sleep after dinner, as usual" (6) – a prelude to the first of their apparently endless long evenings together. The attitude of both daughter and narrator to Mr. Woodhouse repays examination. They have a similarly unsentimental view of him. The narrator informs us succintly that he had "been a valetudinarian all his life, without activity of mind or body . . . and though everywhere beloved for the friendliness of his heart and his amiable temper, his talents could not have recommended him at any time" (he is unsatisfactory, as are most of the Jane Austen parents). Emma faces the same problem. For the moment, since Emma's skilful companion for her. He could not meet her in conversation, rational or playful" (7), but, most remarkably, her love is not simply felt as a duty, but is an active principle which rules this headstrong and critical girl throughout the novel.

Typically, Jane Austen immediately develops this situation in multiple relation to its most likely possible solvent: marriage. Equally typically, the description is focussed and proved by the dramatisation afforded by dialogue. The conversation beginning "Poor Miss Taylor! – I wish she were here again. What a pity it is that Mr. Weston ever thought of her!" (8) is, of course, comic – which is just as well, for with a different tone Mr. Woodhouse's ludicrous worries about James and the "poor horses" would seem a biting demonstration of silly egotism. He can see no reason for a newly married woman to have a "house of her own" – a hint superbly taken up over 400 pages later when Emma faces the same problem. For the moment, since Emma's skilful "exertions" merely steer him round towards a happier end to the evening, we are left with the question as to whether or not to admire her for being so indulgent. As if to determine this, "Mr. Knightley, a sensible man of about seven or eight- and thirty", steps in with the dramatic appropriateness and realistic credibility that we have learned to expect. He quickly earns the right to be called sensible – both feeling and rational – by the cordial tact with which he handles Mr. Woodhouse's hypochondriacal worries and by his pleasant settling of the issue of Mrs. Weston: ". . . but when it comes to the question of dependence or independence! . . ." (10). By now, five pages into the novel, the action is fully set and launched, and the first short chapter not even over yet.

Now consider one of the final episodes. Frank Churchill's intrigue is sustained through a series of hints, half revelations and misunderstandings which interweave with other motifs through the main action and are only fully articulated in his rueful, though still rather chirpy, explanations to Emma in chapter eighteen of volume three. "But is it possible that you had no suspicion?" he says, "I was once very near – and I wish I had" (477) – and we know from his letter to Mrs. Weston that what he wishes is that he had come clean about Jane Fairfax on first leaving Highbury in February, half the book ago. Here the first-time reader may fully understand, for the first time, that his nervous velleities on that farewell visit (which was preceded by a visit to the Bateses): "In short ... perhaps, Miss Woodhouse – I think you can hardly be without suspicion" (2, xii, 260) – were a prelude to his failure to confess something she certainly did not begin to guess, as opposed to a prelude to a failure to propose marriage to her. The control of this strand with so many others – it surfaces also in the crowded texture of the ball at the Crown (3, ii) – is in itself of remarkable fineness and would grace any tale of cross currents in love. But what makes it especially rich – especially Jane Austen's and no one else's – is that it is the *same* scene at the end which confirms in us the feeling that Emma has really had about Frank from the start – and which Mr. Knightley has too firmly articulated. The happy, open lover is, of course, a gentleman: but he will not quite do. He is merely *aimable*.[2] His attitude to Jane, whose superior mind and spirit we have come to admire, is that of the proud possessor of an excellent piece of livestock. His apologies to Emma are interlarded with regular, too regular, exclamations of pleasure: – "Did you ever see such a skin? – such smoothness! such delicacy!" (478); "Look at her. Is she not an angel in every gesture? Observe the turn of her throat. Observe her eyes ..." (479); "I see it in her cheek, her smile, her vain attempt to frown. Look at her" (480). In this appreciation there is a certain glutinous quality which, in its way, harks back to the courtship language of Mr. Elton; and Emma, who could have been bored and affronted, rightly and happily feels that "she had never been more sensible of Mr. Knightley's high superiority of character" (480). All this complexity is immediately apprehensible, and only the formal analysis of it is difficult.

ii

Therefore, I want now to examine and explain a little of the richness by reverting to the problem of what Jane Austen typically selected out of experience to serve her larger enterprise; and to a point made earlier (about *Sense and Sensibility* and by Henry on *Pride and Prejudice*, in chapter five, above) concerning her *creative* use of those artistically conventional ludicrous types whose ludicrousness consists largely in the dependability of their reactions.

The commonplace, indeed the natural, account of the action of *Emma* runs like this: the over-confident heroine, in purposeful contrast to the heroine of *Mansfield Park*, rightly considers herself superior to most of the people around her – to the rather boring and *borné* Highbury, a place "almost amounting to a town" and more really dispiriting than Lionel Trilling's description of it as a "pastoral" location would suggest. Therefore she must find relief for her mind. Therefore she makes the series of wonderful imaginative mistakes of which the book largely consists – and of which no reader needs to be reminded. Later I shall consider the happy exceptions to this pattern, and the nature of her hungry imagination. But first let us re-examine dull Highbury. Apparently it differs from the other dull locales in Jane Austen (nostalgically so very attractive to the twentieth-century reader) mainly in the narrowness with which it confines the protagonists – though there is nothing in it so nakedly unpleasant as there is in parts of *Sense and Sensibility*. Even Box Hill – that genuinely beautiful but not exotic spot – is a considerable outing, and so on. But, of course, as well as being a very credible picture of Regency *moeurs de province*, Highbury is an artistic construct.

According to Flaubert later, everything becomes interesting if you look at it long enough. The truth of this depends on the kind of look we are able to give. Clearly the look of art is magical. Highbury is the very devil of boredom for an intelligent person with nothing much to do. Mr. Knightley, obviously a progressive and improving farmer with his drains and fences and planned cropping and new drills and philanthropy, is a busy man; but Emma has only, in the serious external business of life, the care of her father and the occasional care of the poor:

> They were now approaching the cottage, and all idle topics were superseded. Emma was very compassionate; and the distresses of the poor were as sure of relief from her personal attention and kindness, her council and her patience, as from her purse. She understood their ways, could allow for their temptations, had no romantic expectations of extraordinary virtue from those, for whom education had done so little; entered into their troubles with ready sympathy, and always gave her assistance with as much intelligence as good-will. In the present instance, it was sickness and poverty together which she came to visit . . . (1, x, 86)

This warming and precise passage comes in the middle of an episode where Emma is being particularly complacent and even a little odious in her bossing about of Harriet, and so redresses a balance. But what is further remarkable about it is, that though such intelligent charity was certainly a part of good Christian living for a wealthy woman in England then, this is the only reference to it in *Emma* – one of the few in Jane Austen generally. And it is only a reference; the poor are not dramatically present in all their ugliness and brutality, defiance and gratitude, as they would be in mature Dickens or in George Eliot and Mrs. Gaskell – or even in Charlotte Smith. The "idle topics" quickly reassert themselves in the drama of Mr. Elton and the bootlace, for they are the real business of the book. So our re-acquired admiration for Emma also reminds us of how much the intent gaze of this author habitually omits, as I suggested in chapter one, in the interests of a sharp vision.

What is it to represent nature in a novel? If I want to evoke something I may want to exclude what is next to it in phenomenal circumstance, but irrelevant. I need to include only enough for verisimilitude – and even what I thus include (if I am Jane Austen at any rate) will only rarely be there solely as dressing. Even when we take the weight of Philippa Tristram's interesting observation that, since servants were becoming less and less obtrusive in well-run households of the period, their relative absence in Jane Austen (as opposed to Richardson) is quite natural – an observation crowned by the astonishing anecdote that a little later in the century any lower servant in the Duke of Portland's who was seen by the Duke was automatically dismissed[3] – the lack of accompanying bustle in Jane Austen clearly owes more to art than to nature. As with the material details in *Mansfield Park*, in *Emma* James the coachman will show what a fusspot his employer is; gruel, what a valetudinarian; and the mending of spectacles will encompass a move in an amorous game. This rigorous process, or creative flowering, is precisely what Henry James described by the mild word "selection".

Part of what it achieves is a paradox usually accepted more or less automatically by readers, but not often enough made explicit by critics: that what is tedious and stifling for the protagonists is matter for delight and interest for the audience. To observe this is to observe no more unfamiliar a psychological fact than that we enjoy tragedies. We pursue edifying representations of suffering, as Aristotle first said. Likewise we enjoy the depiction of boredom. It is not to my purpose to speculate again on the causes of this *datum*; but it is necessary to keep it in mind particularly firmly when reading Jane Austen's kind of novel, which so plausibly offers itself as an account of the real and the very everyday.

iii

So, further: what is the relation of such disciplined selection to characterisation by the parade of expected responses? One of the reasons why
Emma is really a, perhaps the, high point of Jane Austen's writing is
that the integration, the seamless use, of comically predictable voices is
at its densest. Consider the misunderstandings surrounding Mr. Elton
and his ambitious marital design on Emma. By the time this is introduced the reader is already highly trained to develop a sympathetic
wariness as to her estimate of things around her. Not only the narratorial direction with its subtle qualifications ("seemed to unite some
of the best blessings of existence"), but the tiniest nuances from episode
to episode accomplish this.

For example, and naturally relevant to Emma's limited environment –
one of the reasons, from the point of view of the solicitious Mrs.
Weston who is early reviewing the prospect of a visit from her new
stepson Frank, why her recent marriage will not badly impair relations
with Hartfield is the "very easy distance" between it and Randalls "so
convenient for even solitary female walking". And equally obviously
Emma is "no feeble character" with her "sense and energy and spirits"
(1, ii, 18). So much for *imagined* inconveniences. But in the next
chapter but one Emma herself is full of her brilliant new idea of
bringing out Harriet from the extremely plain education offered at Mrs.
Goddard's "real, honest, old-fashioned Boarding-school", and one of
the reasons she is able to give herself for undertaking a little character
formation *à la Rousseau* is that, since her father never goes beyond
the shrubbery (and in this rich household there is no suitable female
domestic), she needs a walking companion:

> ... since Mrs. Weston's marriage her exercise had been too much
> confined. She had ventured once alone to Randalls, but it was not
> pleasant; and a Harriet Smith, therefore, one whom she could
> summon at any time for a walk, would be a valuable addition to her
> privileges.... Harriet certainly was not clever, but she had a sweet,
> docile, grateful disposition ... (1, iii, 22)

So the choice is now between two great active rationalising powers: the
characteristic Weston optimism and Emma's genius for having things
her own way. If we add common sense, two to one says that Emma
probably does not absolutely need a companion. And her thought could
not be more lifelike. Sound, practical reasons for doing as one likes are
rarely wanting with clever people.

But in either case we are enabled – by this amongst a hundred, or, as
Harriet herself would express it "five hundred million" other things – to

follow Mr. Elton's courtship with appropriate scepticism and to experience some strict ironies – i.e. we view the action from a different and superior position to that of any of the participants.[4] And what is striking about the climax of the sequence in 1, xiii–xv – especially to the reader of *Pride and Prejudice* and the connoisseur of comic proposals in general – is how like and yet unlike it is to the eruption of Mr. Collins into his book. Both men are vicars, and both masters of a comparable vocabulary of insincere excess. Both also careerists, who after their failure with the heroine go on to a marriage which is anatomised within their novel. Yet Elton has not the fame, the glory, of Collins. And one of the chief reasons for this is that his upsurge is more gradual, and more integrated with the rest of the action. His presence "spruce, black, and smiling" (1, xiii) is, especially in view of John Knightley's brotherly warning to Emma just previous, ominous enough. But he is far from being given a whole *set piece*, or the equivalent of a "new scene at Longbourn". Before dinner at Randalls "Mr. Elton's civilities were dreadfully ill-timed" to a heroine eager to hear about the Frank Churchill who "if she ever *were* to marry" would be the least unsuitable person; but she is rescued by the affable chatter of her host about this son. Elton then returns to his wooing with embarrassing over-familiar nonsense – beautifully observed of a would-be lover, and proleptic of the tone of his actual future wife – about Emma's supposed self-sacrifice over Harriet's cold: "Is this fair, Mrs. Weston? – Judge between us. Have not I some right to complain?" (1, xv, 125). No, none at all *knowingly* accorded by Emma – who perhaps chills him with a Miss Woodhouse look (she thinks he is a little drunk). But again his voice is temporarily submerged by the commotion caused by the new problem of how to get back to Hartfield in face of a few flakes of snow. Mr. Woodhouse is, of course, completely *bouleversé* – and everyone proceeds to act out their own rôle. John Knightley embraces the chance for a sarcastic vision of disaster; Mr. Weston enthusiastically grasps the opportunity for extending even more of his unwanted unpractical good-will and good wine; Isabella is heroically ready to brave the storm in order to get back to her children: and "What is to be done, my dear Emma? – what is to be done?" Mr. Woodhouse exclaims, for, as always, "To her he looked for comfort". What is to be done is that Mr. Knightley goes out to look at the weather and talk to the coachmen, sees that it offers no inconvenience, let alone threat, and reports. The resolution is as precise as the consternation was diffuse:

> Mr. Knightley and Emma settled it in a few brief sentences: thus –
> "Your father will not be easy; why do not you go?"

"I am ready, if the others are."

"Shall I ring the bell?"

"Yes, do."

And the bell was rung, and the carriages spoken for. (128)

This clear-headed efficiency is a kind of moral pointer. Clear speech is always indicative in Jane Austen. But here it is the final piece of sense before Elton's final sticky onslaught in the enclosed carriage. Like his fellow cleric he finds it very difficult to take no for an answer in love. "Believe me, sir, I am far, very far, from being gratified in being the object of such professions", protests Emma still thinking of Harriet. But he replies – with some embarrassing justice – that "adoration of yourself" has been his object, and that "You cannot really, seriously, doubt it. No! – (in an accent meant to be insinuating) – I am sure you have seen and understood me." Even worse, and more Collins-like:

"Charming Miss Woodhouse! allow me to interpret this interesting silence. It confesses that you have long understood me." (131)

There follows Emma's first long, important, day of self-accusation. This is a small, partial, *anagnorisis*, or recognition, including a small newly acknowledged sense of Mr. Knightley's wisdom. But it is swiftly recovered from and ignored in a new morning and with the alacrity of youthful spirits bolstered by her intuition of Elton's not really being in love.

Obviously a lot of the interest of the proposal has been in our enjoying the extended display of Emma's failure to see Elton properly – blinded typically not by Cupid but by the Harriet project; just as through most of the book she fails, often though not always, accurately to intuit what forms itself around her because, setting "up as I do for Understanding" (3, xiii, 427), she is the victim of her own marvellous ideas. More of this later. But what is most notable here is that the proposal does not spring unexpected and undeserved, as it were, out of the action – as does that to Elizabeth Bennet – but is part of a dense counterpoint of motifs around the heroine: or, continuing the metaphor from the previous chapter, a *leitmotif* or a line in a fugue rather than a Collins-type *aria*.

My point is that the predicted responses of dull Highbury are not just a comic background for the main protagonists' lives, not merely a frame. They are interactive with those lives, and each depends intimately on each. This example further indicates another important fact that commentary on Jane Austen's development of 'humourous' comedy tends to overlook, but which, again, is obvious to the simplest reading: that a predictable response is not necessarily a ludicrous one. Mr. Woodhouse's dependence on his daughter is funny, if funny, in a different way from Isabella's defiance of "possible accumulations of drifted snow" to cover the few hundred yards to Hartfield to see little Henry, little John, Bella, George and Emma before the morning. Modern readers may find in Mr. Woodhouse a subtle paternal exploiter as much as a deserving object of filial devotion; but here a mild pathos can also be felt. Further, Mr. Knightley's good sense and swift action is as predictable as anything in the book, but here it is reassuring amidst the dithering – and a trifle moving (it foreshadows, of course, his much larger intervention in favour of poor Harriet at the Crown, for he is made from the first for positive interventions, until his shyness nearly prevents him from proposing to Emma at last).

But whatever the emotional – the human – value and weight of a particular staple and expected response, I guess that the reader's pleasure derives much, and is much involved with, the *anticipation* of its application to a changing situation? When the response is duly exhibited the effect is of satisfaction – a satisfaction perhaps the greater the further the distance travelled by the character in order to adapt the situation to a reigning preoccupation or a ruling passion?

Consider the wonderful familial comedy on the evening of the John Knightleys' first visit (1, xii) – where Mr. Woodhouse and Isabella vie in wrenching everything round, and then back again, to the respective merits of their physicians, rival sea-side towns and the healthiness of Hartfield *versus* Brunswick Square, whilst the Knightley brothers talk good farming business and Emma, aided finally by Mr. Knightley, brilliantly negotiates between possible collisions of obsession. Or *try* to consider the genuine relevance of Maple Grove, Selina etc. to almost anything Mrs. Elton says. We find comparable satisfactions in the encounter with circumstances by stock figures in a great deal of literature: in *Volpone*, say, or in much of Molière. In a more complex mode, the fascination and the terrible unease felt about Shylock is not attributable wholly to his mixture of Jewish outsider and palpable man – something is due to the clash between his comic-rôle mannerisms as gulled miser and father ("My daughter! O my ducats! . . . O my Christian ducats!") and the feeling that he has sustained a truly pernicious loss, like Brabantio in *Othello*.

However, literary and stylistic problems are rarely solved by the adduction of respectable parallels – though they may seem to be; nor by the argument that certain characteristics of a work of art are integrated into it in a lovely manner – they could remain rotten characteristics. The problem here, as I have suggested, is that Jane Austen's novels persist in seeming – in spite of the high economy of selection and elision artfully practised – to be fairly straight representations of everyday reality. How, to re-phrase the question – how on earth – can this accord with the extensive creation and deployment of what is patently an artistic device? – and one that thrives, as it were, on being recognised as such, while at the same time giving the air of being the palpable observation of living things?

iv

With the hope of clarifying this issue I shall consider a challenge to *Emma*'s kind of perfection – so influential on later novels – which is traditional in its terms and assumptions, but as a critique actually much more upsetting than anything likely to be produced by modern versions of scepticism. D.H. Lawrence was dismissive of Jane Austen (see above, page 104); and part of his animus – which has everything to do, like much really telling literary criticism, with his own creative pre-occupations – is likely to have derived from the conviction that:

> ...In the novel, the characters can do nothing but *live*. If they keep on being good, according to pattern, or bad, according to pattern, or even volatile according to pattern, they cease to live, and the novel falls dead. A character in a novel has got to live, or it is nothing.
>
> We, likewise, in life have got to live, or we are nothing.[5]

Now, exactly such patterns are what I have admired in Jane Austen's earlier novels – developed and seen as even more closely woven, and finer, in *Emma*. Yet Lawrence's "even volatile according to pattern" seems a near and even a particularly apt description. So what prevents these works – so evidently alive – from falling dead?

The question looks ineffable, looming with portentous difficulty and the likelihood of mere assertions. Nevertheless, it is possible to avoid the temptation to reply merely dogmatically with 'well, everyone finds them alive, so there' by a further recourse to the specific. I shall consider in a moment the scene structured round Jane Fairfax's significant visit to the post-office in 2, xvi and the typical counterpoint of character this provokes. But first note that Lawrence's challenge raises the whole question of representation in art. Nobody who thinks, just once, on the matter thinks that characters in a fiction are real. Even to formulate the question thus is to destroy it; and it is reserved to contemporary commentators in pursuit of their ideals to say unreflective things such as that "the author adds a less than candid sketch of" Jane Fairfax's "past life"[6] – since there *is* no past life, this is impossible. On the other hand, we can say, as I argued in chapter one, that the ordinary and natural response to Jane Austen's creation of part of England in the early 1800s (in spite of its exclusions) is also epistemologically the most correct. 'So that was what it was like', we exclaim; and this is legitimate since we learn, as I also argued, what and how the past thought and *felt* most directly from documents of this kind – from works of art. (Which is not, of course, to exclude all or any of the other more external and factual records.) Imaginative writers are the most obviously powerful first-hand authorities on the sensibilities of their own times, for the very obvious reason that they *were* the sensibilities of their times. Of course, it is then up to the reader to gauge whether what is written purports to be accurate – realistic – in regard to everyday facts, or not. (That is a part of the present enterprise.)

But the real challenge extending from Lawrence bears a different emphasis: are these characters – these imaginative verbal constructs, these figments – just individuals, just individual manifestations (one-offs), or are they as well in some way representative or universal figures? Actually, they need not be universal to be representative. They could dramatise or illustrate a historically local condition like the 'alienation' 'under capital' of social relations and the consequent 'externalisation and objectification' of these, as is claimed by some neo-marxists (though I do not think they *do*), and still be representative – indeed, they would have to be representative.[7] What Lawrence seems to want is a kind of ideal individuality which denies any typicality and any predictability. I do not think that such pure spontaneity is common even in what Henry James called in this context "untidy life" – most of us, as I have said, perceive through and act out our stereotypes most of the time – and such unpredictable unreflectiveness is certainly not a characteristic of most art. It is nearly a contradiction in fact: for art suggests patterns; and in what is shaped and told we automatically look for a significance greater than the particular – even in the most trifling anecdote, let alone the grandest myth. Merely being alive involves a jumble of sensation; and literary or visual artefacts which only retail the actual (memoirs, photographs etc.) are very likely to meander into literal inconsequence because they are confined and bound in a dogged particular channel – they are just there, nothing follows, and the likely response is 'Oh'. Truth can be stranger than fiction, but also more boring. This is one of the points of Aristotle's observation, echoed down the ages by serious thinkers on art (e.g. Sir Philip Sidney) that:

> ... it is not the poet's function to describe what has actually happened, but the kinds of thing that might happen, that is, could

happen because they are, in the circumstances, either probable or necessary. The difference betweent the historian and the poet is not that the one writes in prose and the other in verse ... [but that] one tells of what has happened, the other of the kinds of things that might happen. For this reason poetry is something more philosophical and more worthy of serious attention than history; for while poetry is concerned with universal truths, history treats of particular facts.[8]

Not, of course, that Lawrence, either in theory or practice, wanted pure unshaped experience. He is obviously reacting to the second rate or worse; to formula work in which everyone or thing has mechanically to represent a larger banality (an entity like 'capital', 'alienation', 'reification' etc. perhaps?). He may well have had *specifically* in mind the lumbering heirs of the great Victorian novelists, such as Galsworthy and Arnold Bennett and their lesser derivatives. But in Jane Austen the patterns, and thus the qualities they evoke, are fresh and subtle. In her work predictability is not mechanical, but full of life and interest (however often we read it).

To take the proposed post-office example: in a society that depends so much as Highbury does on external stimulations for its interests, even the fastidious have to honour the "irresistible form" taken by a new arrival. So in 2, xvi Emma gives an obligatory dinner for Mrs. Elton – of whom in any case the reader desires to hear more after her first eruptions. Here we may note that in order that we may concentrate the better on issues genuinely current, one element of the possible tension in the love story convention – which might have been kept randomly alive in a less assured writer – has been deliberately defused: Mr. Knightley's disavowal in the previous chapter of anything but a friendly interest in Jane Fairfax allows us to take John Knightley's picking her out for sociability – "an old acquaintance and a quiet girl" – as merely pleasant, apparently as it would be in day to day experience, and not boding any family strategy. They talk of the commonplace: he (in the company, of course, of little Henry and little John) has seen her in the rain coming from the post-office that morning and twits her with his slightly barking humour:

> "The post-office has a great charm at one period of our lives. When you have lived to my age, you will begin to think letters are never worth going through the rain for." (293)

He must be all of thirty-five (but a most domestic man). He continues with serious concern for her and her slight embarrassment until the interruption of Mr. Woodhouse, the "kind-hearted, polite old man" (a small narratorial dressing of the balance), widens the conversation to allow a typical display by all present around this subject. Mrs. Weston is concerned with health care. Mrs. Elton surges in with manifestations of importance and assumptions of intimacy:

> "My dear Jane, what is this I hear? . . . You sad girl, how could you do such a thing? – It is a sign I was not there to take care of you." (295)

– (and so on until one begins to dread for those servants whose names she ostentatiously claims to be unable to remember), and even the gentle Jane is forced back on hard, quiet resistance. When the talk becomes general conventional praise of the postal service and modern convenience, and thence chat about handwriting, Emma's sprightliness involves her in the most fearful dramatic irony – for the *averti* reader. She cannot know that by dutifully resolving not to tease Jane about her Dixon fantasy, and bravely raising Frank Churchill's name instead, she is, in fact, talking about that same, very embarrassing, handwriting that we know (or suspect) Jane went to the post-office to collect. But this, flexible and humorous as it is, is far from all there is in these three or so pages. Mr. Knightley says nothing until John Knightley appeals to him about the theory that handwriting runs in families and that Isabella's and Emma's are similar. His apparently casual reply is actually full of importance:

> "Yes," said his brother hesitatingly, "there is a likeness. I know what you mean – but Emma's hand is the strongest."
> "Isabella and Emma both write beautifully," said Mr. Woodhouse; "and always did. And so does poor Mrs. Weston" – (297)

I do not suppose it particularly significant that Mr. Knightley says – "strongest" where "stronger" would be normal; but a hesitation from *him* must give us pause. The preference for Emma is, one supposes, marginally not what his brother might wish to hear; more importantly it confirms our deep wish that he should love her, and thus forms part of a series of unconscious or semi-conscious developing revelations on both their parts which form another and different kind of pattern through the book. His irrational jealousy – which every critic notices – of Frank Churchill even before Frank appears (1, xviii) and afterwards; her wishing him a potential dancer rather than an older man among the "husbands, fathers, and whist-players" at the Crown (3, ii), his dancing with Harriet being "extremely good" after all, their subsequent dance and his wonderful "Brother and sister! no, indeed" which precedes this; her memory of where he was standing on a certain day while

Harriet remembers only Mr. Elton's place (3, iv); their mutually intelligent look – "her feelings were at once caught and honoured" – after she has apologised to Miss Bates about Box Hill in 3, ix, and the instinctive meeeting of hands and his near kiss of her's which follows – rendered in such nervous, exploratory prose:

> He took her hand; – whether she had not herself made the first motion, she could not say – she might, perhaps, have rather offered it – but he took her hand, pressed it, and certainly was on the point of carrying it to his lips – when, from some fancy or other, he suddenly let it go. – Why he should feel such a scruple, why he should change his mind when it was all but done, she could not perceive . . . (386)

– all these constitute a purposeful main design in the novel.[9]

But what I am noticing here is the art by which this *minute* detail about the handwriting is introduced within a crowded scene of comic expected responses. That it could easily be passed over in reading is indicative both of the density of Jane Austen's prose and of the control with which she picks out her themes in seemingly neutral contexts. In fact, no context is allowed to be neutral. It is the zest and depth imparted by such a marvellously complex use of patterns – volatile or otherwise – that effectively rebut the kind of criticism most trenchantly put by Lawrence. Even in the realist novel – perhaps, from a certain point of view, especially there – conventions of representation fruitfully obtain: verisimilitude is, after all, only a version of similitude.

v

Not that Jane Austen does not experiment with representation. The relatively crude stereotypes of Fanny Burney have, after *Sense and Sensibility* at any rate, vanished from her work. But, in addition, there is in *Emma* an experiment which I do not think has been recognised by commentators quite enough as such.

Miss Bates is a famous figure. With educated people at least, she leads, like Mr. Collins again, a quasi-proverbial existence outside the book comparable to that of Falstaff – though not so grand. She is paradigmatic to the novel in being known as the bore who entertains. She is also the person who believes in the perfect suitability of Highbury for human life, and is its laudatrix:

> "We may well say that 'our lot is cast in a goodly heritage'" . . . . "I say, sir," turning to Mr. Woodhouse, "I think there are few places with such society as Highbury. I always say, we are quite blessed in

our neighbours. – My dear sir, if there is one thing my mother loves better than another, it is pork – a roast loin of pork" – (2, iii, 174–5)

Her function within the novel has usually been explained, since Mary Lascelles wrote admirably, in 1939, of the "cobweb lightness and fineness" of Jane Austen's workmanship,[10] by saying that her inconsequencies are an essential means of revealing information and directing the reader's attitudes. Also, of course, she is wonderful as the humble thankful recipient of Mr. Knightley's squirely gifts of apples etc., and as the equally humble and forgiving sufferer from Emma's hot and exasperated effort at wit on Box Hill. But not only does she *not* exhibit – as some of the characters in the novel do – what Dr. Johnson was pleased to find in the Ministers of the Hebrides ". . . such politeness as so narrow a circle of converse could not have supplied, but to minds naturally disposed to elegance":[11] she is further interesting as seeming an unusually naturalistic speaker within Jane Austen's conventions.

It is a common and amiable mistake to think that we talk like people in books, or *vice versa*. The mistake is easily recognised when the book is composed of speeches in alexandrines, like, say, *Andromaque*. It is fairly easily recognised when the speeches are in blank verse – though it is surprising how many people talk a little like Hamlet when pressed. But, again, the novel is a peculiarly deceiving form if we persist in thinking it is *as* naturalistic as it commonly seems. Sometimes it does not really even seem so. It can, in Jane Austen's time as well as any other, be exceedingly mannered. Consider, for example, this effusion supplied by Fanny Burney for Delvile on finding a heroine still steady and sensible at Vauxhall at four in the morning – just after Harrel has shot himself:

> "Amiable Miss Beverley! what a dreadful scene have you witnessed! what a cruel task have you nobly performed! such spirit with such softness! so much presence of mind with such feeling! – But you are all excellence! human nature can rise no higher! I believe, indeed, that you are its most perfect ornament!"
> Praise such as this, so unexpected, and delivered with such energy, Cecilia heard not without pleasure . . . (*Cecilia*, 5, 7)[12]

This is highly conventionalised: like a stage speech, and as much a direction as to how we are to think about Cecilia as a pretence of surface verisimilitude. Jane Austen, as is often said, has a vastly more natural touch. Nevertheless, surely Norman Page is right when in his very useful discussion of Jane Austen's dialogue he mildly says:

... there seems good reason to doubt whether Jane Austen's contemporaries really spoke with the sureness and economy of effect which characterise the speech even of her foolish and vulgar figures.[13]

The "Ers" and "Aahs", grunts and sighs of one's conversation as revealed by tape recorder of TAM would of course make tedious reading (though there persists a sad convention of transcribing some of this into fiction in the interests of a delusive authenticity). Part of the fuller articulacy usual in novels must be to substitute for, or supply, the expressiveness given in nature by glance and gesture, and pitch, *timbre* and volume. So Miss Bates's egregious lack of emotional and mental sureness and economy is indicated by a special appropriate signal in her diction. The signal is that she meaninglessly fails to complete sentences. Mr. Knightley (and others) are quite capable of expressive English *aposiopesis* – as in the phrase about independence alluded to above; and others break off, like Mr. Elton, under the influence of emotion; but Miss Bates is genuinely, consistently, inconsequent. Here is the opening of one of her long speeches in 2, ix (just after poor Emma has been so infuriated by Harriet's dithering over the destination for her purchases at Ford's): the dots are, of course, part of the text:

> "I declare I cannot recollect what I was talking of. – Oh! my mother's spectacles. So very obliging of Mr. Frank Churchill! 'Oh!' said he, 'I do think I can fasten the rivet; I like a job of this kind excessively.' – Which you know shewed him to be so very.... Indeed I must say that, much as I had heard of him before and much as I had expected, he very far exceeds any thing.... I do congratulate you, Mrs. Weston, most warmly. He seems every thing the fondest parent could.... 'Oh!' said he, 'I can fasten that kind of rivet. I like a job of that sort excessively.'" (237–8)

And on it goes – full of information, as Mary Lascelles says, including information about Frank's affected manner – but in marked contrast to the formed speech usual to the other characters. A few lines down there is a further "That, you know, was so very...." and a little later "He would be so very...." both left hanging. This *tic* does sound near to literal transcription – and is something substantially exploited in subsequent literature. Henry James is fond of its use; and it is, for example, part of the distinguished tautened naturalism of Simon Gray's plays (the best contemporary dramatic writing) that characters constantly tail off their speeches into the significant air ...

Later, at the Crown ball (3, ii, 323–3), Miss Bates is punctuated predominantly by a series of breathless dashes. Later still, the style may seem to find its height in the wonderful passage of associative chatter by Mrs. Elton in the strawberry beds at Donwell in 3, vi: but here a distinction must be made, for with Mrs. Elton there is a different convention about the kind of reporting (creation really, of course) assumed. The *entirety* of Miss Bates's incompletions can be assumed to be present, and nature closely rendered. At Donwell, as it might be in a speech of hers, the reader is exposed to the speaker's nature and told by implication of the progress, the enthusiasm turning to boredom and fatigue, of the whole hilarious downgrade pastoral. But Mrs. Elton, "in all her apparatus of happiness, her large bonnet and her basket" (probably such Marie-Antoinette *voulu* excursions were by then a little vulgar, as Mr. Knightley's calm insistence on eating indoors implies) is as it were overheard from a distance, in brilliant *extracts*:

"... Morning decidedly the best time – never tired – every sort good – hautboy infinitely superior – no comparison – the others hardly eatable – hautboys very scarce – Chili preferred – white wood finest flavour of all – price of strawberries in London – abundance about Bristol – Maple Grove – cultivation – beds when to be renewed – gardeners thinking exactly different – no general rule – gardeners never to be put out of their way – delicious fruit – only too rich to be eaten much of – inferior to cherries – currants more refreshing – only objection to gathering strawberries the stooping – glaring sun – tired to death – could bear it no longer – must go and sit in the shade." (358–9)

Here the prose aspires to the condition of the index. If it were taken as a full transcription it would move near to those outer limits of the realm of the naturalistic normally inhabited by Mr. Jingle in *Pickwick*:

"Heads, heads – take care of your heads!" cried the loquacious stranger, as they came out under the low archway, which in those days formed the entrance to the coach-yard. "Terrible place – dangerous work – other day – five children – mother tall lady, eating sandwiches – forgot the arch – crash – knock – children look round – mother's head off – sandwich in her hand – no mouth to put it in – head of a family off – shocking, shocking! Looking at Whitehall, Sir? – fine place..." (ch. 2)

But Miss Bates's diffuseness is un-eccentric. It seems the result of an experiment with direct, unsummarised representation, closer to a copy of nature than is the speech of the equally commonplace people who surround her – but who finish their sentences. This is an extension of artistic range, as opposed, I think, to the evidence Fay Weldon (who daringly says that the part "goes on too long") finds for an "observed" as opposed to an "invented" character – "a slightly spiteful portrait".[14] (Let her speak for herself as a novelist; to me hers seems a confused distinction – and anyway the whole drift of *Emma* after Box Hill runs against the latter notion.)

vi

Enough, for the moment, of Jane Austen's perfected yet still evolving methods. All these descriptions merely concern the medium that creates, and is inseparable from, the possibility of Emma herself. She is Jane Austen's most fully created out-going heroine (temperamentally opposed to Fanny Price and Anne Elliot, and even finer than Elizabeth Bennet), and a moral flower of the novels.

I wish to praise her character.

Not, of course in the banal way that treats her as a real person with whom one may, for example, fall in love; but precisely as the speaker of J.F. Burrows's 21,501 words in a work of art. For she embodies a deeply sympathetic, though obviously vulnerable, positive ethic.

Her great attraction, the exact reverse of "my Fanny", lies in her openness, her *activity*. Every reader is made an expert on her failures – in self-knowledge, in self-control, in discipline, in humility, even in the proper assessment of what she grandly dubs "the yeomanry". And if there were (by some curious freak of obtuseness) a danger that these flaws – which fuel most of the scintillating drama of the book and are often made explicit – might escape someone, somewhere, critics have made it their business to expound them. So we are at liberty to look instead at the virtue implicit in all her mistakes: at their real cause, in fact. Without it the novel would merely be a harder and better *Cranford*.

Like everyone, and especially every main protagonist in a work of art, Emma is faced with choices. It is a commonplace about the book (in relation especially to Jane Austen's other heroines) that she is exceptionally well placed to make them – "handsome, clever, and rich" of course. However dull Highbury is, Emma is its admitted queen – and part of the nearly distracted nature of Mrs. Elton's showing off is in a way a tribute to how unshakable her rival's position is *au fond*. (In fact, Emma would not admit that there *is* a rivalry – and most of the others in the book would have to agree with her.) Above all, she is so placed as to be able to take up in plausible worldly strength that stance towards a woman's lot which is spiritually present in Elizabeth Bennet but not in her circumstances, and for which Fanny Price is unqualified in every way.

This very deliberate elevation, with its attendant temptations, could well be a subject to develop into a tragedy. Emma's characteristically sharp apprehension – "it is poverty only which makes celibacy contemptible to a generous public!" (1, ix, 85) – serves to focus the attention on, to insist on, the areas where her very lucidity misleads her. It is a characteristic of the clever and articulate to seal themselves off from wisdom by the facility, plausibility and apparent comprehensiveness of their formulations. On their way to visit the poor Emma boasts:

> "If I know myself, Harriet, mine is an active, busy mind, with a great many independent resources; and I do not perceive why I should be more in want of employment at forty or fifty than one-and-twenty. Woman's usual occupations of eye and hand and mind will be as open to me then, as they are now; or with no important variation. If I draw less, I shall read more; if I give up music, I shall take to carpet-work. And for objects for the affections, which is in truth the great point of inferiority, the want of which is really the great evil to be avoided in *not* marrying, I shall be very well off, with all the children of a sister I love so much, to care about. There will be enough of them, in all probability, to supply every sort of sensation that declining life can need. There will be enough for every hope and every fear; and though my attachment to none can equal that of a parent, it suits my ideas of comfort better than what is warmer and blinder. My nephews and nieces! – I shall often have a niece with me."
>
> "Do you know Miss Bates's niece? That is, I know you must have seen her a hundred times – but are you acquainted?"
>
> "Oh! yes; we are always forced to be acquainted..." (1, x, 85–6)

How poignant, and cunning, the reference to Jane Fairfax. The passage is often cited – and it is too easy to moralise at Emma's expense on its complacency, to point out how she is proved wrong etc., and how she confuses art with occupation, while the commentator forgets, probably in pleasure at the effect, how very like it is to the sentiments of most twenty- or twenty-one-year olds who are above the mediocre. (Imagine Harriet thinking in anything like this style.) But such blindness could be the prelude to deep suffering. It easily could be, since the world in this novel – like but even more so than the world of a society ruled by laxer social conventions – is diffused with a perpetual contingency. The opportunity for significant personal contact depends on the fall of events rather than the individual will – a fact that, coupled with the dignity, restraint and shyness on both sides, makes for the terrific tension always felt (even while we appreciate the artistically inevitable) as to whether Mr. Knightley will succeed in proposing or not. But although there is suffering in Emma's part – her freedom is also freedom to endure three major episodes filled with self reproach – this, too, is a product of what is admirable in her, and thus accords with no tragedy but a serious comic resolution. For the quality that determines the choices and mistakes she makes is what gives particular piquancy to the speech, and it conduces eventually to happiness rather than grief. She is quite right about the nature of her mind, and absolutely wrong about being satisfied with the tranquil exploitation of "resources". But she has to do *something* with her resources. And it is quite true and partly proper that she is an "imaginist". In dull Highbury, with its lack of life-compelling stimulus save the overrated periodic visits of familiar or unfamiliar outsiders – who are naturally dubious assets when they do arrive – the life in the mind, if you have one, and nothing much else to do, is everything.

Emma's quality – and her tremendous, admirable charm – is that she always chooses what seems to her the *most exciting* option or interpretation available. That this is her implicit criterion – rather than the exercise of her potential good sense and her natural taste – is what makes her so attractive to the reader and, of course, perfect for Mr. Knightley. From it derive all the famous mistakes and occasions for moralising: she must make matches; she must be an itchy reader and never perfect her music;[15] she must cultivate the noble bastard Harriet and rule out Robert Martin; Mr. Elton must marry Harriet; she must fall temporarily in love in a not-too-emotional kind of way with Frank Churchill and he with her; Frank must marry Harriet; Jane Fairfax must be open as well as irritatingly elegant; Jane must be adulterously in love with Mr. Dixon – such a tangle is, as I say, the possession of every reader. But its root is something we should very much approve. For: what could be the alternatives for an intelligent person?

A tone suggested in Mary Brunton represents one kind of alternative. Laura Montreville is resisting the attentions and protection of her predatory adorer Hargrave:

"Let me not hear you – let me not look upon you," said Laura; – "leave me to think, if it be possible," – and she poured a silent prayer to Heaven for help in this her sorest trial. The effort composed her, and the majesty of virtue gave dignity to her form, and firmness to her voice, while she said, – . . . "I dare not trust to principles such as yours the guardianship of this the infancy of my being. I dare not incur certain guilt to escape contingent evil. I cannot make you the companion of this uncertain life, while your conduct is such, as to make our eternal separation the object of my dreadful hope." (*Self-Control*, 1810/11, ch. 5.[16])

It is precisely the point about Emma that she is never in a position to have to protest in this way. In any case she is not pompous (though it should in justice be noted that Laura is capable of more lively tones). But also the strict negative virtue implied – even without its melo-dramatic trapping – is contrary to Emma's whole conception (whereas it would not be to that of Fanny Price, given the difference in quality of language).

Could she then, as a more plausible alternative, more promptly and thoroughly heed the irritant corrective quality of the other superior person in Highbury, Mr. Knightley, and subside into a dull supremacy that would satisfy neither of them? The question is rhetorical, and perhaps a stupid tribute to the vigour of Jane Austen's creation. Really, there are no alternatives, as the subtle insistent detail of the dramatisa-tion of the generous restlessness of Emma's mental process demon-strates. To take a few examples of this: very early on the narrator insinuates that a part of Emma's gratitude to Miss Taylor has been because of the latter's complacency towards her "active, busy" mind. She has been "peculiarly interested in herself, in every pleasure, every scheme of her's; – one to whom she could speak every thought as it arose, and who had such an affection for her as could never find fault" (1, i, 6). Nurture for speedy disaster, one might think. But fortunately Emma is a good person, and one is inclined to see her as Lady Granville saw Lady Osborne at about the same time:

> Lady Francis [Osborne] puzzles me to death. I am tempted to pencher to the admiring side. Granville (who likes her extremely) has been arguing the point of her superiority of character. He says (and I three quarters agree with him), that her conduct is regulated by an uncontrollable determination to follow all her own inclinations. That she is born with good ones is no *merit* of hers.[17]

This is no place to engage in a debate about Nature *versus* Nurture – otherwise the question would arise as to how the debile Mr. Woodhouse could be as it were genetically responsible for his vivid daughter. But the carrying through the novel of the implications of "every pleasure, every scheme" is to the point. Emma is always sharp: so sharp on occasion as even to be able to draw attention to the novelist's own delicate effects. When, for instance, the scheme over Harriet's portrait is in train the characters react to it in succession, in character; and Mr. Knightley, with typical accuracy, says, "You have made her too tall, Emma", but Mr. Elton replies:

> "Oh, no! certainly not too tall; not in the least too tall. Consider, she is sitting down – which naturally presents a different – which in short gives exactly the idea – and the proportions must be preserved, you know. Proportions, fore-shortening. – Oh, no! it gives one exactly the idea of such a height as Miss Smith's. Exactly so indeed!" (1, vi, 48)

This literate/nonsensical essay in Miss Bates-style appreciation might be passed over as part of the Elton gush. But Emma, in the midst of her delusion as to the object of that gush, picks on it (to herself) with a clarity and exact good sense worthy of Dr. Johnson:

> "This man is almost too gallant to be in love. . . . He is an excellent young man, and will suit Harriet exactly; it will be an 'Exactly so,' as he says himself . . ." (49)

It is a comparable mental alacrity in the midst of blindness that, in sensitive retrospective analysis, recognises after the *débâcle* in the carriage from Randalls that "The first error and the worst lay at her door" (1, xvi, 136), but, beautifully, "It was rather too late in the day to set about being simple-minded and ignorant" (1, xvii, 142) – and this is at the same period that detaching Harriet from Robert Martin is still a subject for self congratulation.

Emma wants things to be exciting, to choose, to initiate. She forms part, one might say, of a very familiar tradition of witty young women in fiction (Anna Howe in *Clarissa*, Lady Honoria in *Cecilia*, Miss Milner in *A Simple Story* and Lady Delacour in *Belinda* spring to mind in high-quality work – though the type seems to have been common – and they are followed immediately by the notable Lady Juliana in Susan Ferrier's *Marriage* [1818] and by Lady Cecilia in *Helen* [1834]). But – to generalise – these creations, though usually 'good', are also usually structurally subordinate in that their imperfections and their freedom *contrast* with the real heroine. Emma, with Elizabeth Bennet, is moved to the centre, *is* the real heroine, and therefore revivifies the rôle. Together they are heroines for the future. (How far the future followed them up is another, and complex, matter.) And, as I have said, she is

177

obviously marked off from Elizabeth by her money and status. She is therefore able to act on events, rather than merely to react, however strongly. She is pivotal in combining internal freedom with external independence and being therefore in a position to realise her freedom without threat (and without discipline): she can refuse Elton and merely dally with Frank Churchill; it is, famously, a prompting from within herself that directs her to Mr. Knightley – and she scarcely adopts a passive stance toward him. She is a kind of amatory protestant. And the bustling inward activity of her spirit is constantly brilliant. Consider some more details of her play of mind immediately Frank Churchill arrives:

> Emma wondered whether the same suspicion of what might be expected from their knowing each other which had taken strong possession of her mind had ever crossed his. . . . She had no doubt of what Mr. Weston was often thinking about. His quick eye she detected again and again glancing . . . (2, v, 192–3)

A little later she looks forward to the chance of:

> . . . judging of his general manners, and by inference, of the meaning of his manners towards herself; of guessing how soon it might be necessary for her to throw coldness into her air; and of fancying what the observations of all those might be, who were now seeing them together for the first time. (2, viii, 212)

As the last phrase indicates, Emma assumes that every one is as acute as she thinks herself. Her mind is almost absurdly generous as well as patronising. And she enthusiastically gives to some of the people around her a glamour and vividness which make them worthy to inhabit her own drama. But she is mistaken about this too, and it is of her, gazing idly – no, actively – at the mundane Highbury scene that the narrator brilliantly, and with unusual philosophical overtones, says:

> A mind lively and at ease, can do with seeing nothing, and can see nothing that does not answer. (2, ix, 233)

Such a mind must of course, in one of the broader comic passages of the novel, turn Harriet's undangerous encounter with a few gypsies (children and women) into a drama that might have come out of the more childish parts of Richardson or Fanny Burney, and with Frank, though not on horseback, in the tenor rôle: –

> Could a linguist, could a grammarian, could even a mathematician have seen what she did, have witnessed their appearance together. . . .

How much more must an imaginist, like herself, be on fire with
speculation and foresight! – especially with such a ground-work of
anticipation as her mind had already made. (3, iii, 335)

– and thereby miss the actual exciting clue in the incident which is
Frank's visit to the Bates's, lamely explained as the return of a "pair of
scissars".[18]

In remarking these things I merely pick out strands from a texture the
strength of which every reader will have felt. But the principle behind
them – that Emma is in lively pursuit of any excitement offered by
her limited environment and some which are not offered – naturally
informs the most talked of and most impressive parts of the novel as
well. It is not malice or ill nature that insults Miss Bates on Box Hill,
but restlessness and boredom coupled with an habitual *esprit* – so
that we can see the episode sympathetically as well as through Mr.
Knightley's justified dismay. It is the fresh and spring-like activity of
Emma's approach to her fusty and *gêneant* world which constitutes her
value and explains her charm. The mistakes recede. Unlike the would-
be grander choices made through the imaginative powers of a Victorian
fictional descendant (with whom I have declined to compare Catherine
Morland) – Isabel Archer confronting her destiny in *The Portrait of a
Lady* – Emma's choices are all in favour of enhancement. What she
desires she receives – of course, from the most familiar and the least
expected quarter.

vii

Nevertheless, it would be misleading to conclude this discussion of
Emma with Emma alone. For in this lively comic achievement there is
still something of a parallel and inheritance from the grim outer world
of *Sense and Sensibility*.

It is obvious to all that the didactic intent – a truly respectable thing
which every writer has – is never rammed home or insisted upon in Jane
Austen's work, as it can be in that of most of her predecessors and,
indeed, most of her successors. The moral definitions of her novels are
not *obscure* – they are definitely felt; but at their most important they
reside in the interplay of embodiments of value – frequently negative
embodiments – and usually at the centre, as in *Emma*, imperfect ones –
and not in the remarks of a directive narrator. Nor is any one character
proposed as a 'mouthpiece' – Mr. Knightley is perhaps the nearest to
this, and he is seen often with a very amused eye.[19] Most of this is

received wisdom, and it is one of the reasons why Jane Austen seems so temporally un-local, so unformidable, and so unreservedly entertaining. Nevertheless, an intent is there, and it can be illuminated in this case by considering why it is that the heroine's own love drama is happily concluded in its essentials a good fifty pages before the end of the book? A good deal of the story needs working out, of course: Frank and Jane; Harriet; the practicalities of having to adjust Mr. Woodhouse's system to the shocking news; a poultry raid – and so on. Nor does the interest flag. None the less, Mr. Knightley's proposal could easily, and more traditionally, have come after most of it had been done – or most of it could have been sidelined.

The deep reason for this structure must surely be that the romantic climax is being, literally, 'placed' in a not very romantic world. In spite of the novel's having (to use a word beloved of theatre reviewers) an eponymous heroine, her actions are inextricably linked to her context – a feature that I have tried to echo in this chapter. James Thompson sharply observes that Jane Austen lived at the beginning of a period which was beginning to idealise marriage as an individual "compact of love and affection" as opposed to a contractual and dynastic (or, I suppose, merely useful) business, and that we live at the end of this period.[20] The reader of *Emma* – or of any of Jane Austen – should not really need this observation with its shaky historical ground and its dubious present. As we constantly realise, everything is within the fiction. But although the novel offers the central couple a temporary support, as it were, from the other new couples, this is assumed rather than dramatised; and the Churchills will not be in Highbury and the Martins (embarrassingly enough) not in the same social sphere. So the satisfaction of the ending must be a little muted. Or, rather, "the perfect happiness of the union" among "the small band of true friends" (3, xix, 484) *is* there and felt; but it is equi-present, so to speak, and simultaneous with, the dull and unredeemed environment. Elizabeth Darcy can remove to Pemberley, and Fanny Bertram reform Mansfield – but Emma's privileged position in this deeply original conception scarcely allows of external change – a fact amusingly enforced by her not even changing houses. How definite the novel is being on this point is illustrated by two manifestations of those Highbury leading lights, the Eltons. One might expect Mrs. Elton to fade in bafflement when faced with the betrothals of the two dignified couples in the book. On the contrary, her indelicate coy boasting is even more irrepressible – to their faces: about Jane, who dislikes and resents her, to Emma who adds scorn (now with equanimity) to these feelings: "Do not you think, Miss Woodhouse, our saucy little friend here is charmingly recovered?" (454)

– and on, and, excruciatingly, on. And surely it is a fairly acid piece of anti-Donatism to have everybody married by her husband in his official capacity but with no murmur at all? Sandra Gilbert and Susan Gubar hazard in their usual lively way of novels in this period that "a girl without a benevolent narrator would never find her way out of either her mortifications or her parent's house".[21] But here all is natural, and the narration not a bit over managed. Emma finds herself at last freely and spontaneously choosing to prefer Mr. Knightley's vision of "the beauty of truth and sincerity" – though with a blush for Harriet (3, xi, 404–5) – to her own hectic, wonderful, inner life; and we are deeply moved and believe it. Perhaps this is because unglamorous Highbury remains with us, and there can be no danger, there, of having a sentimental dream. It remains for *Persuasion* to move a heroine right out of this world.

Chapter Eight

Registers of *Persuasion*

"...the fresh-made path spoke of the farmer, counteracting the sweets of poetical despondency, and meaning to have spring again..."

Like Keats Jane Austen died young. Had she lived in the seventeenth century she might have been the subject of one of those plangent formal epitaphs which partly reconcile posterity to the loss of genius – though of nothing so vehement as *Adonais*. Nevertheless, like Keats she created work which is 'late' in a way that has little to do with dates or lifespans. Late, that is, not only in tone and subject matter (the word 'autumnal' inevitably hovers round both artists) but in manifesting so complete a mastery of art as sometimes to dispense with much of what had seemed to constitute that mastery. The abrupt transitions and simple melodies of late Beethoven are, one might argue, apparent crudities only possible to an artist with total confidence in his powers. Pieces of shorthand which form part of wholes more profound and more complex than anything that had gone before. So are the fanfares and chants in *Parsifal*. In such works it is as though an unprecedented control and richness of invention allows a relaxation back into the naïve in pursuit of new depths and new explorations of feeling: or even allows a sophisticated pleasure in the naïve for its own sake – in the peculiar case of Tolstoy's late tales naïvety becomes the source of spiritual value. Accordingly, astonished and gratified by the glittering integrity of *Emma*, the reader of the opening pages of *Persuasion* may be surprised by what seems a reversion to an earlier, simpler, lighter art. But the reader of the final pages is in tears.

i

A more extended comparison may illuminate this phenomenon. Following a remark or reminiscence of Dryden's: –

182

Shakespeare's own Muse her *Pericles* first bore,
The Prince of *Tyre* was elder than the *Moore* . . .[1]

– it was believed for years that *Pericles* was one of the great poet's earliest plays, whereas the parts of it he wrote are probably some of his last work. By contrast, in spite of the questions surrounding the dates of composition of her first novels (see above, chapter two), Jane Austen is so much closer to us in time, her life so much better documented than Shakespeare's, that we know the exact time within which she wrote *Persuasion*: 8 August 1815 to 6 August 1816. We know also that she had begun to "feel unwell"[2] from the illness that was to rob the world of her the following July.

When at a loss for the external sureties of letters, dates on manuscripts, naval actions or other public events mentioned in the text, etc., students of Shakespeare make their appeal to internal stylistic evidence. So Dryden might have had something like the following in mind:

> *Pericles* Hail, Dian! to perform thy just command,
> I here confess myself the king of Tyre;
> Who, frighted from my country, did wed
> At Pentapolis the fair Thaisa,
> At sea in childbed died she, but brought forth
> A maid child call'd Marina; who, O goddess,
> Wears yet thy silver livery. She at Tharsus
> Was nurs'd with Cleon, who at fourteen years
> He sought to murder; but her better stars
> Brought her to Mytilene . . . (5, iii, 1–9)

(Incidentally, the audience has seen all this already.) Just so, were the dates not known, the student of Jane Austen might find an early – though very much more lively – tone in:

> Sir Walter Elliot, of Kellynch Hall in Somersetshire, was a man who, for his own amusement, never took up any book but the Baronetage; there he found occupation for an idle hour, and consolation in a distressed one; there his faculties were roused into admiration and respect, by contemplating the limited remnant of the earliest patents; there any unwelcome sensations, arising from domestic affairs, changed naturally into pity and contempt, as he turned over the almost endless creations of the last century – and there, if every other leaf were powerless, he could read his own history with an interest which never failed . . . (1, i, 3)

Actually, since he is addressing a miracle-dealing goddess, Pericles' prayerful note is more telling than its humdrum verse, out of con-

183

text, suggests; and Jane Austen's sketch of Lady Catherine de Bourgh reincarnated as a man is also subtler than it looks. I think Virginia Woolf, who detected "a peculiar dullness" alongside "a peculiar beauty" in *Persuasion*, was hasty in calling the satire simply "harsh" and "no longer aware of the amusements of daily life".[3] Besides Sir Walter's obvious comic pomp, the passage indicates his boneheadedness ("never took up any book but"), the likelihood of domestic difficulties to be escaped from, his frigidity, and even, fleetingly, his probable tone of voice – "endless creations of the last century". Further, the very baldness of the entry from the favourite volume which follows, with its list of names and births and deaths and places, is surely a very daring solution to the perennial problem of how to introduce the facts of a narrative? Nevertheless, the uncomplicated satirical stance – phrased with all the assured dignity of balanced clauses reminiscent of Fielding – seems to revert back from the complex flexibility of the prose we admire in *Mansfield Park* and *Emma*. And, in accord with this, Sir Walter, unlike Sir Thomas Bertram or Mr. Woodhouse in their different ways, is allowed no subsequent leeway: "Vanity was the beginning and end of Sir Walter Elliot's character; vanity of person and of situation. . . . He considered the blessing of beauty as inferior only to the blessing of a baronetcy; and the Sir Walter Elliot who united these gifts, was the constant object of his warmest respect and devotion" (4). This indeed is his mental beginning and end. He undergoes only two changes: the external degradation (which he is, infuriatingly, too stupid to feel) from the "real respectability" of his position and responsibility as a (more or less) functioning county magnate to the "heartless elegance" of a flatterer of the Irish aristocracy in Bath; and the modification of his view of the name Wentworth from its denoting "nobody . . . nothing to do with the Strafford family" (1, iii, 23) to its being a "well-sounding name" (2, xii, 248). One would have to have a richly compassionate view of human nature to find him a caricature, but he is rendered with such decisive, unrelenting strokes as to put him in the company, as it were, of John Thorpe, Robert Ferrars and Mr. Collins – even of Lord Merton in *Evelina*. And the same is true of Elizabeth, although in the curiously fluctuating tones of the first three chapters – which I shall discuss shortly – it momentarily seems that she might have been developed into a new Maria Bertram, or even an ungenerous Emma.

So it is all the more exciting to discover, in the cases of both artists, that these simpler earlier modes co-exist with things far more widely expressive. One of the most thrilling moments in art – probably because it is conjectured to be the moment when Shakespeare *himself* took over the hitherto pedestrian and amusing fable (the argument is circular, but never mind) – is when Pericles, a humbler Lear, confronts the storm:

> The god of this great vast, rebuke these surges
> Which wash both heaven and hell; and thou that hast
> Upon the winds command, bind them in brass,
> Having call'd them from the deep! O, still
> Thy deaf'ning, dreadful thunders; gently quench
> Thy nimble sulphorous flashes! O, how, Lychorida,
> How does my queen? Thou stormest venomously;
> Wilt thou spit all thyself? The seaman's whistle
> Is as a whisper in the ears of death,
> Unheard . . . (3, i, 1–10)

Such verse, especially when framed by an affectionate pastiche of the mediaeval poet Gower, who acts as chorus, operates as a kind of resounding, super-competent recall or *resumé* of Shakespeare's mature tragedies. One feels he could write like this on command. But it itself gives way to – serves as the frame for – the sublime and magical distillate of the late plays, dramatised in this case in the recognition by an almost destroyed and extinct Pericles of his lost daughter, Marina, in the fifth act:

Pericles   . . . I am great with woe
> And shall deliver weeping. My dearest wife
> Was like this maid, and such a one
> My daughter might have been: my queen's square brows;
> Her stature to an inch; as wand-like straight;
> As silver-voic'd; her eyes as jewel-like
> And cas'd as richly; in pace another Juno;
> Who starves the ears she feeds, and makes them hungry
> The more she gives them speech . . . (5, i, 105–13)

Succeeded by:

>   . . . thou dost look
> Like Patience gazing on king's graves, and smiling
> Extremity out of act. (137–9)

And:

> O Helicanus, strike me honour'd sir!
> Give me a gash, put me to present pain,
> Lest this great sea of joys rushing upon me
> O'erbear the shores of my mortality,

> And drown me with their sweetness. O, come hither,
> Thou that beget'st him that did thee beget;
> Thou that wast born at sea, buried at Tharsus,
> And found at sea again . . . (190–7)

This, in its context of solemn music, flickers and pulses toward that area of feeling that T.S. Eliot, talking of the later plays, called "a fringe of indefinite extent, of feeling which we can only detect, so to speak, out of the corner of the eye and can never completely focus; of feeling of which we are only completely aware in a kind of temporary detachment from action" and which is the nearest we can get in art to "a condition of serenity, stillness and reconciliation".[4] It is, admittedly, some distance in kind from Jane Austen's own apotheoses – though not so far as the superficial glance would have it. But my present purpose is to suggest that her late work exhibits also that combination of the secure and known and tried, the inherited and evolved, the early and the middle styles, so to speak, with the new and tentative and innovatory, which is characteristic of a 'late' manner. In her, too, something deeper seems to be sought, and found. To explore this I return to the start of *Persuasion*.

ii

It is a pity that it is called *Persuasion*. The title, which Henry Austen chose out of several, has made readers unduly highlight, or sometimes even wish into being, instances of a social process not more common in this novel than it would be in any passage of normal experience, or imagined experience (c.f. my remarks on titles in general, below, chapter four, pp. 70–1). If we are neither anchorites nor psychopaths we spend our lives persuading or being persuaded, importantly or trivially – it is often hard to tell in advance which – every day of the week. And Cassandra talked of another, more neutrally satisfactory title, *The Elliots*. But this accident is only one instance of a certain sublime lack of finish in the work. The rewriting and remodelling of the cancelled chapter in which Captain Wentworth proposes (originally 2, x[5]), rather paradoxically offers us a unique example of the brilliance and swiftness of Jane Austen's second thoughts. More of this later: but it is paradoxical because the rest of the text clearly had not the advantage of that long indwelling and detailed revision – the "many perusals" of which Henry Austen speaks – which makes for the technical perfection of so much of her other work. I think, as I have hinted, that this shows quite strongly before the action settles into Anne's point of view

in chapter four. The tart bravura of the opening description of Sir
Walter is succeeded, immediately, by a curiously ambivalent narratorial
voice. Unimportant as this later becomes (and generally clear as it
already is) the reader may wonder who is speaking in:

> Be it known then, that Sir Walter, like a good father, (having met
> with one or two private disappointments in very unreasonable ap-
> plications) prided himself on remaining single for his dear daughter's
> sake. For one daughter, his eldest, he would really have given up any
> thing, which he had not been very much tempted to do.... His two
> other children were of very inferior value. Mary had acquired a little
> artificial importance, by becoming Mrs. Charles Musgrove; but Anne,
> with an elegance of mind and sweetness of character, which must
> have placed her high with any people of real understanding, was
> nobody with either father or sister: her word had no weight; her
> convenience was always to give way; – she was only Anne.
>   To Lady Russell, indeed, she was... (1, i, 5)

Here, perhaps the "good father", and certainly the "other children were
of very inferior value", are either straight accounts of what Sir Walter
thought, or devastatingly sarcastic in being the reverse of the truth. In
either case they sort uneasily with the scornful and emotional tone of
the rest – which is brimming with narratorial judgement. The passage
lacks the perfect pitch of the openings to *Mansfield Park* and *Emma*,
though it has a comparable drive. Similarly: Lady Russell is in the
event one of the least realised of Jane Austen's secondary characters –
compare Mrs. Jennings or Mrs. Norris. And one of the reasons for this
might be that the description of her at the beginning of chapter two is
so relatively lengthy and unfocussed. The question is of Sir Walter's
retrenchment:

> She was a woman rather of sound than of quick abilities, whose
> difficulties ... in this instance were great, from the opposition of two
> leading principles. She was of strict integrity herself, with a delicate
> sense of honour; but she was as desirous of saving Sir Walter's
> feelings, as solicitous for the credit of the family, as aristocratic in her
> ideas of what was due to them, as any body of sense and honesty
> could well be.... She had a cultivated mind, and was, generally
> speaking rational and consistent – but she had prejudices on the side
> of rank and ancestry; she had a value for rank and consequence
> which blinded her a little. Herself, the widow only of a knight, she
> gave the dignity of a baronet all its due; and Sir Walter ... was as
> being Sir Walter, in her apprehension entitled to a great deal of
> compassion and consideration ... (11)

This gives her conflict twice in principle and then twice in practice. It would surely have been honed had Jane Austen lived.

It may seem ungrateful to pick on these petty blemishes; but not, I think, if we see them as part of that relatively careless fecundity which I am trying to suggest. So in the next paragraph but one Lady Russell exemplifies in her advice the conflict of which we have just been told:

> "... it is singularity which often makes the worst part of our suffer-ing, as it always does of our conduct. ... for, after all, the person who has contracted debts must pay them; and though a great deal is due to the feelings of a gentleman ... there is still more due to the charac-ter of an honest man." (12)

This is dense with point. We observe how even the best people in this *milieu* (save one) jumble together prudential arguments – not breaking ranks – with ethical ones. In retrospect we recognise that a dislike of "singularity" is exactly one of the things that might lead Lady Russell to exert pressure against a young girl's marriage to an obscure naval officer – and thus undesignedly cause "the worst part of [her] suffer-ing". In prospect, as it were, we see that in Lady Russell's second and conflicting argument, she, of all people, heralds the main moral drift of the book. This kind of packed accuracy, so different from, yet almost simultaneously co-existent with, the brilliant acidity of the first sketches of Sir Walter, *is* the sort of tight writing which had been developed in the first two Chawton novels.

Yet there is also something fresh in this prose. I do not want to raise a host of irrelevant critical devils – side issues – by using the term 'poetic'.[6] But some of the language of the opening has a kind of free, resonant, evocative quality which signals a new opening out in Jane Austen. I have already quoted the sad little syllables which everyone remembers, and that lay down the *donnée* from which the action so tensely and wonderfully evolves upward: "– she was only Anne". But consider also how an evocative impulse even redeems for a moment – with something like pity – the possible situation of the otherwise thoroughly repellent Elizabeth:

> Thirteen years had seen her mistress of Kellynch Hall, presiding and directing with a self-possession and decision which could never have given the idea of her being younger than she was. For thirteen years had she been doing the honours, and laying down the domestic law at home, and leading the way to the chaise and four, and walking immediately after Lady Russell out of all the drawing-rooms and dining-rooms in the country. Thirteen winters' revolving frosts had

seen her opening every ball of credit which a scanty neighbourhood afforded; and thirteen springs shewn their blossoms, as she travelled up to London with her father, for a few weeks annual enjoyment of the great world. She had the remembrance of all this; she had the consciousness of being nine-and-twenty . . . (1, i, 6–7)

Que ces vains ornements, que ces voiles me pèsent! says Phèdre – and a more self-aware Elizabeth, with THIRTEEN tolling out in her life, might well evoke a comparable sympathy were the novel to continue in this vein. But sympathy has more urgent objects, and she retires beside her father as another exemplar of the sterile pride which the novel is concerned to supersede.

Every reader, every commentator, has felt this supersession. It is now time to link my suggestions about the evolving manners of the prose with a more systematic consideration of the meanings for which they are evolved. For, of course, these are intimately connected, indistinguishable.

iii

"A great deal is due to the feelings of a gentleman . . . still more due to the character of an honest man". It is actually a commonplace piece of morality.

Is *Persuasion*, then, a cosy story, as most of our democratic contemporaries would have it, about the triumph through action and superior amatory charm of the professional classes/middle classes/imperial classes/*bourgeoisie*/new nineteenth-century man – etc. – over a defunct aristocracy or gentry? Oddly, in view of the fatuous nature of these descriptions, yes – this is what it is about. But nothing like so simply, or so cosily, as the description of Captain Wentworth as "a modern-minded man"[7] would suggest. We need to be particularly careful not to patronise the past – the baneful tendency of a civilisation which mistakes high technological advance for an advance in social forms – when reading a novel that is, a bit surprisingly, so apparently sympathetic to the more automatic prejudices of our own local culture. To do so is to make its meanings less delicate, less interesting and less searching than they can be; whereas they are, as usual with Jane Austen, easily available in their full intensity to the alert reader in their own terms.

First the navy: it, like much else in the novel, is predominantly seen and valued through Jane Austen's most faultless centre of consciousness, and probably her most attractive. Whereas the action of *Emma* encompasses the complex feat of perceiving through a mind that is energetically wrong-headed and itself the subject of corrective change, that of *Persuasion* is viewed by someone refined, experienced and almost always gently right. Someone, too, with none of the vestigial coldness or period reserve which hangs (on the whole unjustly, as I have argued) round Elinor Dashwood or Fanny Price.

There is no point in adding here to the chorus of praise and love that generations have lavished on Anne Elliot. Pictures of perfection may have made Jane Austen feel sick and wicked (a charming reaction indeed[8]); but *this* picture is as far as could well be from that pained and strained correctness of contemporary 'vartue' so often present in other novelists of the period. Anne's Christian resignation is felt as particularly sympathetic and *beautiful*. There are several reasons for this. It is felt partly, obviously, because she is carefully denied the fresh physical charm of a conventional heroine. Partly, I guess, because she is encountered in close tandem with a narratorial commentary which is uninhibitedly sharp (as we have seen) – and is thus both guaranteed from any taint of sentimentality, and protected *in situ*, as it were, from the danger of the reader feeling over-defensive on her part in relation to the characters who slight her. Mary's selfish whinings at Uppercross and the blundering nature of the amiable patronage offered by the other Musgroves, for instance, are framed and contained within narratorial summaries distinguished by a kind of tolerant scorn, which enable us to contemplate peacefully Anne's reacting with no anger at all – not even private resentment – to questions like "Dear me! what can *you* possibly have to do?" (38, and see particularly 37, 40, and 45–6 in 1, v–vi).

Partly because, whatever the depths of estrangement and suffering her experience threatens or skirts, it is seen as progressively and realistically rewarded – in this world. Partly because, even when diagnostic strokes reminiscent of Fanny Price are introduced:

> ... excepting one short period of her life, she had never, since the age of fourteen, never since the loss of her dear mother, known the happiness of being listened to, or encouraged by any just appreciation of real taste. (1, vi, 47)

– this doubly poigant deprivation (the short period must have been when she knew Commander Wentworth) is faced without a hint of self-pity and with no straining after virtue. The passage continues:

> In music she had been always used to feel alone in the world; and Mr. and Mrs. Musgrove's fond partiality for their own daughters' performance, and total indifference to any other person's, gave her much more pleasure for their sakes, than mortification for her own. (*Ibid.*)

So, "Well done, Miss Anne! very well done indeed! Lord bless me!" –
we are reasonably content.

And partly – to complete this abstention from praise of Anne –
because the fine innovatory manner, implicit with metaphor, which
evoked the futility of Elizabeth's life of precedence, can be used to put
some affectionate distance between us and her sister in her moment of
happiness:

> Prettier musings of high-wrought love and eternal constancy, could
> never have passed along the streets of Bath, than Anne was sport-
> ing with from Camden-place to Westgate-buildings. It was almost
> enough to spread purification and perfume all the way. (2, ix, 192)

Now, one important result of the attractiveness of this portrait is that
the reader is powerfully induced to accept the navy, and Captain
Wentworth, at Anne's own high positive valuation. Most readers are
very ready to do so. After all, whatever our soberer judgements may
protest about imperial exploitation, secret police, draconian hanging
laws, the condition of Ireland, doggish poverty, brutal conditions
of labour etc., the Regency is widely perceived as one of the most
glamorous periods in English history. Even some of its very abuses
(soberly considered) are admired. The fine clothes and lavish establish-
ments; dandies who wore specially designed yellow leather boots for the
day's reading; the cruel but exciting sports; the self-abnegation of
servants; the sexual licence of the Prince's court; Brighton; the wicked
Lord Byron – such a list thrills every English heart quite as much as
it thrills Hollywood. On the genteeler side, Jane Austen's novels are
themselves part of the traditional picture – in the same selective way as
early Dickens is part of our picture of life two decades later. But
at the emotionally generative centre of this glamour is the great, un-
ambiguous, world-shaping victory won against the looming threat of
Napoleonic despotism – an unprecedented victory, and unparalleled
until the defeat of Hitler's Germany and Japanese aggression in this
century (which latter was, however, followed by a period of national
decline and a tide of sapping guilt, not yet stemmed, as opposed to a
period of expansion and blooming confidence). And at the centre of
that victory was the navy.

So we tend to be predisposed. We tend not to speculate, as does
Charlotte Smith, for example, in *The Old Manor House* (1794), that
these officers had to man some of their ships from press gangs; or that
the ships themselves were, from one angle, mere cruel gun platforms,
spattered in blood. We tend also perhaps to bring willy-nilly to the
reading our knowledge of Jane Austen's cherished and distinguished

naval brothers – forgetting in the process her very unillusioned portrait of the rum-flavoured coarseness of Lieutenant Price. Most love stories are about falling in love: one of the original features of *Persuasion* is that it is about staying in love against hope. Anne's view of the navy may thus at times seem partially at odds with the probable whole truth, as it is at odds with that of another good woman's view of the eruption of the victorious navy into civil society – which rather resembles Sir Walter's:

> Well, last night was the completest of failures [at Buckingham Palace]. Elbowed by the navy, numberless queer figures ... in the midst of a dull rout. . . . Talleyrand crawled past me ... like a lizard along a wall . . . [9]

So the question arises: what is Anne's view a view of?

Of course, it is of a real body of men, credible officers; and it receives the warming dramatic endorsements of which every reader is aware – the Crofts' exemplary marriage and lovable manners, Harville's grave decency, the warmth and freedom of their chat. And despite what has just been hinted, it is almost universally observable that professional military men tend to be the most humane and affable of persons in civil life. The more disciplined and effective their killing, it seems, the more admirable and principled their private existence. Perhaps Jane Austen is indirectly getting near to this *nexus* – though my speculation is fanciful in relation to a fictional character – in Captain Wentworth's half-humorous objections in the naval discussion at Uppercross to having women on board ship – his "feeling how impossible it is, with all one's efforts, and all one's sacrifices, to make the accommodations on board, such as women ought to have" (1, viii, 68–9).

But it is a passing remark of Admiral Croft's that draws closer attention to the relationship between fiction and the probable real. Reporting Wentworth's attitude to the engagement of Louisa and Benwick, he says to Anne, who is as usual on secret tenterhooks for information – ("I hope his letter does not breathe the spirit of an ill-used man"):

> "Not at all, not at all; there is not an oath or a murmur from beginning to end."
> Anne looked down to hide her smile. (2, vi, 172)

Very slight, and primarily amusing about the Admiral. But I have heard it objected – by a naval man – that these sailors do not swear enough to be real naval men. 'Who cares?' the literary person replies, 'they are refracted through the consciousness of a refined woman (or, rather, two), and, besides, the oaths designed to terrify and compel early nineteenth-century seamen on the *Asp* or the *Laconia* would hardly be likely to be produced in the drawing-room. Unlike the Admiral, our criterion of excellence in art is not the simple naturalistic one of wondering where the relevant object was built or whether we would "venture over a horsepond in it".' This is very well, and no one can be sorry that Jane Austen eschewed the rather tiresome half-hearted *verismo* of Captain Mirvan in *Evelina* or the more authentic antiquated violence of naval manners in Smollett. But the objection is also useful in pointing to the real axis of *Persuasion*: If we want to discover the purport of the navy we must not consider it as primarily a piece of realistic drawing – though it may be that – but as a term in a love story. Anne admires what she sees, as well as seeing what she admires.

All love stories, however tender, are also stories of shifting power relations. And this is one of the most nervous and wonderful in English. D.W. Harding's argument, previously alluded to, that *Persuasion* – like *Mansfield Park* in its more straightforward way – is a version of the Cinderella tale[10] helps to describe a powerful truth. Anne starts the book ignored, shelved, her talents useless; and her necessary resignation to this state is more poignant – for the reader – in that it is both enforced and facilitated by the reflection that, in a way, she has only herself to blame. *Her* relatives are not wicked, only cold and self-obsessed. Perhaps the most vulnerable feature of her position in the subsequent tense reaquaintance with Wentworth is that, having broken their engagement years ago, her delicacy dictates that she deny herself the right of simple enquiry about the subject the most important to her in the world. Indirection and overhearing in hedge-rows is her temporary doom. No proper reader ever wanted her to come out with something like "How is Captain Wentworth? Is he married or engaged? I used to know him, you know!" Instead her wise passivity is subject to constant *shocks*, as when on meeting Mrs. Croft she is reassured about the latter's ignorance of the past: –

> . . . and consequently full of strength and courage, till for a moment electrified by Mrs. Croft's suddenly saying, –
> "It was you, and not your sister, I find, that my brother had the pleasure of being acquainted with, when he was in this country."
> Anne hoped she had outlived the age of blushing; but the age of emotion she certainly had not . . . (1, vi, 49)

"Electrified" must have been a very strong word in an age not familiar with electricity.

But every reader will have entered into Anne's suspenseful existence.

What I wish to emphasise is the change in the shifting dynamic of the amount of authority given by each lover to each during its progress. This starts to alter for the reader, in a subtle way, just after their first, confusing, meeting at Uppercross. Anne has found a typical consolation in being able to convince herself that she welcomes his reported opinion that he "should not have known her again". His words "were of sobering tendency; they allayed agitation; they composed, and consequently must make her happier" – a brave, dim happiness. Then, as the narration steps away for a moment from Anne into a description of Wentworth, the case seems to be closing:

> He had not forgiven Anne Elliot. She had used him ill; deserted and disappointed him; and worse, she had shewn a feebleness of character in doing so, which his own decided, confident temper could not endure. She had given him up to oblige others. It had been the effect of over-persuasion. It had been weakness and timidity.
>
> He had been most warmly attached to her, and had never seen a woman since whom he thought her equal; but, except from some natural sensation of curiosity, he had no desire of meeting her again. Her power over him was gone for ever.
>
> It was now his object to marry . . . (1, vii, 61)

But the reader of novels must know that her power cannot have gone[11] – and quickly recognises that this is no monovocal account, but a fine passage of free indirect speech which hovers between narration and his slightly schoolmasterly thoughts. Accordingly his protestation to himself about power is swiftly undermined – a page later – by the impartially narratorial:

> From this time Captain Wentworth and Anne Elliot were repeatedly in the same circle . . . Whether former feelings were to be renewed, must be brought to the proof . . . (1, viii, 64)

Wentworth's version of his own situation is too much in what we are now discovering to be his character: impulsive, confident and decided. And the lovely complicated plays on decision and persuadableness which constitute much of his immediate subsequent relation with Louisa – including his slightly ponderous allegorical eulogy on a hazelnut (1, x, 88) – follow from this characteristic, until they find their resolution and nemesis in the half comic melodrama on the Cobb.

But before that episode there are some moments when his decided character, his character as a good officer, is displayed to us to advantage through Anne's gratified and (to use a favourite word with the later Jane Austen) fluttered reactions. The two most often discussed – I suppose because they are so touching and urgent – are characterised by his strength and his silence: his freeing of her neck from the incumbrance of the naughty and unstirring little Walter Musgrove (1, ix, 80); and the considerateness – almost painful to Anne in its proof of "pure, though unacknowledged friendship" – of his putting her into the Croft's gig – "Yes, – he had done it." (1, x, 91). These are appropriately muscular deeds: but they hardly surpass in vividness the tantalising physical quality of the social placement in the scene where he listens to Mrs. Musgrove's "fat sighings" over "poor Richard" (a scene most often made the centre of a slightly tiresome debate over whether or not Jane Austen's freedom from sentimentality can extend to a certain amount of callousness). "Fat sighings" is itself – in its surprising freeing of the adjective from routine connotation – a phrase in the same 'late' manner as "revolving winters". Its context is remarkable for a kind of delicate symbolism. Wentworth "almost instantly" seats himself on the other side of Mrs. Musgrove from Anne:

> They were actually on the same sofa for Mrs. Musgrove had most readily made room for him; – they were divided only by Mrs. Musgrove. It was no insignificant barrier indeed. Mrs. Musgrove was of a comfortable substantial size, infinitely more fitted by nature to express good cheer and good humour, than tenderness or sentiment; and while the agitations of Anne's slender form, and pensive face, may be considered as very completely screened, Captain Wentworth should be allowed some credit for the self-command with which he attended to her fat sighings over the destiny of a son, whom alive nobody had cared for.

Anne's attractive form is screened in this bustling world by the commonplace; and, lest we miss it, this is reinforced by the terms of what appears to be a piece of general realistic wisdom:

> Personal size and mental sorrow have certainly no necessary proportions. A large bulky figure has as good a right to be in deep affliction, as the most graceful set of limbs in the world . . . (1, vii, 68)

This grasping of the creative intelligence at the piquant collocation – so nearly a discord – of Anne's slender physical grace with Mrs. Musgrove's ordinary bulk, Wentworth's self-control as a good Captain ashore with the wry narratorial commentary, and each with each, is a quality that helps to make *Persuasion* peculiarly haunting – and, imperfect as it is, in some ways finer even than *Emma*.

iv

The episode on the Cobb is the hinge of the novel. So far, the tide of happy attractiveness has flowed all Wentworth's way. He and his fellow captains seem as sensitive as they are sensible – though it is notable that, with Benwick, Anne modestly "feeling in herself the right of seniority of mind", quickly adopts the rôle of mentor and gives him a serious reading list which amusingly does not include novels and might even have satisfied the objector in *Northanger Abbey* (though we later learn that she admires at least *Cecilia*). The Cobb chapter – the climax and close of the first volume – opens with a fine economical piece of writing typical of developed Jane Austen. The point about her ordinary people, as we have seen, is that they have no interests outside themselves, narrowly defined. So Henrietta's response to the beauties of Lyme – just celebrated by the narrator in famous and uncharacteristic passages of moved lyrical description – is to chatter on wonderfully about how they, the doctors, and the sea air would suit poor dear Dr. Shirley – meaning that he should have the grace to remove from Uppercross and allow Charles Hayter to be his curate. Like Anne the reader is amused by this innocent egotism: but immediately the comic surface is disturbed by a fresh entry which is to help, in the most natural coincidental manner, to shift further the balance in the relationship between her and Wentworth. A young man – a civilian – appears and:

> ...as they passed, Anne's face caught his eye, and he looked at her with a degree of earnest admiration, which she could not be insensible of. She was looking remarkably well; her very regular, very pretty features, having the bloom and freshness of youth restored by the fine wind which had been blowing on her complexion, and by the animation of eye which it had also produced. It was evident that the gentleman, (completely a gentleman in manner) admired her exceedingly. Captain Wentworth looked round at her instantly in a way which shewed his noticing of it ... (1, xii, 104)

The writing here is perhaps a bit too carefully explanatory; and the new entrant is forgotten, for the moment, in the drama of silly Louisa's fall. But from this point Anne stops being the underdog.

It says a great deal for our sense of the gravity of Anne's progress that the fall and its immediate results are not ludicrous. I refer not to the description of physical events, but to the fact that, as one critic says, "in a society supposedly dominated in practical matters by the male we have, besides three women in various states of collapse, two experienced opponents of Napoleon and a young squire dependent on the clear-headedness of a retiring young woman". The concomitant of a decided and very positive character like Wentworth's is expected to be presence of mind and alacrity in action. He and Benwick are veterans of sea battles which must have been hell on earth, with one's companions blown to pieces or bayonetted or burnt alive on every side, and the constant menace of the sea itself. Yet:

> "Is there no one to help me?" were the first words which burst from Captain Wentworth, in a tone of despair, and as if all his own strength were gone.
> "Go to him, go to him," cried Anne . . .

And:

> . . . every thing was done that Anne had prompted . . . while Captain Wentworth, staggering against the wall for his support, exclaimed in bitterest agony,
> "Oh God! her father and mother!"
> "A surgeon!" said Anne.
> He caught the word; it seemed to rouse him at once . . . (1, xii, 110)

The progression has been made and confirmed from "she was only Anne" to "no one so proper, so capable as Anne" for practical action. No wonder that the relation between her and Wentworth is now one, at least, of parity.

I am not suggesting that we are invited to mock these naval figures. What a closer look seems to confirm is that their function is not so much to represent the real navy in 1814 – though for the flower of the service they may do this – as to provide an embodiment of a *sensibility different from* that of the gentry who form the subject of Jane Austen's previous work. The navy is a good, apt, candidate for this, but not the inevitable one. (So much may be obvious to every reader: but reflection on it should certainly prevent the easy retrospective organisation of these officers into a representative group, and their identification with some newly emergent 'objective' historical tendency, or interest in the state.) What Anne primarily admires is the honesty of honest men – or, in her own resounding and touching formulation, "the frank, the open-hearted, the eager character". And one should not forget that this is very much *her* valuation. As I have said, she is credibly and creditably in love. Wentworth is of so delicate a sensibility that he will not visit Louisa for weeks after the accident for fear of upsetting her (an at first obscure move in the plot, since of course Benwick is very much present): – but this has nothing to do with his being an officer. What now emerges, to the reader's delight, is the recognition that Anne's admiration for the naval character does it honour – more, though differently, than Sir Walter might imagine – rather than *vice versa*. Wentworth is very attractive and deservedly successful – he has made well over half a million pounds in today's money from prizes in the wars and is likely to make more – there is no false consciousness about the desirability of funds.[12] But Anne is the superior character (as she is the last person in the book outside her immediate family to recognise). She is as superior, in her way, as Mr. Knightley is to Emma, and almost as often right. (The only area in which their judgements on occasion waver is, pleasantly, where their affections are deeply engaged.) And in her modest form we recognise, if anywhere in this novel, the 'mentor' figure of whom literary scholars like to write.[13] Nevertheless, the novel now adds a subtler test of her conviction: and this is carried out in Jane Austen's counter to the navy, her experiment with Mr. Elliot.

v

Mr. Elliot is often thought of as an artistic failure, and further evidence of the unpolished nature of *Persuasion*. It is objected that he convinces neither the reader nor the heroine. But the creative argument could not do without him.

By the time Anne leaves Lyme the reader can balance against her continued subjection to her anxious love for Wentworth the new and exciting pulse of her having two other possible admirers, Benwick and Mr. Elliot. Even in the lovely melancholy prose of her solitary farewell to Uppercross at the beginning of the second volume – where nature co-operates with feeling in a moment of stillness rare in Jane Austen's quick narratives – even there the sad November atmosphere is lightened somewhat by counterbalancing words such as "softened", "relenting", and "breathings". But it is Mr. Elliot who is to be crucial. There is no need to rehearse here the stages of their acquaintance – enacted in the telling context of Sir Walter's sadly pretentious establishment at Camden-place. The point about Mr. Elliot is that he poses a powerful, as it were reactionary, alternative to the naval alternative, a re-embodiment of what we have previously learnt from Jane Austen to admire in a man. To refer to Mr. Knightley once more:

> Every thing united in him; good understanding, correct opinions, knowledge of the world, and a warm heart. He had strong feelings of family-attachment and family-honour, without pride or weakness; he

lived with the liberality of a man of fortune, without display; he judged for himself in everything essential, without defying public opinion in any point of wordly decorum. He was steady, observant, moderate, candid; never run away with by spirits or by selfishness, which fancied itself strong feeling; and yet, with a sensibility to what was amiable and lovely, and a value for all the felicities of domestic life, which characters of fancied enthusiasm and violent agitation seldom really possess.

Or is this Mr. Darcy as polished by the love of Elizabeth Bennet? Admittedly it is the opinion of the conventional Lady Russell (2, iv, 146–7), but before the denouement Anne can counter it effectively only because her feelings are pre-engaged – a fact against which we might care to balance *our* impressions of Mr. Elliot. It is true that there are one or two false notes – struck in Jane Austen's mature mode. The hostility to Mrs. Clay, although welcome, is a little too obviously self-interested. Mr. Elliot's way of finding new capital by the old expedient of marrying beneath him is a deal less glamourous, anyway, than that of capturing French ships. Anne's suspicion of Sunday travelling is nothing like so unusual or prim as the vision from our particular cultural *enclave* makes it seem – even Boswell was reluctant to do it, and perhaps we may notice, peering out sometimes, that many in the world remain jealous of their sabbaths.[14] But these are flaws that it would have been very easy to explain and cleanse in a different upshot. The Mr. Elliot we experience dramatically tallies with Lady Russell's account. Even his perhaps excessive regard for rank is theorised with genuine plausibility:

Anne smiled and said,
"My idea of good company, Mr. Elliot, is the company of clever, well-informed people, who have a great deal of conversation; that is what I call good company."
"You are mistaken," said he gently, "that is not good company, that is the best. Good company requires only birth, education and manners, and with regard to education is not very nice. Birth and good manners are essential; but a little learning is by no means a dangerous thing in good company, on the contrary, it will do very well. My cousin, Anne, shakes her head. She is not satisfied. She is fastidious. My dear cousin, (sitting down by her) you have a better right to be fastidious than almost any woman I know; but will it answer? Will it make you happy? Will it not be wiser to accept the company of these good ladies in Laura Place...? (2, iv, 150)

This is from the man who also approves of and sympathises with Anne's visits to her old school friend in the face of Sir Walter's frigid ridicule, and who – late on and always too late for him – manifests at the concert a fine Austenian charm – (if Anne had been Isabel Archer she would have married him):

> "I am a very poor Italian scholar."
> "Yes, yes, I see you are. I see you know nothing of the matter. You have only knowledge enough of the language to translate at sight these inverted, transposed curtailed Italian lines, into clear, comprehensible, elegant English. You need not say anything more of your ignorance..." (2, viii, 186)

It would be aggressively anachronistic to deny that this is attractive. Especially when it is coupled for Anne with the prospect of being able to undo the harm done by her father to a name of which she, too, is proud, by becoming a proper successor to her mother at Kellynch.

Of course, this Elliot counter-thrust is not fully worked out. It is not allowed to be in such a relatively short novel. It is perhaps a tribute to the urgency with which the new values dramatised in the book interested Jane Austen, to her eagerness to occupy new ground – or perhaps it was a combination of that with failing health – that this powerful re-creation of the idea of the perfect traditional gentleman – "completely the gentleman" from his entrance – this potential reinvigoration of the stance so easily and wittily dismissed in its decadent husk-like incarnation in Sir Walter Elliot, is so abruptly dropped. He is a Sir Walter given sense, and reconsidered without external comic flourish; a kind of false Grandison (as Jocelyn Harris remarks[15]) – and not yet unmasked. Interestingly, he is never seen in dramatic, scenic competition with the open-heartedness of the new men. It is possible that Jane Austen felt herself momentarily in danger from the familiar spell. At any rate, Anne's early unease: "He certainly knew what was right. ... yet she would have been afraid to answer for his conduct. She distrusted the past, if not the present. ... Mr. Elliot was rational, discreet, polished – but he was not open. ... Mr. Elliot was too generally agreeable" (2, v, 160–1) is *not* sufficient to neutralise him and make him merely a plot device for sustaining the tension and making Captain Wentworth jealous. Very late on – in the wonderful rush of events that overtake Anne around the concert, and after that fruitful jealousy has been provoked and he himself has virtually proposed – it is still necessary for her to inoculate her feelings with emphatic doses of her true love. Mr. Elliot cannot be a cipher:

It was altogether very extraordinary. – Flattering but painful. There was much to regret. How she might have felt, had there been no Captain Wentworth in the case, was not worth enquiry; for there was Captain Wentworth: and be the conclusion of the present suspense good or bad, her affection would be his for ever. Their union, she believed, could not divide her more from other men, than their final separation.

Prettier musings of high-wrought love and eternal constancy . . . (2, ix, 192)

I have already remarked on the teasing tone of what follows.

So Mr. Elliot goes on to share the fate of many distinguished characters in literature (and politics). He threatens the structure he is supposed to serve; therefore, like Satan in *Paradise Lost*, Gilbert Osmond in *The Portrait of a Lady*, or, nearer home, Henry Crawford, he must be authorially destroyed. He gets the double treatment – perhaps in its way another tribute to his polished power – of a past that labels him "black at heart, hollow and black" (2, ix, 199) (as opposed to merely cold and selfish like, for example, John Dashwood), and of a present that leads to his confusingly motivated departure with Mrs. Clay (which would hardly prevent Sir Walter's marrying again). He suffers, in short, a *genre* change.

His underminer, Mrs. Smith – as undeservedly indigent as her namesake, the good novelist Charlotte – has an additional serious subsidiary function in the main fable, as one would expect in a novel by Jane Austen. She obviously furnishes an object for the exercise of Anne's kind and loyal heart, but also she corrects her idealism in a way that can only make so very good a heroine even more likeable. Anne's pious version of the experience of professional nurses: –

"What instances must pass before them of ardent, disinterested, self-denying attachment, of heroism, fortitude, patience, resignation – of all the conflicts and all the sacrifices that ennoble us most. A sick chamber may often furnish the worth of volumes." (2, v, 156)

– is countered, clearly from the experience of a less airy world, a world more like Portsmouth in *Mansfield Park*, with:

". . . I fear its lessons are not often in the elevated style you describe. Here and there, human nature may be great in times of trial, but generally speaking it is its weakness and not its strength that appears in a sick chamber; it is selfishness and impatience rather than generosity and fortitude, that one hears of. There is so little real friendship in the world!" (*ibid.*)

This interplay is reassuring to our sense of the credible; and in a longer work much might have been done with a world of Smiths, William Elliots, and Clays (perhaps *Sanditon* could have come to encompass similar figures). But here the need to return to the great main theme dictates an expedient shift back in artistic time to a much earlier, naïve, and unashamedly fictionalising manner: even a pre-*Northanger Abbey* manner, reminiscent possibly of the confident clear satirical handling of Sir Walter, but much more egregious since it is a rather Burneyesque melodrama.

I have the impression that it is only Critics who *mind* about these novelistic abruptions in *Persuasion*. They are the kind of thing any reader – sophisticated or otherwise – takes in her stride. This itself is another tribute to the moving power of the main narrative, to the final parts of which I now return.

vi

The trajectory of Anne's progress to ascendancy over the feelings of her lover would be simple were it not for her habitual self-doubt. And a lot of this, both the progress and the doubt, finds its expression in the later manner I have tried to describe. In conclusion I shall point to a few more instances of this manner, and to its continued co-existence with other, earlier registers.

Anne is sufficiently aflutter when Wentworth first appears at Uppercross:

> ... it would soon be over. And it was soon over. In two minutes after Charles's preparation, the others appeared; they were in the drawing-room. Her eye half met Captain Wentworth's; a bow, a curtsey passed; she heard his voice – he talked to Mary, said all that was right; said something to the Miss Musgroves, enough to mark an easy footing: the room seemed full – full of persons and voices – but a few minutes ended it. Charles showed himself at the window, all was ready, their visitor had bowed and was gone ...
>
> "It is over! it is over!" she repeated to herself again, and again in nervous gratitude. "The worst is over!" (1, vii, 59–60)

The prose is as breathless as the occasion. But it is calm compared with that of the complex scene at Molland's when the possibility of harmony with Wentworth is swiftly becoming alive again for Anne. Here she trembles on an edge of tension for which there is available no set,

202

confident, eighteenth-century vocabulary of thought and feeling, no detachment. Captain Wentworth is glimpsed outside:

> For a few minutes she saw nothing before her. It was all confusion. She was lost; and when she scolded back her senses she found the others still waiting for the carriage, and Mr. Elliot (always obliging) just setting off... (2, vii, 175)

When she recovers a little, conscious control is still not absolutely re-established:

> She now felt a great inclination to go to the outer door; she wanted to see if it rained. Why was she to suspect herself of another motive? Captain Wentworth must be out of sight. She left her seat, she would go, one half of her should not be always so much wiser than the other half, or always suspecting the other of being worse than it was. She would see if it rained. She was sent back, however, in a moment by the entrance of Captain Wentworth himself... (*ibid.*)

It is fruitfully unclear as to whom the rationalising about the rain is addressed — herself or her companions. Nevertheless, this *is* her moment:

> She had the advantage of him in the preparation of the last few moments. All the overpowering, blinding, bewildering, first effects of strong surprise were over with her. Still, however, she had enough to feel! It was agitation, pain, pleasure, a something between delight and misery. (*ibid.*)

Such reactions from a dignified person who so notably kept her head at Lyme are bound to move us. In previous work only the half-voluntary meeting of Mr. Knightley's hand with Emma's has a comparable spontaneous feel to it (*Emma*, 3, ix, see above, p. 169). Yet, as there, barriers are broken and happiness is in sight:

> Captain Wentworth was not comfortable, not easy, not able to feign that he was. (176)

Immediately coals of fire are heaped on his head by his companions' directly reported chatter about how pretty, very pretty, Anne is, and how intimate with the family her good-looking cousin.

Now Anne, still tremulous but rising in confidence, is able to do "what she believed right to be done" at the start of the next chapter and greets Wentworth as he enters the octagon for the concert under the chill eyes of Sir Walter and Elizabeth — "How do you do?" (2, viii, 181). It is one of those moments when future happiness is determined by doing the right, courageous, little thing – like Emma's equally principled determination to brave Mr. Knightley's confession of love for Harriet in the sunlit evening shrubbery at Hartfield. But here it is Wentworth's speech that is embarrassed and self-betraying. We are told of "sentences begun which he could not finish – his half-averted eyes, and more than half expressive glance" (185); but before this we have registered, precisely from the manly decideness of his opinions on Benwick and Louisa, that he is preoccupied with one subject only. It is a beautiful demonstration of that state in which whatever we talk about circles back again and again into what we do not want to mention: – The Musgroves are "'only anxious with true parental hearts to promote their daughter's comfort. . . . more than perhaps –' He stopped." Well, there is a disparity of mind between the two, and mind is essential. "Fanny Harville was a very superior creature"; and "A man does not recover from such a devotion of the heart to such a woman – He ought not – he does not." (182–3). Everything is ready for the happy ending.

From the basis of these dramatic passages of semi-conscious behaviour, Jane Austen derives in the last three chapters, two of them the re-written ones, the most luminous state of complex harmony in the whole of her work. For instead of ingeniously but simply overcoming the remaining problems of time, place and communication – as she had briskly done in the comical, linear earlier style of the earlier draft – she evolves a striking kind of indirect climax which is peculiarly moving partly because it is structured, with a kind of confident arbitrariness, to contain so many different strands of thought and feeling.

I think admirers of Jane Austen find the end of *Persuasion* so uniquely beautiful because of this combination of registers. There is, as its constant medium, a sustained tension of the breathless and exciting kind described. Anne, always in public, has to resort with fearful daring – in the first gathering at the White Hart and before Captain Wentworth is invited to the Elliots by Elizabeth – to a kind of coded utterance (semaphore) to indicate that she would rather be with him than anywhere in the world. He stalks around and catches a word with her (2, xi). She – at the second gathering, and again amidst a social buzz nearly all of which, of course, is painfully pertinent to their situation – is constantly aware of him writing, perhaps watching, perhaps hearing, while she talks to Captain Harville. But simultaneously, beside this – at the centre of it, with an effect of mutual heightening and deepening – is the elegant, rational, collected, emotional, collected, impassioned discussion of the relative natures of women and men and their destinies in society. This celebrated conversation is one of the most convincing intellectual interchanges in any novel. It arises directly out of the circumstances and characters of the speakers – it is not at all like an authorial disquisition or a homily from a main character *à la* Grandison. Rather, it recalls the discussion about the relative capacities of men and women in love from *Twelfth Night* where (2, iv) Orsino and Viola make comparable direct, feeling, statements in an atmosphere also consisting of delicious tangents. And near *its* centre is a humorous but entirely un-flippant exchange which it is difficult not to read as very near to the author's heart, and as recalling, in a less playful vein, chapter five of *Northanger Abbey*: – "Songs and proverbs, all talk of women's fickleness. But perhaps you will say, these were all written by man", says the unliterary Harville. "Perhaps I shall" replies the very well-read Anne:

> "Yes, yes, if you please, no reference to examples in books. Men have had every advantage of us in telling their own story. Education has been theirs in so much higher a degree; the pen has been in their hands. I will not allow books to prove any thing.
> "But how shall we prove any thing?"
> "We never shall. We never can expect to prove any thing upon such a point . . ." (2, xi, 234)

The point for the reader is, of course, that this is experienced as one of the dramatic heights of female fiction – intent on proving quite a lot – and wonderfully dependant on its heroine's (not yet its hero's) being able to speak out and continue to be the initiator of events. So the almost final determining move in the fraught psychological action is at once a superior play of mind and a kind of commentary on the context – the novel – in which it appears.

Registers change again: Anne's assertion of the unenviable lot of loving longest, while men can be active and decided in the larger world, precipitates the most directly emotional proposal in Jane Austen. (For intensity only Darcy's blundering first avowal compares with it.) With that effect of the strong, assured disposal of means which I have argued to be characteristic of 'late' art, there is a reversion, absolutely natural to the action, which it was not in *Mansfield Park*, to the old letter form – recalling the infancy of the novel but here more literally and vividly "written to the moment" than ever before. Wentworth's letter is potent exactly in that it is a running commentary, artless, uncomposed.

This is direct realism. But, of course, it is far from really naïve. It is part of an extended moral realism which is expressed in a virtuosic variety of ways. Registers change again: in an unemphasised contrast to the perfect clarity at the end of *Emma* – where total truthful accord between the lovers is posited by Mr. Knightley, and the narrator decorously withdraws with the assurance of "the perfect happiness of the union" – *Persuasion* proceeds to its close with a series of tranquil qualifications which make for less overt certainty but even greater conviction. Their spirits "dancing in private rapture", the rediscovered lovers discuss the past, and Anne amusedly finds that Wentworth's recall is pleasantly imperfect: – "to my eye you could never alter" he claims. Nor are the irrecoverable years forgotten or entirely redeemed by present happiness. Recalling 1808 Wentworth asks:

> ". . . if I had then written to you, would you have answered my letter? would you, in short, have renewed the engagement then?"
> "Would I!" was all her answer; but the accent was decisive enough. (2, xi, 47)

The accent almost resembles late Henry James, and in a beautiful touch (and his piece of serious wit) Wentworth recognises that "Like other men under reverses . . . I must learn to brook being happier than I deserve". But then, with another abrupt shift of mood and mode, a bright narrator appears, or reappears, to round things off:

> Who can be in doubt of what followed? When any two young people take it into their heads to marry, they are pretty sure by perseverance to carry their point, be they ever so poor, or ever so imprudent, or ever so little likely to be necessary to each other's comfort. This may be bad morality to conclude with, but I believe it to be truth . . . (2, xii, 248)

This is the triumphant note of *Northanger Abbey*, or of the too swift closing of *Mansfield Park*. It advertises its own finality, and, in an obvious way, its own fictionality. The difference is that in this very complex, fine effect, it is not final. After everything else has been rounded up in cheerful style – completing the circle to an earlier art – the main subject demands a more reflective voice.

Jane Austen, unlike a great many novelists, confidently wrote right up to her present. We may know that the era after 1815 was, after Napoleon's last doomed eruption that summer, one of peace and great prosperity for England – with just enough action to keep its navy happy and expanding for Empire. But neither heroine nor author of this book can have seen things so certainly. Therefore, the last happy ending has a richer and deeper emotional appeal than any that had preceded it. And, of course, this is not separable from the freshness and the danger of what has been embraced or the manner which has evolved to express it:

His profession was all that could ever make her friends wish that tenderness less; the dread of a future war all that could dim her sunshine. She gloried in being a sailor's wife, but she must pay the tax of quick alarm for belonging to that profession which is, if possible, more distinguished in its domestic virtues than in its national importance.

THE END

Payment of "the tax of quick alarm" ensures that for the reader any imagined future cannot now be felt as shelved or static – withdrawn into a fictional ideal; which is perhaps why it resonates again and again and again in the mind.

Chapter Nine

Small Talk on *Sanditon*

This chapter, written as an epilogue on Jane Austen's final beginning, develops the method of chapter five into a conversation that aims to be, appropriately, a little more informal. But, while Henry still represents a scholarly and professional voice, Alec – the layman and former sceptic – has become an enthusiast for Jane Austen. He reads everything about her.[1] He even claims to dream of her. They meet one morning in Henry's book room...

Alec Verifiability? The dream felt true. Its tone convinced. The power of intuition, you know.

Henry Its tone? You claim that you knew it was really Jane Austen because of the tone?

Alec Yes. The emotional tone. After all, it's through *that*, that we decide on the truth or falsity of things. Two and two may be defined as four within a system, but they also feel *not five*. And with meanings related to the world or our inner experience – symbolic meanings of all kinds – we ultimately choose what fits, what harmonises. Reason takes us a vast way, you'll say... but it can't finally determine what we choose as correct, as feeling right. At least this is so for all practical emotional convictions. . . . Anyway, Jane Austen was real enough to me in the small hours of the night. Moreover, what she had to say about *Sanditon* was characteristically sober, decisive and sensible. Actually, she referred to it at first as *The Brothers*, being more than a little piqued at the way in which the world – from Henry Austen onwards – pins down her posthumous publications with only one of her working titles, and then proceeds to interpret it in that questionable light – *Northanger Abbey*, *Persuasion*, and now this. She...

Henry   Ah, *Sanditon*! How fascinating! How everyone admires the sheer gallantry of those two months in 1817 – when the dying genius produced and provisionally corrected in so short a span a work of such vigour and *élan*! And how touching the detail that she – dissembling, no doubt, the wasting disease which was to kill her four months later – dated her work so precisely from January the seventeenth to March the eighteenth. Quite amazing! I am unabashedly one of those academics who confidently see in this work a NEW DEPARTURE! How typically brilliant it is that, aware as she must have been of failing health and of the impotence of the medical profession in her case, she should produce a vigorous and amused satire on the very subject of health and hypochondria. Typically brilliant, too, that this – following her positive embrace of the vital social movements of the time exemplified through the naval careers in *Persuasion* – should be a critique of a section of that ebullient entrepreneurial capitalism that flourished in the new security following the victorious conclusion of the wars with France. Flourished, in particular, in exploitation of the expanding leisure of the monied classes – the process thus ironically reaping the fruits of the labours and dangers of a Captain Wentworth and a Captain Harville and even a Captain Benwick, so to speak. How brisk everything is! How strong the *genius loci* of Sanditon! How finely invented, for example, is Mr. Parker's choice of name for his spanking new house in the new development. Sanditon, I remember, is "his Mine, his Lottery, his Speculation and his Hobby Horse; his Occupation his Hope and his Futurity". I always think, by the way, that in this light-hearted context we should, nevertheless, ponder the deft intrusion of a grave Christian implication in the words "Hope" and "Futurity". The new building, with its splendid ambivalent view of the Ocean and experience of "the Grandeur of the Storm", is called "Trafalgar House" – a name only to be regretted because "Waterloo is more the thing now". What splendid ironies! Yet Mr. Parker is no rapacious villain ...

Alec   Are there *any* villains in Jane Austen? Henry –

Henry   ... Mr. Parker is a kindly family gentleman, and insistently amiable – even though he seems to have capitalised his inheritance and ventured into the unknown of property development. It is only with Lady Denham, more traditionally conceived, a bit like Mrs. Jennings, as "born to Wealth but not to Education", that we begin to see – through Charlotte in chapter eight – a far less amusing and possibly sinister side to the enterprise. Her meanness – "when Rich people are Sordid" – is likely to have become infectious, pervasive.

Alec   Henry – A moment, please. How sadly you remind me of the
ease with which academic criticism becomes a fluent and self-sustaining
'discourse', taking mere seeds for flowers on which to descant. To
praise *Sanditon* so glibly and so highly – to assume that all the
intentions that may be divined are realised in what little we have – is
surely to detract from the wonder of the completed novels. To give *it*
such importance is dangerously close to evidence that the reader, or
critic, has not possessed the true nature of the previous, polished,
achieved, work. Virginia Woolf's speculation – which I remember from
The Common Reader – that had she "lived a few more years
only . . . stayed in London, dined out, lunched out, met famous people"
and so forth, Jane Austen would have

> . . . devised a method, clear and composed as ever, but deeper and
> more suggestive, for conveying not only what people say, but what
> they leave unsaid, not only what they are, but what life is . . .

– would have become, in effect, more like Virginia Woolf's idea of
herself, an "ur-Woolf" in Janet Todd's happy phrase – this speculation
always strikes me as pleasantly presumptuous and – especially the
lunches with famous people! – a bit twentieth-century-ludicrous.
Nevertheless, surely the further remark that the "stiffness and bareness"
of the first chapters of *The Watsons* show her great predecessor as:

> . . . one of those writers who lay their facts out rather baldly in the
> first version and then go back and back and back and cover them
> with flesh and atmosphere . . .

– contains a lot of intuitive sense? Jane Austen's main point last night
was even more severe. She was a rather indignant shade – though not
exactly King Hamlet. She wondered how the very fluid and as yet
unarticulated structure of her sketch could ever lead to confidence as to
its fulfilment – let alone to bland completion by another hand – even
that of the beloved Anna Lefroy, who gave up an attempt in the 1840s.
In fact, the 1975 version by 'Another Lady' – what cheek in itself! –
which I've read, tamely makes Sidney Parker the quipping hero; Sir
Edward the crudely ludicrous and weak villain; more or less
reintroduces a version of the Steele sisters from *Sense and Sensibility* in
the shapes of the Beauforts; and leaves the health resort material just
about where it was, except for a good deal of loving period detail. I
don't think Jane Austen had read it . . .

As it was she granted that her *donnée* – yes, she used that word – was
different, and that she had left Charlotte a much more than usually
objective, uncharacterised pair of eyes onto the action – merely the

sensible child of markedly conservative parents setting out to interpret the world, and much less vitally a central sensibility than those in her previous work. Of course she mentioned the recent *Persuasion* particularly in this respect; but she also *alluded* to her lifelong practice of meticulous rethinking and careful revision. – She granted further that the world Charlotte sees exhibits an even more radical deracination of the rural gentry than that achieved by, or in, Sir Walter Elliot. But she said – and I confess it's curious how these remarks fit in with my feelings when I read the current interpretations of the book by Brian Southam and Tony Tanner – that she disliked being viewed either through the glasses of the big kind of nineteenth-century novel that came after her, or through twentieth-century nostalgia for a rooted past. It is no accident, she said, that the older Heywoods, far from being a solid and easy incarnation of traditional rural virtue – gentry Adam Bedes or Gabriel Oaks *avant la lettre*, as it were – are staid old sticks with far too many children for their means, through whose lack of curiosity about the world she'd hoped to offer a comic contrast to the bustle of Mr. Parker, rather than a solemn corrective to it. –

... So when I awoke I looked up the passage where the Heywoods are characterised in chapter two, and I think this is what she may have had in mind ... [he reaches for the volume, and reads]:

> Mr. and Mrs. H. never left home ... their movements had long been limited to one small circle; and they were older in Habits than in age. – Excepting two Journeys to London in the year, to receive his Dividends, Mr. H went no farther than his feet or his well-tried old Horse could carry him, and Mrs. Heywood's Adventurings were only now and then to visit her Neighbours ... (MW 373)

Why is that horse old? Give me the freshness of new Sanditon any day! Yet Tanner, as I remember, determinedly assumes that the dividends must be for "work done and things produced". I challenge any admirer of Henry Tilney, or Mr. Knightley – let alone Wentworth – to say that this worthy pair are meant to represent any kind of distinction. Sidney Parker might have provided a proper contrast to his brother – yes, *The Brothers* – but 'might' must, annoyingly, be the key word in any discussion. The authoress, in spite of all I did to evolve the dream, wouldn't be drawn.

Henry I grant that critical readings can be overdone. And that Charlotte herself is very little present except as coolly amiable and rational, and a little prim, like Fanny Price without the sensitive inwardness. Yet surely there is criticism of the bustling commercial ethos of Sanditon itself? – Criticism of Mr. Parker's Jingle-like advertising speeches? – Criticism of all kinds of details like the importation of grotesque luxury goods such as "Blue Shoes and nankin Boots" into the rural community? – Implied criticism of the new Buildings, Mall, and Crescent? – even admitting that Jane Austen usually admired new buildings and open situations, and that we think houses of that period as especially fine. And criticism, too, of the Parker sisters busybodying hypochondria, which veritably creates a bogus commodity out of which their family may profit? Surely all this heralds "an entirely new phase in Jane Austen's development" as Mr. Southam would say? Even though, since it precedes nothing, this is hard to establish?

Alec There's something in all that, perhaps. There *might* be. But *how* new is this matter? And since when do we think of Jane Austen as writing the kind of 'condition of England' novel so familiar to us from those massive works that succeed her – the works of Dickens, George Eliot, Mrs. Gaskell, Trollope and so on and on – up until now really? Aren't you in danger of imposing an anachronistic convention on our authoress? At any rate I seem to remember her in my dream as amused and a little flattered at all the pleasant and loquacious wish-fulfilments of her twentieth-century admirers, but objecting somewhat in *these* terms: If she had wished really to take on a new locale as her new subject she would have thought a seaside health resort a timid choice. Hadn't she already, she would enquire of these admirers, rendered the vanities of Bath? – twice: and with the un-looked-for result of making that town attractive to posterity. Hadn't she shown the beauties of Lyme? Or, for that matter, the squalor and the vitality of Portsmouth? On the point of the heroine being cast into a *milieu* away from home, did not the structures of *Sense and Sensibility, Northanger Abbey* and, very immediately, *Persuasion,* display some interest in this? Indeed, was an idea recalling *Evelina* new? If entrepreneurial spirals had been an important interest, was she completely ignorant of London – might she not have chosen to set her action there, at the centre of things? In any case she could direct my modern attention to a book published in 1990, Phyllis Hembry's *The English Spa 1560–1815,* which shows that the "new 'leisure industry' was well under way in the eighteenth century, as small landowners and gentry competed in the spa game". Did we think of her as tardy in her observation? More definitely, isn't the comic opportunity provided by quackery and hypochondria taken very often, and very legitimately and variously, in art? Didn't we like, or count, Mr. Woodhouse and Isabella? But, though she doesn't mention him in

her work, did we assume that she was unaware of the medical
burlesque in Smollett's novels? – of Ferdinand, Count Fathom's
disguises, or of *Humphry Clinker*? More definitely still, did not the
promise-all structure of Volpone's posture as a quack:

O health! health! the blessing of the rich! the riches of the poor! who
can buy thee at too dear a rate, since there is no enjoying this world
without thee? ... 'tis this blessed *unguento*, this rare extraction, that
hath only power to disperse all malignant humours that proceed
either of hot, cold, moist, or windy causes.... To fortify the most
indigest and crude stomach ... applying only a warm napkin to the
place ... for the vertigine of the head, putting but a drop into your
nostrils ...

– did not this, which she quoted from the second act of Jonson's play,
seem of a family with her notation of Mr. Parker's similarly quasi-
scientific eulogy of Sanditon in chapter two? – Hers is actually the much
funnier passage, I think, because of its human warmth. Listen. He
values the place as dearly as modern therapists do their art – everybody,
however well, needs curing by its means:

He held it indeed as certain, that no person could be really well, no
person, (however upheld for the present by fortuitous aids of exercise
and spirits in a semblance of Health) could be really in a state of
secure and permanent Health without spending at least six weeks by
the Sea every year. The Sea air and Sea Bathing together were nearly
infallible, one or the other of them being a match for every Disorder,
of the Stomach, the Lungs or the Blood; They were anti-spasmodic,
anti-pulmonary, anti-sceptic, anti-bilious and anti-rheumatic. Nobody
could catch cold by the Sea, Nobody wanted Appetite by the Sea,
Nobody wanted Spirits, Nobody wanted Strength. – They were
healing, softing, relaxing – fortifying and bracing – seemingly just as
was wanted – sometimes one, sometimes the other ... (373)

And the spelling of "anti-sceptic" might be a joke inside the text. In
any case ...

Henry Yes – I think it most likely merely evidence of lack of revision,
for the Greek roots of the two words are quite distinct. But I suppose
that in your main contention you *might* be right, now that you put it so
definitely – though I don't think a dream – really, a *dream!* – gives you
any authority. No, it's *your* scepticism that persuades me. The
description of *Sanditon* as a new departure is a bit melodramatic and
tinny, when looked at. Nor can one see it – as your 'Another Lady' in

the 1975 continuation does – as "unrepentant . . . escapism" from "our servantless world". So, yes, I think *I* now have something of a literary historical nature to offer – something I've often thought, but which, on reflection, supports your argument against the novelty of the piece. Funnily enough, everybody seems to observe it, at the same time as going on about said novelty.

Alec   Something, perhaps, about the high incidence of literary pastiche and comment in the work – unequalled since the *Juvenilia*, and since *Northanger Abbey* – which, of course, she'd been looking at closely the year before?

Henry   Precisely. There's the quite striking literary critical interest by which Charlotte is allowed to doubt the sincerity of Burns's art through her idea of his life. More dramatically: it should be obvious to anyone who knows the *œuvre* that Sir Edward Denham tries to be a Henry Tilney, but ends up as a grotesque and exaggerated version of Captain Benwick – being corrected by the heroine. And his silly sub-romanticism, his dangerous sympathy with the Lovelace tradition, is often noticed. Actually his description of the ideal novel in chapter eight, put down in the text as the troublingly perverse result of an isolated and not very bright *misreading* of Richardson and "sentimental Novels", sounds to me like a description of *The Monk* – which would ally him to John Thorpe. But surely this satire is at its most amusing – and most lifelike, I fear – in the previous chapter? Unable to remember, probably because there aren't any, Scott's beautiful lines on the sea – "That Man who can read them unmoved must have the nerves of an Assassin" – Sir Edward substitutes Woman, twice:

> Oh! Woman in our Hours of Ease –

And:

> Oh! Woman in our hours of Ease (397)

I haven't seen it noticed, though it *must* have been intended to be, that the couplet continues:

> Uncertain, coy, and hard to please.

Wonderfully undercut. But it's not just Sir Edward who puts us in mind of earlier satiric modes. After rejecting one of the later volumes of *Camilla* in the Circulating Library, Charlotte herself quite famously perceives Clara in literary terms. Let me see. [He takes up Alec's copy.] Chapter six. She could:

...see in her only the most perfect representation of whatever Heroine might be most beautiful and bewitching, in all the numerous volumes they had left behind them ... she could not separate the idea of a complete Heroine from Clara Brereton ... (391)

One who can read this unreminded of *Northanger Abbey* must have the nerves of ...

Alec Quite so. But I think you may also argue – you've mentioned Benwick – that this recall of past modes and joke-types is quite consistent with Jane Austen's latest practice in *Persuasion*. Last night she ...

Henry Oh, yes. Last night.... Hah. But the recall of past modes *in itself* isn't, obviously, any kind of evidence of innovation. More like up-dating, really. I feel that there is, appropriately, quite a lot of pleased reminiscence of Jane Austen's whole career in this last little book. [He waves at the volume.] The grand dubious sententiousness of the opening sentence of chapter three: "Every Neighbourhood should have a great Lady" (375) – doesn't this remind one of "It is a truth universally acknowledged, that a single man in possession of a good fortune, must be in want of a wife ...", which we've had the pleasure of discussing in the past? But ... yes ... in chapter seven there's a rather notable resurgence of the playful narrator so beautifully evident near the end of *Persuasion*, in volume two, chapter seven of that book:

I make no apologies for my Heroine's vanity. – If there are young Ladies in the world at her time of Life, more dull of Fancy and more careless of pleasing, I know them not, and never wish to know them. (395)

Though the *idea* here is similar to that in chapter eleven of volume two of *Emma*, where the narrator recommends joy in the passage beginning "It may be possible to do without dancing entirely ...", the further *play* with the idea of a Heroine – with the idea of a fiction where, a page later, a sight of sycophancy may be "very amusing – or very melancholy, just as Satire or Morality might prevail" – is in that somewhat shorthand late-early manner, involving some resuscitation of earlier modes, and therefore directly continuous with *Persuasion*. You see?

Alec Yes. It's been my point too. But ... Anne Elliot ... the characterisation ...

Henry   Yes. Well, that *is* your point as I understand it. There just isn't enough to go on. At the periphery, as in *Persuasion*, there are sketches, at least, for a whole range of characters who seem to be there in order to rehearse their amusing responses – rehearse their harps, their concern with garden produce, their meanness and propensity to wag a will – to borrow a phrase from Samuel Butler – and their health obsessions. Although Diana Parker's furthering of charities as far afield as Burton-on-Trent and York seems to me to predict Mrs. Jellyby in *Bleak House*; and her confusion over Mrs. G. has a positively Pooterian bathos, all this is scarcely new in kind to Jane Austen. But it – surprisingly – has no air of staleness. Not at all. There are, for example, all those vigorous list of names and epithets, which give the air of a bustling workshop of fiction. And at the centre there is the wonderful sea-wind briskness of Mr. Parker, and a fine un-moralised energy in *some* of Charlotte's responses, notably her being amused at the close of chapter four by:

> ... standing at her ample Venetian window, and looking over the miscellaneous foreground of unfinished Buildings, waving Linen, and tops of Houses, to the Sea, dancing and sparkling in Sunshine and Freshness. (384)

And the pleasure and energy is elsewhere too – in the literary devices and pastiche, of course, but also in Mr. Parker's reservations about Arthur:

> It *is* bad ... [to] sit down at the age of 1 and 20, on the interest of his own little Fortune, without any idea of attempting to improve it, or of engaging in any occupation that may be of use to himself or others. (388–9)

Arthur's cocoa threatens to rival Mr. Woodhouse's gruel. However, and this is what is truly sad, there is, as I think you were about to suggest, no correspondingly deep centre to the book. No Anne Elliot. And, in spite of the commentators you have mentioned – with whom I *had* thoughtlessly gone along, as it were – little solid evidence of a substantial controlling thematic concern. To revert to what I was just saying about the earlier work: Is not Charlotte – at a venture – really more like Elinor Dashwood than anyone else in Jane Austen's novels? A ready judger, with feeling? But even then she's comparatively thin. A satisfactory centre *might* have developed – even a displaced one, not Charlotte ... but ... I agree with you ...

Alec   Yet. ... Yet there *is* something there, isn't there? A special *Sanditon* feel, so to speak? We don't sense just a rewrite or a rehash, as 'Another Lady' so evidently does. We haven't mentioned the mist.

Henry Mist?

Alec Yes. What Robert Liddell called "the famous *chiaroscuro* in the last chapter". In a book so full of bright weather there is *the* most striking ending – or breaking-off. Not unlike a dream, if you'll pardon me, in its specificity amidst vagueness, its odd magic. There's a drama about perception when Charlotte at last approaches Sanditon House which arrests every reader. First it is – perhaps significantly – difficult to see in "the close, misty morning" what kind of a vehicle the suddenly arriving Sidney Parker is driving – in the opposite direction. Then.... Listen:

> ... an outside fence was at first almost pressing on the road – till and angle *here*, and a curve *there* threw [the boundaries] to a better distance. The Fence was a proper Park paling in excellent condition; with clusters of fine Elms, or rows of old Thorns following its line almost every where. – *Almost* must be stipulated – for there were vacant spaces – and through one of these, Charlotte as soon as they entered the Enclosure, caught a glimpse over the pales of something White and Womanish in the field on the other side; – it was some-thing which immediately brought Miss B. into her head – and step-ping to the pales, she saw indeed – and very decidedly, in spite of the Mist; Miss B. – seated ... (426)

And, just on:

> Miss Brereton seated, apparently very composedly – and Sir E.D. by her side. – They were sitting so near to each other and appeared so closely engaged in gentle conversation, that Charlotte instantly felt she had nothing to do but to step back again, and say not a word. – Privacy was certainly their object. – It could not but strike her rather unfavourably with regard to Clara ... (*ibid.*)

But she is inclined to tolerance, and, Mrs. Parker having seen nothing, in her "moralising reflection", she largely thinks of:

> ... the extreme difficulty which secret lovers must have in finding a proper spot for their stolen Interviews. – Here perhaps they had thought themselves so perfectly secure from observation – the whole field open before them – a steep bank and Pales never crossed by the foot of Man at their back – and a great thickness of air, in aid – . Yet here, she had seen them. (427)

Truly remarkable, isn't it, the air of mystery within those unusually stressed spatial relations? You might want to relate it to contemporary

Gothick writing perhaps, but I'd say it's almost Henry Jamesian in its sense of implicit revelation. And, of course, the thing about the mist is that it's either just a naturalistic trimming – which I can't believe – or *purely* metaphoric: *it* accomplishes no deception, doesn't actually impede anything, but is, rather, literally atmospheric, in that it serves to suggest a whole new uncertainty in the action and in our estimate of how Charlotte perceives this. But, alas, the fragment ends a few sentences afterwards – with Jane Austen's final telling joke, about the portraits of Lady Denham's husbands.

Henry So you're suggesting that we might, after all, be witnessing a whole new departure for Jane Austen? Not to do with her analysis of society primarily, but in a fresh nineteenth-century prose symbolism?

Alec Hold on, Henry . . . symbolism? Sanditon's mist is delicately and strangely evocative, like the autumn land at Uppercross. But to find a really resolute *symbolism* the spirit has rarely so far to go. Let me give you an example from another kind of art. Do you know the Gare d'Orsay in Paris, recently converted into the grandest of modern galleries? There you see a *symbol*, composed, by a mixture of event and intent, with beauty and deliberation! A fine mid-nineteenth-century station, erupting into the city at the railhead. Around it in black-bronze tribute the statuary of Industry, Commerce and Colonial Empire. Now within it, a svelte museum of art, starting with the work of Jane Austen's day and going onward in time to moderately recent abstractions on an upper floor. And within all this, mark, underground and vital, is a hub of the best modern railway network in Europe. How complicated, how refined, and how simple an embodied symbol of Art, Industry and Technology . . . ! It has, *pari passu*, most of the connotations some people would like to read into *Sanditon* – commerce, art, bustle, and the observation of bustle. But in novel writing this sort of bold signification, where things definitely stand for things, rather resembles the contemporary mode of Benjamin Constant. . . . Do you remember those fine passages in *Adolphe*, where for ever and again in the hero's painful egocentric process of parting from his mistress Ellenore, the psychological point is accompanied and reinforced, so naturally yet so *evidently*, by the surrounding description? To take the most explicit instance: do you recall in particular that painful winter walk in chapter ten? – I happen to have a copy with me. . . . The vocabulary is limited and austere, like Racine [He produces the book and reads, self-consciously]:

C'était une de ces journées d'hiver où le soleil semble éclairer tristement la campagne grisâtre, comme s'il regardait en pitié la terre qu'il a cessé de rechauffer. . . . Le ciel était serein; mais les arbres étaient sans feuilles; aucun souffle n'agitait l'air, aucun oiseau ne le traversait: tout était immobile, et le seul bruit qui se fit entendre était celui de l'herbe glacée qui se brisait sous nos pas. "Comme tout est calme, me dit Ellenore; comme la nature se résigne! Le coeur aussi ne doit-il pas apprendre à se résigner?" Elle s'assit sur une pierre . . .

Well, we understand clearly enough that the stony chill embraces his heart, and that the grass crunched underfoot bears some relation to *hers*. . . . Do we want to say that Jane Austen would have written somewhat like this if she'd really wished for a new vein of symbolic suggestion closely related to the progress of the action, for a new – hackneyed phrase – departure? Well, that she *might* have done so – might in the strong sense – the uses of external description and the weather in all her books, but most notably at Sotherton in *Mansfield Park*, at Box Hill in *Emma*, at Uppercross and Lyme in *Persuasion*, bear witness. But the artistic ambience is so different. . . . *Adolphe* was published, after nine years in manuscript, in 1816. It was immediately translated into English, I imagine because of its author's intellectual and political prominence. But I don't suppose Jane Austen read it. She had declined to meet Mme. de Staël years before – hadn't wanted lunch with a famous person on that occasion – and could well have felt that the external morals of *Adolphe*'s subject are too easily taken sympathetically for granted. It was George Eliot's copy that was, according to Oscar Browning, "interlined and marked by her in every page, and thumbed so as almost to fall to pieces".

Henry Is there much comparison, then?

Alec Well, certainly in another aspect the novels have in common the desire and capacity to apply large analytical categories to the experience they dramatise. Could you look out that general passage about the Parkers' mental character late in *Sanditon* while I find something comparable in *Adolphe*? . . . Yes, here we are, chapter four – Constant . . . thank you Henry . . . how professional . . . [Henry has returned the copy of *Sanditon* open at chapter ten] . . . Constant generalises on the experience of his couple directly:

Dès qu'il existe un secret entre deux coeurs qui s'aiment, dès que l'un d'eux a pu se résoudre à cacher à l'autre une seule idée, le charme est rompu, le bonheur est détruit. L'emportement, l'injustice, la

219

distraction même, se réparent; mais la dissimulation jette dans l'amour un élément étranger qui le dénature et le flétrit à ses propres yeux.

Adolphe is full of this kind of compressed compelling wisdom; whereas in *Sanditon* Jane Austen ties a similar categorical lexicon more closely in with the description of her personages. In the case of the Parkers:

> It was impossible for Charlotte not to suspect a good deal of fancy in such an extraordinary state of health. – Disorders and Recoveries so very much out of the common way, seemed more like the amusement of eager Minds in want of employment than of actual afflictions and releif. The Parkers, were no doubt a family of Imagination and quick feelings – and while the eldest Brother found vent for his superfluity of sensation as a Projector, the Sisters were perhaps driven to dissipate theirs in the invention of odd complaints. . . . the rest of their sufferings was from Fancy, the love of Distinction and the love of the Wonderful. – They had Charitable hearts and many amiable feelings – but a spirit of restless activity, and the glory of doing more than anybody else, had their share in every exertion of Benevolence – and there was Vanity in all they did, as well as in all they endured. (412)

Compare . . .

Henry Alec! I'm glad you read that *out*: for while it may be true that in her confidence in and appeal to general concepts Jane Austen has much in common with the leading edge of French sensibility in that age, she – and probably Constant, too, come to think of it – have more in common with eighteenth-century writers than they have with the way in which *we* normally express ourselves. This in spite of, or as well as, her command of most of the means and methods of modern art. As I heard you speaking I first of all thought I remembered Swift in the phrase "vent for his superfluity of sensation" – it has his commercial, agricultural, possibly even physical kind of metaphorical vigour: but, above all, of course, it's Dr. Johnson we hear in "eager minds in want of employment. . . . Imagination and quick feelings . . . invention. . . . Fancy . . . love of distinction . . . restless activity. . . . Vanity in all they did, as well as in all they endured". It's really the vocabulary of *Rasselas* applied to a modernising age.

Alec Thank you. So I'm afraid we haven't, with the best will in the world, been able to evolve much substantial argument in favour of new phases, ventures, departures – or anything comparably exciting for the literary critic –

. . . Nevertheless as to the question of symbolism: my point about that wonderful mist is precisely that it is tantalising and suggestive; it is different from our example, Constant, just because it's so vague *and* so obviously important; not obscure, but mysterious. It hasn't the patent, clear, narrowing, cohesiveness of the French prose. And I don't think you'd find that in the eighteenth century, any more than you'd find the more exploratory evocations of barely conscious feeling in *Emma* and *Persuasion*. Maybe its very strangeness is the factor that impels the critics, on laying down their books, to all their speculations? But meanwhile what a blessing that Jane Austen's . . . what should one call it? . . . ease? . . . clarity? . . . her clarity ensures that *she* is never perfectly secure from observation! – Yes here, I have seen her.

Notes

INTRODUCTORY: JANE AUSTEN'S EASE – AND CRITICISM

1 Alison G. Sulloway, *Jane Austen and the Province of Womanhood*, Philadelphia, 1989, xvii, 109. This may well sound too strange to be representative. But much more interesting and better-equipped minds than Alison Sulloway's are involved in such critical afflatus. Jocelyn Harris's view in *Jane Austen's Art of Memory*, Cambridge, 1989, is that Jane Austen constantly echoes and alludes to very many previous authors in literature and philosophy, in detail from Chaucer onwards (it sounds almost as learned as Milton), and that therefore awareness of this and them gives a new edge to reading her. This is – somewhat paradoxically – rather close in its distancing effect to the thesis of James Thompson's *Between Self and World: The Novels of Jane Austen*, Pennsylvania University Park and London, 1988, which is that we positively *need* Marx's theories, as mediated through Georg Lukács and Frederick Jameson, to understand the alienation and consequent reifications of personal relations peculiar to the early capitalist structure of Jane Austen's time: understand them, that is, in a way that Jane Austen could not.

The effect of all these arguments is, as I urge elsewhere, to elevate the critic into the source of a necessary intervention between the immediacy of response naturally felt in reading Jane Austen (or a lot of good artists) and the reader's interpretation of it. Yet actually the historical adductions, in Thompson's otherwise often acute and interesting book, are quite mild and trite (as often with theorists).

On a very different front, Deirdre Le Faye in her revision and enlargement of W. and R.A. Austen-Leigh's *Jane Austen: A Family Record*, London, 1989, partakes of the same heady but chilling sense that the scholar is indispensable: "... neither her life ... *nor her works* can be understood without reference to the lives of the other Austens." (x, my italics – i.e. without reading Le Faye).

2 See: Marilyn Butler, *Jane Austen and the War of Ideas*, Oxford, 1975; new edn., with new Introduction, 1988, xxxvi, xxxviii, xl, xli. The comparison here is largely with Maria Edgeworth, on whom Professor Butler has written the definitive critical biography (Oxford, 1972).

Alistair M. Duckworth in *Jane Austen: New Perspectives. Women and Literature*, Vol. 3, N.S., ed. Janet Todd, New York and London, 1983, 48.

Michael Williams, *Jane Austen: Six Novels and Their Methods*, Basingstoke and London, 1986.

3 Butler, *Jane Austen and the War of Ideas*, xxxi.

4 For instances of this in Jane Austen's language see: K.C. Phillipps, *Jane Austen's English*, London, 1970; Norman Page, *The Language of Jane Austen*, Oxford, 1972; and Stuart Tave, *Some Words of Jane Austen*, Chicago and London, 1973. Recently Myra Stokes, in *The Language of Jane Austen*, Basingstoke and London, 1991 (a repeat title presumably dictated by the series in which her interesting, though rather critically unsophisticated and sometimes innaccurate, book appears) adds some useful observations to these, notably those in her first chapter about mealtimes in the period, and the division of the day into before and after dinner – morning and evening – with the afternoon, if mentioned, being commonly the time of our early evening (during which, in a telling example, Mr. Knightley proposes to Emma).

5 An aggravated form of this situation – aggravated only somewhat by the greater distance into the past – is described and analysed by Wilbur Sanders in his book about Shakespeare, *The Dramatist and the Received Idea*, Cambridge, 1968. Here he shows that what is compelling in the plays (especially *Macbeth*) is precisely what was *not* available to the commonplace wisdom of the age. Similarly, investigations of late eighteenth-century ideology and literary convention, fascinating in themselves, can too easily assume in Jane Austen a passivity which, on any kind of reflection, is *obviously* alien to her highly critical mind.

6 *London Review of Books*, Vol. 12, No. 13, 12 July 1990.

7 In *A New Mimesis: Shakespeare and the Representation of Reality*, London and New York, 1983, A.D. Nuttall does exactly this, rather brilliantly (though the feminists and new historicists against whom he argues seem to pay little attention). But it takes just over half of his book.

On the other hand, some quite intelligent academic reactions to Jane Austen find it rather hard to survive the theoretical (feminist, neo-marxist, sub-freudian etc.) climates in which they are occasionally found: in e.g. Mary Poovey, *The Proper Lady and the Woman Writer: Ideology and Style in the Works of Mary Wollstonecraft, Mary Shelley, and Jane Austen*, Chicago, 1984; Thompson, *Between Self and World*; Claudia Johnson, *Jane Austen: Women, Politics and the Novel*, Chicago, 1988.

8 For those not familiar, the remarks are as follows: to Anna Austen (later Lefroy), Jane Austen's niece, 9 September 1814: [you have set your story in] "... such a spot as is the delight of my life; 3 or 4 Families in a Country Village is the very thing to work on ...", *Jane Austen's Letters*, collected and ed. R.W. Chapman, Oxford, 1932, 2nd edn. 1952, 401.

To J. Edward Austen, her nephew, 16 December 1816, in comparison and contrast to his "strong, manly, spirited Sketches, full of Variety and Glow" – "... the little bit (two inches wide) of Ivory on which I work with so fine a Brush, as produces little effect after so much labour ..." (*ibid.*, 469).

9 For these see Andrew Wright and others, 'Jane Austen Abroad' in John Halperin, ed., *Jane Austen: Bicentenary Essays*, Cambridge, 1975, 298–317.

10 Some descriptions and hypotheses about the non-political nature of English society, even when fully industrialised, are offered in Ross McKibbin's *The*

Ideologies of Class: Social Relations in Britain, 1880–1950, Oxford, 1990.

11 E.g. John Cannon and other of the historians and statisticians he discusses in *The Aristocratic Century*, Cambridge, 1984.

12 *An Introduction to the English Novel*, London, 1951, Vol. 1, Part III, ch. 2.

13 In the introduction to his edition of *Persuasion*, Harmondsworth, 1965. Harding's most celebrated contribution to the study of Jane Austen, and justly so, is his 'Regulated Hatred: An Aspect of the Work of Jane Austen', *Scrutiny*, VIII, March 1940, 346–62. This was one of the decisive factors in discrediting a merely Janeite appreciation.

14 In an unpublished doctoral dissertation for London University (1990) Glenys Mary Stow convincingly shows that Jane Austen extended an inheritance, consonant mainly with Dr. Johnson's moral thought, of a vision of "companionate" marriage; marriage, that is, of people who are equal in their individuality rather than bound in the hierarchic, patriarchal and possibly exploitative union implicit in a rival tradition – and in cliché.

15 *Independent on Sunday*, Review, 20 January 1991, 29. But a contrasting part of the modern picture is painted by Zvi Jagendorf who describes himself and his wife as deriving at least some distraction during the Iraqi missile bombardment of Jerusalem from reading *Emma*. 'Jerusalem Diary', *London Review of Books*, Vol. 13, No. 5, 7 March 1991.

16 Cf. "Nothing, of course, will ever take the place of the good old fashion of 'liking' a work of art or not liking it: the most improved criticism will not abolish that primitive, that ultimate test", Henry James, 'The Art of Fiction'.

17 'Jane Austen: Novelist of a Changing Society' (1980) in *Collected Essays*, Vol. 1: *The Englishness of the English Novel*, ed. G. Singh, Cambridge, 1983, 27–8.

2 EARLY WORKS, TRADITIONS, AND CRITICS I: *LADY SUSAN* AND
THE SINGLE EFFECT

1 Since 1989 it has been displayed, on long term loan from Mr. Peter Michael, in the library of Queen Mary and Westfield College, London.

2 For a discussion of this point and all the dates see B.C. Southam, *Jane Austen's Literary Manuscripts*, Oxford, 1964, 52–62 and *passim*.

3 The main disagreement is between Q.D. Leavis, 'A Critical Theory of Jane Austen's Writings', *Scrutiny*, x, 1941–2; reprinted in *Collected Essays*, Vol. 1, who favours 1798, and Southam, *Jane Austen's Literary Manuscripts*, 42–52, 136–48, who favours 1793–4. Southam may well be right, though his argument, being based on "internal evidence" as to "style, subject matter, and treatment", is less scientific than it looks, and nothing can be proved either way. Marvin Mudrick in *Jane Austen: Irony as Defense and Discovery*, Princeton, 1952, concedes with reluctance a date before 1801.

4 This happens especially with some popularising feminist writers, e.g. the strident, inaccurate and tendentious Dale Spender in *Mothers of the Novel*, London, 1987, and many of the introducers of the shabby, unedited Pandora reprints with which that work was associated. But it can happen also in comparatively respectable books, e.g. those by Jane Spencer and LeRoy W. Smith cited in n. 5 below.

5   I have in mind particularly the following. They are very uneven in value, but I have confined my sense of this fact to putting a star beside work of real critical interest. Of course, the categories overlap, and in addition there are other works in which the most useful remarks are made in passing and in pursuit of different aims, e.g. by Barbara Hardy in *A Reading of Jane Austen*, London, 1975.

Literary relations:
*Mary Lascelles, *Jane Austen and her Art*, Oxford, 1939.
"Q.D. Leavis, 'A Critical Theory of Jane Austen's Writings', and 'Jane Austen: Novelist of a Changing Society'.
Henrietta Ten Harmsel, *Jane Austen: A Study in Fictional Conventions*, The Hague, 1964.
Frank Bradbrook, *Jane Austen and her Predecessors*, Cambridge, 1967.
Kenneth Moler, *Jane Austen's Art of Allusion*, Lincoln, Nebraska, 1968.
Jane Spencer, *The Rise of the Woman Novelist*, Oxford, 1986.

Political, Ideological, Social etc.:
*Marilyn Butler, *Jane Austen and the War of Ideas*.
Warren Roberts, *Jane Austen and the French Revolution*, New York, 1979.
Mary Evans, *Jane Austen and the State*, London and New York, 1987.
Park Honan, *Jane Austen: Her Life*, London, 1987.

Feminist concerns:
*Margaret Kirkham, *Jane Austen: Feminism and Fiction*, Brighton, 1983.
LeRoy W. Smith, *Jane Austen and the Drama of Woman*, London, 1983.
Claudia Johnson, *Jane Austen: Women, Politics and the Novel*.

6   A good example is *A Preface to Jane Austen*, Christopher Gillie, London, 1974, revised edn. 1985.

7   Quoted in *Jane Austen: The Critical Heritage*, Vol. 2, *1870–1940*, ed. B.C. Southam. London, 1987.

8   *Jane Austen*, London and New York, 1975.

9   Honan, *Jane Austen: Her Life*.

10   Although this can be bracing and educative. Q.D. Leavis's arguments in 'A Theory of Jane Austen's Writings' seem to me to offer the instructive paradox of being wrong but also much more interesting than most writing on Jane Austen.

11   See *The Novel in Letters*, ed. Natascha Würzbach, London, 1969.

12   *Letters*, 322, 344.

13   *Jane Austen's 'Sir Charles Grandison'*, ed. B.C. Southam, Oxford, 1980.

14   Compare an interesting, rather parallel, argument by Patricia Meyer Spacks that in *Lady Susan* Jane Austen gives women (especially but not only the heroine) power and the ability to control events through letter writing in contrast to the passive and merely emotive manifestations of the staple heroines of minor eighteenth-century fiction – "these women mobilize their forces, internal and external", *Persuasions: Journal of the Jane Austen Society of North America*, 16 December [Jane Austen's birthday] 1987, 88–98.

15   John Loftus, in *Comedy and Society from Congreve to Fielding*, Stanford, 1959, points out the conceivable sources of some of Richardson's effects in early eighteenth-century 'sentimental' middle-class drama – e.g. Rowe's *The Fair Penitent* and Charles Johnson's *Caelia*.

16 E.g. by Walton A. Litz in *Jane Austen: A Study in her Artistic Development*, London, 1965, 40–1.
17 Cf. "... by sheer style she plays on reality", Spacks, in *Persuasions*, 92.
18 "Jane Austen, *ob.* July 1817", July 1917, reprinted in *Critical Heritage*, Vol. 2, 258.
19 *Jane Austen: Irony as Defense and Discovery*, 138.
20 Deborah Kaplan in 'Female Friendship and Epistolary Form: *Lady Susan* and the Development of Jane Austen's Fiction', *Criticism*, Spring 1987, Vol. 29, No. 2, 163–78.
21 It is perhaps to avoid this that Mudrick makes out the shape of a tragedy, or Litz argues that it is a "literary" dead-end, broken off because the conception of the heroine is too simple, too much of a mere term in an antithesis between "Art" and "Nature" – *Jane Austen: A Study in her Artistic Development*, 41–5.
22 Though this is explained and justified in terms of contemporary intentions in John Mullan's *Sentiment and Sociability: The Language of Feeling in the Eighteenth Century*, Oxford, 1988. He argues that this is precisely what Dr. Johnson was admiring when he said of Richardson, "you must read him for the sentiment" – i.e. for the uplifting use of *exempla* in a moral commentary which justifies the whole fictional enterprise (57). I think we are now *unlikely* to be able to read in this way; and am unsure whether the purity and discipline demanded would ever actually be available to many more readers than Johnson himself.
23 Frank Bradbrook in *Jane Austen and her Predecessors*, 122–3. Taken up by Margaret Drabble in her readable introduction to *Lady Susan. The Watsons. Sanditon*, Harmondsworth, 1974, 13. See also Roberts, *Jane Austen and the French Revolution*, 128. The comparison is slightly extended in an unpublished thesis for London University by Evelyn Farr, but there also made little of (1989). There is an article by Simon Davies – 'Laclos dans la littérature anglaise du XIXe siècle', in *Laclos et le Libertinage*, Univ. de Picardie, 1983, 255–64, which treats also of *Vanity Fair* and of Swinburne's *A Year's Letters* (or *Love's Cross Currents*, also epistolary and often compared with Laclos) and *Lesbia Brandon* (which I have been unable to obtain).
   It is important as I write to emphasise that *Les Liaisons Dangereuses* is a great French novel, to be distinguished from the heavy-handed adaptation for stage and screen by Christopher Hampton. For one of the distortions involved in the latter, see Marina Warner's observation on the film – in *The Don Giovanni Book: Myths of Seduction and Betrayal*, ed. Jonathan Miller, London, 1990, 93–107 – that Mme. de Merteuil is made (in a post-freudian manner) to dominate Valmont as a *mother* – which would actually interlace quite nicely with Lady Susan's domination of Frederica.
24 Q.D. Leavis, 'A Critical Theory of Jane Austen's Writings', and others, e.g. Southam, responding to her.
25 For the love of French culture see, e.g. Honan, *Jane Austen: Her Life*. For the tragic nature of Laclos (and Mozart) see Brigid Brophy, *Mozart the Dramatist: the Value of His Operas to Him, to His Age and to Us*, London, 1964, revised edn. 1988.
26 For an account of the historical (not literary) forms out of which the content had been drained to produce this situation, see the conclusion to Maurice Keen's *Chivalry*, New Haven and London, 1984.

27 E.g. by Deborah Kaplan, 'Female Friendship and Epistolary Form', and Patricia Meyer Spacks, in *Persuasions*.
28 Reprinted in *Critical Heritage*, Vol. 2, 171–3.

3 EARLY WORKS, TRADITIONS, AND CRITICS II: *NORTHANGER ABBEY*
AND OTHER NOVELS

1 1778, Vol. 1.
2 *The Life of Samuel Johnson, LL.D*, 1791 (additions 1793), Oxford edn. ed. R.W. Chapman, 1953, 1371. The quotation is from *Cecilia*, Bk. 7, i (the hero Delvile is writing).
3 I gather that there *are* very few readers of *The Wanderer* (1814). But certainly *Camilla* deserves to be more widely frequented.
4 In 'Madame D'Arblay', *Edinburgh Review*, LXXVI, Jan. 1843. He continues – in what is really a very sympathetic account – to quote her on Johnson's praise of Sheridan's refusing to allow "his lovely wife to sing in public": "The last of men was Dr. Johnson to have abetted squandering the delicacy of integrity by nullifying the labours of talents."
5 *The Life of Samuel Johnson*, 1370, 1373. For a general discussion of this subject see Peter L. De Rose, *Jane Austen and Samuel Johnson*, Washington, 1980.
  It is of incidental interest that Boswell also mentions as a debtor Henry Mackenzie. Mackenzie is the author of the "very clever essay" in the Edinburgh periodical *The Mirror* "about young girls who have been spoilt for home by great acquaintance" which Mrs. Morland proffers as cold comfort to her daughter on her abrupt and abashed return from Northanger. No doubt Mrs. Morland is supposed to be unaware that he was also the author of the dangerously Sentimentalist *The Man of Feeling* (1771) – John Mullan has some interesting pages in his *Sentiment and Sociability*, 114–46, on the wavering and slightly sour relations of the "hard headed" "Scottish Addison" to the cult of feeling of which he was so celebrated an exponent, and which he yet came to feel to be divorced from useful reality.
6 Léonie Villard, *Jane Austen and her Work*, 1915; London, 1924, 187. But cf. Mary Lascelles: "while there are common readers and imperfect novels it should not die", *Jane Austen and her Art*, 55. And in 'Critical Realism in *Northanger Abbey*' A.D. McKillop offers a fairly extensive representative scattering of the works and kinds of work that might be alluded to in the novel (reprinted in *Jane Austen: Twentieth Century Views*, ed. Ian Watt. Englewood Cliffs, N.J., 1963).
  Incidentally, the revival by some critics and writers in the late twentieth century of a (usually psychoanalytically sophisticated and burdened) up-dated version of the Gothick fantasy type gives additional reason for attending to the obvious justice of Jane Austen's comical critique of its dangers in *Northanger Abbey*. No doubt she would be almost as surprised at the notice given by modern critics to some of the writers she indulgently despised as Pope must be by the reprinting – because he mentions them – of the authors he thought he had condemned to the eternal oblivion of dullness in *The Dunciad*.
7 E.g. in '"Regulated Hatred" Revisited' in *Jane Austen: 'Northanger Abbey' and 'Sense and Sensibility'. A Casebook*, ed. B.C. Southam, London, 1976,

122–7. Southam, in a kind of reply to D.W. Harding's famous essay, quotes material about contemporary riots which he says puts Henry in a "very curious light" and makes us, as opposed to Catherine, think him "condemned out of his own mouth". This argument is difficult to follow. Incidentally, I wonder what Southam makes of Henry's "quiet driving" – which seems an almost infallible indication of virtue in novels. It is compared with John Thorpe's here, just as Lord Orville's is opposed to the rowdy speeding of Mr. Coverly and Lord Merton in *Evelina*.

There also some hostile pages on Henry in *The Madwoman in the Attic* by Sandra M. Gilbert and Susan Gubar, New Haven and London, 1979, 138–40 – characteristically abstracted from the mood or tone of the text, but also characteristically stimulating.

In *Ghosts of the Gothic: Austen, Eliot, and Lawrence*, Princeton, New Jersey, 1980, 149 ff., the fanciful and energetic Judith Wilt finds Henry too self-indulgently satirical, and thus a threatening transposition of the 'lover-mentor' of eighteenth-century fiction. – Some modern commentators are keen to identify types like 'lover-mentor', 'reformed flirt', 'learned girl' etc. in order to assert that there is a considerable tradition of fiction – especially female fiction, though Richardson can get rather massively in the way here – out of which Jane Austen wrote (c.f. Spencer, *The Rise of the Woman Novelist*). It is implied in the more vulgar manifestations of this (e.g. Spender, *Mothers of the Novel*) that she, though in a mysterious way prestigious, had not a vast amount to add.

On General Tilney's degree of "villainy" see also Andrew Wright, *Jane Austen's Novels: a Study of Structure*, London, 1954; Frank J. Kearful, 'Satire and the Form of the Novel: the Problem of Aesthetic Unity in *Northanger Abbey*', *English Literary History*, xxxii, 1965, 511–27; also the works, already cited, of Ten Harmsel, Litz, Moler and Butler.

8   But this is a leading case where it is necessary to protect Jane Austen for the common reader from even first-rate specialists. Marilyn Butler in *Jane Austen and the War of Ideas*, effectively claims that we need to know a great deal about the intellectual and literary climate around Jane Austen before we can properly understand her: xxxi and 166–7, 215, 228, 232–3, 248, 294, 296 and *passim*). As I have said, I think this a mistake – a perhaps involuntary exaltation of 'research' which issues (interestingly) in what seems like a diminished respect and liking for the artist.

Cf. Kate Fullbrook's witty and feeling discussion of Jane Austen's position as an artist *vis-à-vis* 'politics' in her excellent 'Jane Austen and the Comic Negative' in *Women Reading Women's Writing*, ed. Sue Roe, Brighton, 1987, 39–41 and *passim*.

9   See C.S. Emden 'Northanger Abbey Re-dated', *Notes & Queries*, 195 (1950), 407–10, and Kenneth Moler's discussion of this in *Jane Austen's Art of Allusion*, 28–31.

10 Compare the phrasing of Henry Pye, that unfortunate Poet Laureate, when predicting the decline of novel reading in 1792:

> The only persons of the present day, who at all devote their attention with ardour and perseverance to the reading of compositions of fictitious distress, (and I believe their number, especially among the higher ranks, decreases every day,) are those usually called romantic young women,

who dedicate much of their time to the study of the numerous tales, with
which the press continually furnishes our circulating libraries . . .

From *A Commentary Illustrating the Poetic of Aristotle*. Or compare the
phrasing of Anna Seward recommending, in 1787, "the moral, the pious"
Richardson as the true antidote to "the trash, daily pouring out from the
circulating libraries". Both quoted by Geoffrey Day in *From Fiction to the
Novel*, London and New York, 1987, 125–6, 146.

    I owe the following example from *George Bateman* to Linda Bree.

11 Day, *From Fiction to the Novel*, 27 ff. is obviously wrong in saying that
Fanny Burney was here the first novelist to call her fiction a "novel", cf.
e.g. Coventry, quoted above.

12 Like the fine passage in chapter five of Maria Edgeworth's *Patronage*
(1814), in which the "just representations of the life and manners or of the
human heart" to be found in "Miss Burney – Mrs. Opie – Mrs. Inchbald"
are defended against fashionable preferences for Continental writers.
Nevertheless (as in what I have quoted from *Belinda*), Maria Edgeworth's
own confidence and tone elsewhere about the novel tended to the fitful and
playful rather than to the forthrightness of *Patronage*. According to
Marilyn Butler she was "dissatisfied with the intellectual standards of the
novel as she found it" (*Jane Austen and the War of Ideas*, xxxvii). *Que
faire*? In 'Ennui' (written 1804; published 1809) Lord Glenthorn, nobly
self-exiled from his impressive real Gothic castle (which initially reminds
him of Mrs. Radcliffe), warns the reader:

> If, among those who may be tempted to peruse my history, there should
> be any mere novel readers, let me advise them to throw the book aside at
> the commencement of this chapter; for I have no more wonderful
> incidents to relate, no more changes at nurse, no more sudden turns of
> fortune . . . (xxi)

Actually this is quite good advice, for by this stage the really excellent
things in the tale – which are not those he mentions – are over, and mere
morals are beginning to be drawn. It is unclear how we are meant to take
it: it is certainly not seriously clever in the way *Northanger Abbey* is. (But
then Maria Edgeworth was never a golden artist like Jane Austen; rather, a
highly intelligent woman who fictionalised brilliantly, especially in shorter,
amusingly didactic, works which dramatise the compulsive behaviour of
otherwise quite admirable people, such as 'Almeria', 'Ennui', 'Emilie de
Coulanges', 'The Modern Griselda', 'The Absentee' and 'Manoeuvring' –
mostly *Tales of Fashionable Life*. Though much later there is the sparkling
Helen of 1834, a full-length novel with the beginnings of some really
inward character conflict in its Cecilia. I wonder by the way if the title of
'Manoeuvring' – written in 1808 – and the key use of the word in *Lady
Susan* reflect the current French wars? – in his very amusing *Memoirs* of
campaigns with the Directorate and Napoleon Lieutenant-General Marbot
uses it frequently).

    The tradition of bemused defence – among lively writers at any rate –
was long lived. As late as 1874 Wilkie Collins found it worthwhile to
vindicate novels in a highly satirical passage reminiscent of *Northanger
Abbey*. In a country-house library in *Man and Wife*, chapter 17, the "Solid

Literature" of "Histories, Biographies and Essays" etc. is supposedly distinguished from "Light Literature" which is "the Novels of our own day". "We" would be "satisfied" with ourselves if found consulting the former and "ashamed" if "publicly discovered" reading fiction – "indulging a vice". But this is, of course, a "common and curious form of human stupidity". Henry James famously took up the same theme – but that, and the fact that many readers might still testify to the same inward perpetual lingering doubts about fiction, is another story.

13 John Mullan argues interestingly (*Sentiment and Sociability*, 98 ff.) that in the eighteenth-century debate about the moral status of novels the terms remain the same while only the works to which they are applied differ: e.g. in the case of Richardson *versus* Fielding each side accuses the other of arousing harmful passions and asserts its own inculcation of virtuous thought and feeling. Thus there is an uncertainty as to the true "target" of anti-novel strictures, especially since any work which illustrates virtue triumphant – *Pamela* perhaps – has to evoke the appropriate, possibly titillating, threat. And even the apparently pro-Richardsonian *Female Quixote* involves a satire on "that lexicon of [feminine physical] gestures whose articulacy is so important to Richardson".

14 The more so because the up-dating to include *Belinda* is one of the only certain revisions of *Northanger Abbey*. It is obviously not plausible that Jane Austen did this only in order to mock Maria Edgeworth's disclaiming Advertisement – in which she offers a "Moral Tale . . . the author not wishing to acknowledge a Novel" because often novels disseminate "folly errour and vice". (For a discussion of this whole question see Butler *Maria Edgeworth*, 305 ff. and *passim*.)

    I think David Lodge in 'Composition, Distribution, Arrangement: Form and Structure in Jane Austen's Novels', in *The Jane Austen Handbook*, ed. D. Grey, B.C. Southam and A.W. Litz, New York, 1986; reprinted in *After Bakhtin*, London, 1990, 116–28, is the only critic to find Jane Austen's defence of the novel as a *genre* "highly equivocal". He also thinks it the only work of hers that "lends itself to a deconstructive reading" because we are denied "sure ground for interpretation and discrimination". But he does not follow this up, being more intent on applying Bakhtinian categories. I feel that if anyone did they would be driven to a tiresome highlighting of the odd weakness and discrepancy, rather than moving in sympathy with the amusingly shifting lights I am trying to describe.

15 The relationships with periodical literature are also more complicated than is usually assumed. The joking reference to Richardson's contribution to the *Rambler* (No. 97): "as a celebrated writer has maintained . . . no young lady can be justified in falling in love before the gentleman's love is declared" (1, iii), actually cuts both ways. Richardson, heavily in praise of the *Spectator*, is criticising the modern display of charms at Tonbridge and Bath – "showy girls" like Isabella – but, in the old-fashioned courtship he describes with playful solemnity as a contrast, it is clear that, in fact, the young lady knows very well what is going on: "She is perhaps not an absolute stranger to the passion of the young gentleman". So Jane Austen is really joking with her fellow novelist, not about him.

    Evidently the sentiment about priority in love was traditional. It recurs, for example, in *Uncle Silas*, again in humorous, if sinister, form.

16 For more comment on the continued duty to use this indispensable literary
    term without any more self-consciousness than is absolutely inescapable in
    a post post-structuralist climate, see Raymond Tallis's admirable *In
    Defence of Realism*, London, 1988. This is a very witty, clean and
    powerful assessment, from the philosophical point of view, of modern
    literary "theory" (even if it does, in passing, dauntingly say that "... one
    has to be almost pathologically self-confident to believe that one's own
    contribution to, say, the vast corpus of studies on Jane Austen is an
    essential or even useful mediator between the artist and her potential
    readership" [160]). See also below, ch. 4, n. 1 and ch. 7.
17 On this topic one *has* deeply to agree with LeRoy Smith's rhythmic remark
    that "the most important step [for heroines] is to develop self-awareness
    and self-knowledge through self-evaluation", *Jane Austen and the Drama
    of Woman*, 40. Smith habitually writes as though he were a psy-
    chotherapist who approves of Jane Austen – a method and tone full of
    unacknowledged and unargued assumptions common in modern campus
    criticism and shared sometimes by e.g. Claudia Johnson, *Jane Austen:
    Women, Politics and the Novel*. But John K. Mathison makes a more
    useful point, earlier, in his 'Northanger Abbey and Jane Austen's con-
    ception of the value of fiction', *English Literary History*, xxiv, 1957,
    138–52, where he argues, in effect, that even bad novels can help people
    grow up: "To the reader of *Northanger Abbey* it becomes abundantly clear
    that the trashy horror stories supplied by Isabella were educationally useful
    to Catherine, if only because of the difficulties and confusions in which
    they involved her ..." [146] Still, this is a trifle weak, I think, and does not
    address the question of what kind of novel Jane Austen had in mind in the
    chapter-five defence, which he quotes straight.
18 *Computation into Criticism: A Study of Jane Austen's Novels and an
    Experiment in Method*, Oxford, 1987, 129–32. For further discussion of
    this book see below, ch. 7.

4 EARLY WORKS, TRADITIONS, AND CRITICS III: IMPLICATIONS OF THE SECOND CHAPTER OF *SENSE AND SENSIBILITY*

1 How this process in turn stands in relation to the language, the world, and
   our other experiences is, of course, the difficult philosophical problem (or
   series of problems) about literary art which has eluded any but temporary
   dogmatic solution since Aristotle at least. As I said in chapter one, it is
   decidedly not the intention of this work to offer any general theory.
     However, on the question of realistic representation in general I am
   pleased to note in passing the sanction given by a sophisticated contemporary philosopher, Bernard Williams, who says (in describing Hilary
   Putnam's description of "internal realism") that:

   > We have the idea that we live in a world that exists independently of us
   > and our thoughts. This idea may be called realism. Almost everyone
   > shares it, and even those whose philosophies seem to deny it really
   > accept it in some form – some literary theorists, for instance, who say
   > that we can never compare our texts to 'the world' but only to other
   > texts. (*London Review of Books*, Vol. 13, No. 3, 7 February 1991)

This would obviously allow the kind of argument I am conducting, as well as, for example, an argument about Naturalism. (See further John Ellis, *Against Deconstruction*, Harvard, 1984, and Raymond Tallis, *In Defence of Realism*, and *Not Saussure*, Basingstoke, 1988.)

The present subject of *patterning* in representation will surface again several times, in similar but slightly different conditions (usually the mysterious relation of fictional verisimilitude to repeated and predictable comic devices) in the discussions of *Sense and Sensibility*, *Pride and Prejudice* and *Emma*, below *passim*. A formulation of a similar problem in contemporary critical *langue du bois* underlies much of John A. Dussinger's *In the Pride of the Moment: Encounters in Jane Austen's World*, Columbus, Ohio, 1990: "Although previous scholarship has generally assumed a mimetic model to describe Austen's characterization, this approach has been at odds sometimes with a parodic art that calls attention to literary analogues and deliberately subverts trusting the text." (13) As this suggests, Dussinger employs an eclectic quiverful of the current terms of art ("discourse... privilege... dialogic... perceiving the subject... parodic intertextuality... metonym... symbol... alienation etc., etc.) to make his general point − which is that encounters in Jane Austen show the characters acting in character.

A potentially livelier epistemological line could be provided by Richard Handler and Daniel Segal in *Jane Austen and the Fiction of Culture*, Tucson, 1990, were the authors not so literal as critics, and culturally remote. They are ethnographers and anthropologists who consider − in quite a bland and clever way − that Jane Austen is not committed to any particular doctrine about her society (e.g. Conservative, feminist etc.), but a "comparativist" who "creates conversations, negotiations, and confrontations in which any voice or perspective can call into question the completeness of any other" (10). They then assert − *via* an anti-positivist attack on simple divisions between "ethnography and literature" (or science *versus* fiction) − that she thus enables her reader to realise the "contingency" of social rules and "the polysemy of social action" (165) in the real world. Obviously to accept such a view would be to bypass peaceably, and usefully, a lot of rhetorical debate and implausible assumption (e.g. James Thompson's in *Between Self and World*, as described in n. 1 to ch. 1 above). But if the claim is meant to be more, and more absolute than, a way of resaying − from a different angle − that the novels are very complex, it is surely unacceptably relativistic, endlessly end-deferring, and even nihilistic. (It would also militate, of course, against the preservation of the felt sense that Jane Austen is close to the modern reader − and thus be Anthropological in a defeating way.)

2 Farrer, "Jane Austen, *ob*. July 1817"; and Claudia Johnson in her, in this case, sharp and excellent but sometimes extreme account in *Jane Austen: Women, Politics and the Novel*, 49.

Poovey, *The Proper Lady*, is cogent and interesting, though I think too pessimistic and abstract, when, talking of the idea of a "perfect society" *versus* "realism" in the novels, she says of *Pride and Prejudice* and *Sense and Sensibility* that: "Austen is able to effect an aesthetic resolution of what is essentially a moral dilemma because the realistic elements... are so carefully contained... Austen simply does not explore to the full the social and psychological implications of her realism . . ." (202) Of course, this argument depends on the assumption that simple imitative realism is what Austen is primarily after here: it will be obvious that I think the case more complex than that, and not readily yielding to such blunt either/or terms.

3   See, for variations of the preceding: Bradbrook, *Jane Austen and her Predecessors*; Moler, *Jane Austen's Art of Allusion*; Jan Fergus, *Jane Austen and the Didactic Novel*, Totowa, New Jersey, 1983; Spencer, *The Rise of the Woman Novelist*.

In *Jane Austen*, London, 1988, 77–8 and 98, Tony Tanner gives a useful brief summary of the intense contemporary focus on the second word of the title, generated mainly by the existence of the school of "sensibility" novels, and its relation to the philosophic debate about an innate "natural" moral sense – partly derived from the speculations of Shaftesbury, Hutcheson and Rousseau on this important matter – as opposed to the "nurture" school derived from Locke's theory that consciousness is a *tabula rasa* on which education has to work. The interested reader will note that Elinor habitually invokes both schools – as in her judgement on Mr. Palmer quoted below ("not . . . so . . . unaffectedly ill-natured or ill-bred") – whereas, of course, Marianne inclines (fairly moderately, in fact) to the natural – see also below. But it, typically, inhibits reading to get very involved in annotations of a philosophic debate: inhibits a natural response, I mean – which is why I make no attempt to offer or reproduce an account like Tanner's here.

See also Butler, *Jane Austen and the War of Ideas*; and for more detailed recent work Janet Todd, *Sensibility: An Introduction*, London, 1986, and Mullan, *Sentiment and Sociability*.

4   Tanner, *Jane Austen*, ch. 3, *passim*, is ingenious on the prevalence of secrecy in this book – without quite doing justice to the prevalence of secrecy in life.

5   Butler, *Jane Austen and the War of Ideas*, 190.

6   Cecil Seronsay was probably the first to mention *King Lear* in relation to the Dashwoods in 'Jane Austen's Technique' in *Notes & Queries*, 200 (1956), 303–5.

The sentimental/ruthless use of a child is amusing. Nevertheless, it must be said that childhood is one of the areas that Jane Austen obviously chose not to treat – and which later became a marvellous subject in novels. With the partial exception of Fanny Price (and her sister Susan) in *Mansfield Park*, children are of interest only insofar as they offer such pretexts as this (which may be matter for rather guilty relief in the late twentieth-century reader).

7   'Miss Austen's Six Novels' in *English Women of Letters*, 1862; reprinted in *Critical Heritage*, Vol. 1, 176 ff. And Alisdair Duckworth's *The Improvement of the Estate*, Baltimore and London, 1974, 85–91, is interesting about the hard monetary values involved in these calculations.

In *Jane Austen: Real and Imagined Worlds*, New Haven and London, 1991, 43–65, Oliver MacDonagh – writing from the historian's point of view, though somewhat casually and thinly as to literature – concludes, after a review of Jane Austen's own relations to cash, that in *Sense and Sensibility* "Money constitutes a sort of underlying beat below the narrative" – an interesting stress.

One should add in justice to John Dashwood that Fanny is really the leader throughout. In their formidable, witty and deeply tendentious section on Jane Austen in *The Madwoman in the Attic*, Sandra M. Gilbert and Susan Gubar also make a comparison with *King Lear* (120) – but their polemical position (with strong reference to Shakespeare) that Jane Austen is "in revolt against the conventions she inherited" leads them to think that "her reversals imply that male traditions need to be evaluated and reinterpreted", and so their emphasis lights unfairly on poor John in contrast to the "evil daughter" (*sic*) in the play. It is often a natural adjunct to the feminist case that the power behind the throne (or rocking the cradle) in past marriages, and which is still very observably a part of common experience, be discounted, its having been previously too complacently invoked by liberal conservatives – Mrs. Humphry Ward, for example. (For a sensible specific account of some historical circumstances in England see Jeanne Peterson, *Family, Love and Work in the Lives of Victorian Gentlewomen*, Indiana, 1989.)

In further justice to John we may also learn that the dowager Duchess of Manchester, who became a widow in 1739, lived on an annuity of £2,000 – about half the income of the family – until 1786, near on fifty years (see Cannon, *Aristocratic Century*, 126).

8 Marvin Mudrick, for example, in *Jane Austen: Irony as Defense and Discovery*, has some brilliant pages on the subject (71 ff.) in the course of his vivid account of Marianne (and Elinor).

9 See Johnson, *Jane Austen: Women, Politics and the Novel*, 52.

10 Probably. An article in the *Westminster Review* of October 1853 which is attributed to George Eliot judges that in spite of her excellence and truth to life "Miss Austen" must still be "classed in the lower division" because her work does not "admit the soul into that serener atmosphere . . . which ought to enlarge the domain of thought, and exalt the motives of action". Reprinted in *Critical Heritage*, Vol. 1, 145–6. This kind of thing is as much Victorian orthodoxy (the reviewer/George Eliot is actually quoting Bulwer Lytton) as is the twentieth-century admiration of tough-mindedness. I guess that it is actually what some modern readers feel, but do not care to say.

11 Mudrick, *Jane Austen: Irony as Defense and Discovery*, ch. 3, *passim*, and Tanner, *Jane Austen*, 82. Claudia Johnson also wants to extend Marianne's penitent reference to "self-destruction" to mean something far grander and more disastrous than it does – *Jane Austen: Women, Politics and the Novel*, 64. And cf., earlier, Gilbert and Gubar, *The Madwoman in the Attic*, 156–7, who leave a creative vagueness about "the unfettered play of her [Marianne's] imagination seeming to result in a terrible fever".

12 A reflection by Fontane – so affectionately admired by Thomas Mann – on his own methods in the middle of *Before the Storm*, 1878, is both illuminating in itself and indicative by comparison of how developed natural and fluent an artist Jane Austen was, even in her early work:

> . . . however right it may be to condemn the presentation of single figures wearing their thoughts and actions like labels stuck to their coats, and to laud instead that art which inspires the reader's own imagination to the creative development and completion of what is merely indicated and hinted at, this just rule may be waived when, as here, the exhibition of

finished figures one beside the other is intended to represent little more than a *portrait gallery* offered to the reader less for the sake of the pictures themselves than for that of the *place* where they are to be found. (Trans. R.J. Hollingdale, Oxford, 1985, 136)

The distinction is interesting, and could be applied *mutatis mutandis* to *Sense and Sensibility* if "place" is taken to apply to the general *ambience*; but, of course, Jane Austen is far too sophisticated to set it out thus explicitly.

13   *Jane Austen: Irony as Defense and Discovery*, 63 ff.

14   Mrs. Leavis's idea in her introduction to the novel, reprinted in *Collected Essays*, Vol. 1, 147–61, that Cassandra Austen was the "model" for Elinor and Jane for Marianne puts this in an even more attractive light. In which case a speculative biographer should surely conclude (which I have not seen done) that there was an important occasion in Jane Austen's life in which she was near a fire, was scolded or snubbed by an aggressive older woman whom she intensely disliked, and was bravely and cogently defended by Cassandra (or wished to be). Though one does not think easily of Cassandra as like Mary Crawford...

15   *Jane Austen and the War of Ideas*, 191 ff. – but according to Butler we are meant to think that, in spite of Elinor's being "shaken by her feelings", this is correct. Consequently, overall the reader is in danger of finding Elinor "frigid", and thus defeating the novel's conservative didactic purpose.

16   For example, as well as Marilyn Butler (above), though on different sides, Kenneth J. Moler, *Jane Austen's Art of Allusion*, 70–1, thinks that it "ironically" shows that you can be too sensible ("irony" is a useful word for critics, like "paradoxically"), while Mudrick, *Jane Austen: Irony as Defense and Discovery*, 83–5, pushes his characteristically exciting account to the point where "irony" fails and Elinor and her creator are guilty of "flagrant inconsistency" they both being "almost in love" with Willoughby – a flamboyant idea.

It is obviously hard for poor Elinor to win once she is seen as the simple embodiment of a principle – though Jan Fergus, *Jane Austen and the Didactic Novel*, ch. 2, conducts a painstaking defence, especially against the piratical Mudrick whom she finds "perverse" and "exasperating" (40). In fact, all commentaries arguing from a slip seem to me slightly averted from probability, slightly absurd, in that they pretend to detect inadvertence in a part of the novel where it is least likely to occur, where Jane Austen is most likely to be writing carefully and deliberately. One slip about Elinor's feelings might be credible even in so habitually controlled a novelist, revising over the years. But a series of them? – and at so fraught a juncture?

5   QUESTIONS ABOUT *PRIDE AND PREJUDICE*

Most references are in, or implied in, the text. See opening of the chapter.

1   The primary modern model for this is Erich Heller's brilliant chapter on *The Magic Mountain* in his book on Thomas Mann – *The Ironic German*, London, 1958 – which contains its own demurs to Plato, Dryden and Friedrich Schlegel. But also (relevant for me) in this interesting critical form

is Henry James's practice in '*Daniel Deronda*: a Conversation' of 1876. James creates his characters more fully, though lightly, but his use of three speakers recalls that of Hume in his Dialogues on natural religion. Other precedents are supplied by memories of some of Oscar Wilde's critical essays; of Landor; of Vernon Lee; and of parts of Gide's *Corydon*.

2 No claim is made – in the manner of some contemporary academics – to be reinstating a dialectical, Platonic, 'open' model for criticism in favour of the more authoritarian Aristotelian one allegedly implied by ordinary critical monologue. However, the allusions made by the speakers to ideas other than their own are all genuine – often from works cited elsewhere in this book – and it will be obvious to the observer of modes of speech and the flow of ideas that some of the references and language of both questioner and answerer lightly echo and refer to numerous contemporary schools of critical thought – and are therefore dated fairly firmly as being of the late 1980s and the 1990s. But (although I have tried to be fair) it is almost needless to say that there is no intent to suggest that there is full representation of any particular critical position or creed.

3 In chapter three of *Shakespearian Negotiations*, Oxford, 1988, Stephen Greenblatt describes wit contests in *Twelfth Night* and finds expressions of displaced sexuality in "the subject" with all the verbal "chafing" and "friction"/"erotic heat" displaced to off-stage. I find this quite usefully suggestive for Jane Austen's practice in *Pride and Prejudice* and elsewhere.

4 See, primarily, chapter ten of the Austen-Leigh *Memoir* for Jane Austen's "parental interest in the beings she had created". The traditions relevant to *Pride and Prejudice* are: that a favourite colour of Jane Bingley's was green; that Kitty Bennet married a clergyman who lived near to Pemberley; but that Mary had to be content with one of Mr. Philips's clerks and remain near Meryton. One wonders what the older Bennets, variously, made of this. See also R.W. Chapman, *Jane Austen: Facts and Problems*, Oxford, 1948, 122–4.

5 Ch. 2, vi and xii. Trans. Charles Johnston, London, 1977; Harmondsworth, 1979.

6 MANSFIELD PARK, FANNY PRICE, FLAUBERT, AND THE MODERN NOVEL

1 As she remarked herself her works contain no extras such as:

> ...a long chapter of sense, if it could be had; if not, of solemn nonsense, about something unconnected with the story; an essay on writing, a critique on Walter Scott, or the history of Buonaparté or anything that would form a contrast...

– on *Pride and Prejudice*, letter to Cassandra Austen, February 1813, *Letters*, 300–1. Commentators have taken it from here.

2 Page 166.

3 For example, the sociologist Mary Evans uses it for the title of the first chapter of her alert *Jane Austen and the State*. And, even more recently, it supplies the highly academic John A. Dussinger with his title for *In the Pride of the Moment: Encounters in Jane Austen's World*.

4   London, 1987, x.
5   From her introduction to an edition of *Mansfield Park*, 1957; reprinted
    by B.C. Southam in *Jane Austen: 'Sense and Sensibility', 'Pride and
    Prejudice', and 'Mansfield Park'. A Casebook*, 236–42.

    For another descriptive collocation of views up to its date – as well as
    those of the author – and especially an interesting account of the con-
    temporary political and intellectual climate in which the visit to Antigua
    might be assumed by its first audience to render the virtuous Sir Thomas
    more flexible and more humane, under the influence of the Evangelicals,
    and therefore more in tune with his serious young dependant and Edmund
    (e.g. "Did you not hear me asking him about the slave trade last night?" 2,
    iii, 198) – see Avrom Fleishman, *A Reading of 'Mansfield Park': An Essay
    in Critical Synthesis*, Minneapolis, 1967.
6   Nabokov in *Lectures in Literature*, London, 1980, 30.

    Farrer in 'Jane Austen. *ob*. July 1817', 264.

    Amis, 'What Became of Jane Austen', 1957, reprinted in Southam,
    Casebook, 243–6. Incidentally, Sir Kingsley's character as a critic of Jane
    Austen seems to me to tally closely with his character as a novelist:
    brilliant as a deflatory satirist; courageous and honest in the most appealing
    and admirable way; but somewhere painfully and obscurely occluded,
    stifled in the spirit.

    Trilling, '*Mansfield Park*' in *The Opposing Self*, New York, 1954, also
    reprinted in Southam, *Casebook*, 216–35 (see especially 219).

    Perhaps the most extravagant – though one feels that they are also meant
    to be sophisticated and to some extent playful – descriptions are those of
    Nina Auerbach in 'Jane Austen's Dangerous Charm: Feeling as one ought
    about Fanny Price' in *Jane Austen: New Perspectives*, ed. Janet Todd,
    208–21. Here Fanny, "the controlling spirit of anti-play", is compared to
    a Romantic anti-hero, and is a "centre of fierce inactivity", a "monster",
    "predatory", "cannabilistic" and so forth – all of which is fitting to a novel
    which is "a dark realisation of an essentially Romantic vision".

    Another thoroughly modern way of resolving the problem – and others
    – is proposed by Isobel Armstrong in '*Mansfield Park*', Harmondsworth,
    1988. She insists forcibly on – and seems moderately pleased by – the
    inevitability of "unease", though not, it is insisted, relativism, in "a text
    [i.e. this novel] in dialogue with itself"; – "We find ourselves asking
    questions rather than providing answers" (95 ff.). However, the present
    writer is too afraid perhaps of the undertows of life, and too anxious to
    reconstitute some certainty in our culture to be willing to welcome the
    willed deferral and suspension – for an unspecified time – of present
    meanings in favour of some "radical reading" to come. C.f. the
    Anthropological views of Handler and Segal, alluded to in ch. 4, n. 1.
7   January 1813, *Letters*, 298.
8   Hubert Teyssandier comfortably, if abstractly, says that "...the stock
    figure of the angelic heroine acquires verisimilitude and is seen to go
    through the real sufferings of existence", 'On *Mansfield Park*' in *The
    Nineteenth Century Novel: Critical Essays and Documents*, ed. Arnold
    Kettle, London, 1981, 88.

    More interesting is a phrase in Bernard Paris's *Character and Conflict in
    Jane Austen's Novels*, Detroit, 1978, where Fanny's goodness is called

"that of a terrified child" (49). Paris's Horneyan "Third Force" psychological analysis leads him to extend this into the argument that Fanny's vindication in the novel is evidence of Jane Austen's own "psychological limitations" and "blind spots" about her "defensive strategies" (62). Obviously such analysis is kind of lively; but also obviously it depends on a view of art as more easily subject to simple categories than it is – there is talk of the characters being "at once aesthetic, illustrative, and mimetic", and so treatable as "real human beings". This in turn leads to a daring last chapter in which "The Authorial Personality" – i.e. Jane Austen – is diagnosed as finally, in *Persuasion*, "to be emerging from embeddedness and to be embracing life".

9   There are numerous related terms for the same, leading, but essentially elusive phenomenon (its identification in each case depends very much on taste or subjective judgement; where some would identify it others sometimes would prefer to detect only indirect reported thought). In *The Dual Voice*, Manchester, 1977, Roy Pascal describes the evolution of the French phrase by Bally and others early in this century. But Nabokov, *Lectures in Literature*, uses "oblique speech"; M.M. Bakhtin in *The Dialogic Imagination*, as translated by M. Holquist and C. Emerson, Austin, Texas, 1981 – but written in Russia in the 1930s – has "hidden speech"; Graham Hough in 'Narrative and Dialogue in Jane Austen', *Critical Quarterly*, Vol. 12, No. 3, 1970 offers "coloured style"; J.F. Burrows, *Computation into Criticism*, likes "thought idiolect"; and Lennard J. Davis in *Resisting Novels*, New York and London, 1987, prefers "free indirect discourse" – etc. See also further comments below, in part two of this chapter.

10 *Jane Austen*, ch. 5.

11 *Jane Austen and Her Art*, 201.

12 Tanner, *Jane Austen*, 172. Hardy, *Jane Austen's Heroines*, London and New York, 1984, 65. Actually many commentators quote and admire these speeches. Frank Bradbrook, *Jane Austen and her Predecessors*, invokes the *Rambler* itself. Kenneth J. Moler, in *Jane Austen's Art of Allusion*, and in 'The Two voices of Fanny Price' in Halperin, *Bicentenary Essays*, 172–9, detects, not so admiringly, Hannah More. By far the best admiring account, in which a significant moral "openness" is detected in "the greatest rhapsodist in Jane Austen", is by Barbara Hardy in *A Reading of Jane Austen*, 58–65.

13 It was perhaps memories of the latter that lent the admirable vigour to Elizabeth Bowen's remarks in her essay on Jane Austen in *Impressions of English Literature*, ed. W.J. Turner, London, 1944 that: " . . . she applies big truths to little scenes – so no scene stays 'little' under her hand. . . . Not only the charm but the strength of Jane Austen's novels resides in their being so innately grown-up . . ." (246)

14 In her interesting book *Jane Austen: Feminism and Fiction*, Brighton, 1983, 101–2, which, among other things, criticises powerfully the notion that Fanny is to be taken straight-faced as a conduct-book heroine, compares Jane Austen with Mary Wollstonecraft, and argues that a "feminist point of view" may be positively connected with the "style of an eighteenth-century moralist". (The same strong argument is to be found in 'Feminist Irony and the Priceless Heroine of *Mansfield Park*' in *Jane Austen: New Pespectives*, ed. Janet Todd, 231–47.)

15   For example, on the literary side by Elaine Showalter in *The Female Malady: Women, Madness and English Culture*, New York and London, 1987; or on the literary-biographical by Jean Strouse in *Alice James*, Boston 1980.

16   To Cassandra Austen, January 1813, *Letters*, 298. Note also the relatively small number of chapters in this volume – thirteen as opposed to the eighteen and seventeen that flank it – an aid to narrative pace, I suppose. (In pages it is about three-quarters of the length of the others.) In these external organisational terms *Emma* alone, in three volumes, and *Persuasion*, in two, have perfectly symmetrical structures.

17   *Jane Austen*, 159

18   *Lectures in Literature*, 41.

19   For Henry, see *Letters*, 378. For Cassandra, see the memories of Jane Austen's goddaughter, Louisa Knight (Lady George Hill), quoted in Austen-Leigh/Le Faye *A Family Record*, 181.

20   Gratitude as a motive for entering into any contract, including marriage, seems to me to have a good deal of inherent psychological force and plausibility – for either sex.
    The idea of its respectability as a reason and sanction for marriage in the mouths of moralists certainly spans Jane Austen's period. Dr. John Gregory in *A Father's Legacy to his Daughters*, 1774, emphasises that it and, unsurprisingly, "esteem" should be the *female* requirements. Actually, he seems to think that the combination more or less equals "love". Equally, at the other end of the period, in Maria Edgeworth's *Helen*, 1834, we are to admire Lady Davenant's having been converted from romantic love for an unworthy suitor by the man who becomes her husband:

> He went deeper and deeper into my mind, till he came to a spring of gratitude, which rose and overflowed, vivifying and fertilising the seemingly barren waste. (Ch. 7).

Nevertheless, although gratitude is given considerable weight in Jane Austen's works – perhaps especially, and naturally in view of the circumstances of the action, in *Pride and Prejudice*, with its slightly Richardsonian resonance, as above – it is not, obviously, seen as a *sufficient* condition for the ideal union (particularly, of course, where the gratitude is primarily an economic matter).

21   'Jane Austen, *ob.* July 1817'.

22   The feeling is comparable to that in the reader at the end of *Daniel Deronda*. We are likely to want, but cannot have, the marriage of Gwendolen to Deronda – the interesting, glamorous, erring one linked to the representative of intellect and virtue. But the logic of the respective books demands a tension between this desire and the deeply held moral purpose. Accordingly, we are likely to resent a little the lucky virtuous figures, Mirah and Edmund.
    Jane Austen is here working on a more complex plot, or emotional shape – of which the Marianne thread in *Sense and Sensibility* is a forerunner – than that she chooses in the straighter happy endings of, for example, *Pride and Prejudice*, *Emma* and *Persuasion*.
    The best short account of how Mary Crawford's charm almost survives against heavy moral odds – "we are constantly aware of it, partly under its spell, even though the text is strewn with hints of its corruption" – is in

Denis Donoghue's elegant and probably very influential essay 'A View of *Mansfield Park*' in *Critical Essays on Jane Austen*, ed. B.C. Southam, London, 1968 (reprinted in Donoghue's *England Their England*, New York, 1988).

In her roguish tale *Mansfield Revisited*, London, 1986, Joan Aiken blithely cuts the knot by having Henry guiltless – the victim of the scorned Maria's slander; and Mary a dying, repentant, saint.

23 *The Dialogic Imagination*, 263.
24 From Burrows, *Computation into Criticism*, 30.
25 1906. Quoted by Southam in *Critical Heritage*, Vol. 2, 75.
26 See, for example, the merely dutiful reference made by Barbara Smalley in her *George Eliot and Flaubert*, Athens, Ohio, 1974.
27 This essay can be most easily found, together with some other references by James to Jane Austen, in *The Critical Muse: Selected Literary Criticism of Henry James*, ed. Roger Gard, Harmondsworth, 1987.

It is interesting that James's half-patronising, half-nostalgic image in 'The Lesson of Balzac' of her "over the work basket" with "her tapestry flowers", dreaming, in moments later "picked up" as little stitches of artistic truth, is prefigured at the end of *Washington Square* (which was excluded from the New York edition) where the limited triumph of the rather old fashioned heroine concludes:

> Catherine, meanwhile, in the parlor, picking up her morsel of fancy-work, had seated herself with it again – for life as it were.

28 *Lectures in Literature*, 10.
29 A triumph of laborious technique – especial admiration for which seems a first-rate indicator of poor, over-literary, taste.
30 To be found in *Contre Sainte-Beuve* etc., ed. Clarac and Sandre, Paris (Pléiade edn.), 1971, 586 ff.
31 *The Dual Voice*, 102.
32 *Ibid.*, 11–12. Vargas Llosa, *The Perpetual Orgy*, 1975; trans. and published in New York, 1986.
33 *The Dual Voice*, 34. A stabler recognition of Jane Austen's use does, however, seem to be filtering through within English studies. Norman Page, especially, has an able and unfanatical discussion of her employment of the mode in *The Language of Jane Austen*, 121 ff. He stresses particularly the relation and proportion of it to the "tone" and "viewpoint" of the novels. And in *After Bakhtin*, 126, David Lodge says that Jane Austen "was the first English novelist" to use free indirect speech "extensively" (in the useful short explanatory essay, 'Composition, Distribution, Arrangement' already referred to).
34 It is, incidentally, my impression (as only a very rusty Latinist) that Livy, in his dramatisations of the disputes of Republican commanders in 216 BC – written at the very beginning of our era – employs something not dissimilar to free indirect speech. Here, for example, is one of the disputes leading up to the disaster of Cannae (Fabius was Dictator; Minucius, Master of the Horse):

> Even before this, success and popularity had rendered Minucius intolerable enough; but now his behaviour went beyond all bounds of moderation and decency, and he bragged about his defeat of Fabius even

more than his so-called defeat of Hannibal. That Fabius, sought out in times of stress as the one and only match for the victorious Hannibal, should now, by popular vote, be made equal to a junior officer [i.e. Minucius himself] – he, a dictator, brought to the level of his master of Horse – and that too, in a country where mere masters of Horse had been in the habit of cringing like curs before the dictator's terrible rods and axes: why, the thing was unprecedented in all history! Such was the result of his own dazzling valour and success! He was determined, therefore, to follow where his fortune led, if the dictator persisted in the dilatory and do-nothing tactics which gods and men had alike condemned. (*Histories*, xxii, 27, trans. Aubrey de Sélincourt.)

35 *Lectures in Literature*, 50.
36 She is an example, perhaps, of what Jonathan Culler, in *Flaubert: The Uses of Uncertainty*, Ithaca, N.Y., 1974, has in mind when he asserts that Flaubert introduced deliberate irrelevancies into his work, in the interest of assuring the reader of the indeterminacy of the universe.
37 October 1813, *Letters*, 344.
38 Not just for us. It was precisely this economy that appealed to some of Jane Austen's contemporaries. Of *Pride and Prejudice* Annabella Milbanke (later Lady Byron) wrote in May 1813: "It depends not on any of the common resources of novel writers, no drownings, no conflagrations, nor runaway horses, nor lap-dogs and parrots, nor chambermaids and milliners, nor rencontres and disguises. I really think it the *most probable* I have ever read." And William Gifford, the editor of the *Quarterly Review* reported with pleasure to John Murray that there are: "No dark passages; no secret chambers; no wind-howlings in long galleries; no drops of blood upon a rusty dagger . . ." Accordingly, Richard Whately (later Archbishop of Dublin) judiciously praised this new "accurate and unexaggerated" "Flemish"-style realism in his excellent review of *Northanger Abbey* and *Persuasion* for the *Quarterly* of January 1821. – All quoted or reprinted in Southam, *Critical Heritage*, Vol. 1, 8 and 87–105.

However, this is a good place to note Martin Green's powerful qualifying literary/historical argument in *Dreams of Adventure, Deeds of Empire*, London and Henley, 1980, in which he articulates very challengingly an alternative to the "domestic" or "Great Tradition" novel (represented superbly by Jane Austen) – in fictions more explicitly having to do with adventure, expansion, action, Empire. . . . *This* different kind of novel or tale he sees as usually artistically less perfect and internally less profound, but nevertheless publicly and politically at least as formative and important. His argument runs through Defoe, Scott, Cooper, Tolstoy, Mark Twain, Kipling and Conrad, with many fascinating excursions into history, myth, and lesser writers. The book is in sophisticated and thoughtful contrast to the enclosed atmosphere of much academic critical writing.

39 See, Southam *Casebook*, 240; as also Q.D. Leavis's 'A Critical Theory of Jane Austen's Writings'.
Macaulay wrote eloquently:

Shakespeare had neither equal nor second. But among the writers who, in the point we have noticed [the "true representation of human nature"], have approached nearest to the manner of the great master, we have no hesitation in placing Jane Austen, a woman of whom England is justly proud. She has given us a multitude of characters, all in a certain sense, common-place, all such as we meet every day. Yet they are all perfectly discriminated ... ('Madame D'Arblay', *Edinburgh Review*, LXXVI, January, 1843, 561).

7 EMMA'S CHOICES

1 There is a comparable buried charge in "seemed" as used by Maria Edgeworth in *The Dun* (1802) where the bawd Mrs. Carver seems to be "touched with compassion" for the innocent sixteen-year-old Anne, and sustains five pages of excellent charitable behaviour until she reveals what she is – yet we are not surprised.

2 In *The Idea of the Gentleman in the Victorian Novel*, London, 1981, Robin Gilmour gives an interesting, acute and un-nostalgic account of this key idea and ideal.

As to *aimable versus* amiable: Maria Edgeworth has her (French, of course) Marmontel prefer the English sense in the near contemporary *Ormond*, 1817 – so the topic seems to have been current. Norman Page remarks in *The Language of Jane Austen*, that it was a habit of that age to be alert to, and discuss, the meanings of such concepts and their appropriate definition. A sympathetic example of this can be found from life, as it were, in the letters of (the extremely *grande dame*) Harriet Granville, a large selection of which is available in *A Second Self (1810–45)*, ed. Virginia Surtees, Salisbury, 1990. With Mr. Knightley's: –

> "He [Frank] may be very 'aimable,' have very good manners, and be very agreeable; but he can have no English delicacy towards the feelings of other people: nothing really amiable about him." (1, xviii, 149).

– we may set her judgement on Mme. de Lieven:

> It is every thing that makes a person amiable which is wanting in her – gentleness, sweetness, cheerfulness, kindness, abnégation de soi. There is a great deal of decorum and propriety ... (89)

And note the French here.

3 *Living Space in Fact and Fiction*, London, 1989, 38 ff.; 59.

4 The common meaning of 'irony' or 'ironic' nowadays is either odd/ amusing or sarcastic. But it scarcely needs noting again how very fond critics of Jane Austen are of the term.

5 'Why the Novel Matters', published posthumously in *Phoenix*, London, 1936, 537.

6 Janet Todd, *Women's Friendship in Literature*, New York, 1980, 290.

7 See Thompson, *Between Self and World*, 13 ff. Mary Poovey, *The Proper Lady*, is on much the same trail when she argues that "romantic" love flatters "bourgeois" society because it disguises the system of "economic and political domination" by "foregrounding" personal relations which actually do not "materially affect society". Particularly it disguises the exploitation of women (237–9). This is very neat and grand; but like so much of this materialist stuff it seems out of touch with the real as

experienced in Jane Austen's novels; *or* the real real. To feel *paranoia* on behalf of (some of) the past is a poor way of understanding it. To do Mary Poovey justice, she admits that her "ideological bias" is ahistorical and recognises that such "hindsight" may impair her "sensitivity" (245).

Perhaps English readers feel less remote from Jane Austen on these matters than some Americans apparently do?

8 *Poetics*, ch. 9; trans. T.S. Dorsch, Harmonsdworth, 1965.
9 For a more systematic and fuller account of these sequences see my *'Emma' and 'Persuasion'*, Harmondsworth, 1985.

For a convincing analysis of various technical modes involved see Hough, 'Narrative and Dialogue in Jane Austen', 201–29.

10 *Jane Austen and her Art*, 177. It is an academic vulgarism to think that the more recent critical work is the better it is.
11 *A Journey to the Western Islands of Scotland*, 1775, ed. R.W. Chapman, Oxford, 1930, 95.
12 *Cecilia* was published in 1782. Of course, more naturalistic speech than this occurs in many novels before it – including more naturalistic polite speech – as well as the obvious uses of dialect from at least Defoe onwards, and the use of genteel vulgarisms, of which the dialects of the Steele sisters in *Sense and Sensibility* are the important expressive example in mature Jane Austen (see above, ch. 4).
13 *The Language of Jane Austen*, 117.
14 *Letters to Alice on First Reading Jane Austen*, London, 1984, 72.
15 She too fitfully, and amusingly, knows this fault: "She did most heartily grieve over the idleness of her childhood – and sat down and practised vigorously an hour and a half." (2, vii, 208).
16 Page 37 in the Pandora edition, London, 1986.
17 Surtees, *A Second Self*, 183.
18 Though it is confusing for critics to speculate about the relations between the life and works of a writer, it is hard to forego the description of Emma as a creative person, though shockingly lacking in the necessary discipline. (Her idea of an interesting consequence of the death of Mrs. Churchill is the revelation of "Half a dozen natural children, perhaps – and poor Frank cut off!" – 3, vi, 357).

In which case we *could* say that, unlike Tolstoy and Joyce (for instance), Jane Austen did not start with autobiography and then move into a wider and more distanced, more 'objective' creation, but, very remarkably, the other way round.

A speculation of comparable intellectual dubiety which, none the less, gives some enjoyment to Jane Austen fans is the classification of her heroines into headstrong (H) and obedient (O), and the evenness, or symmetry, of the resulting pattern, or graph. Taking the works in order of probable completion we get: H (*Lady Susan*); O (*Northanger Abbey*); H & O (*Sense and Sensibility*); H (*Pride and Prejudice*); O (*Mansfield Park*); H (*Emma*); O (*Persuasion*). H O H/O H O H O.
19 J.F. Burrows convincingly questions the sage-like character often given to Mr. Knightley in his expanded analysis, *Jane Austen's 'Emma'*, Sydney, 1968.
20 *Between Self and World*, 18.
21 *The Madwoman in the Attic*, 169.

8   REGISTERS OF *PERSUASION*

1   Quoted by F.D. Hoeniger in his introduction to the 'Arden' edition. London 1963, lxiii. The question is complicated by the general agreement that the first two acts, and some of the rest, are the work of the prolific 'inferior hand' (Day in this case, probably) – which is why I shall take my example of poorer writing from late in the play.

As the first phrase of her title suggests, the strenuous Nina Auerbach in 'O Brave New World: Evolution and Revolution in *Persuasion*', *English Literary History*, 39, 1972, 112–28, also invokes later Shakespeare. However her argument is not about ways of writing or creative pressure. Rather, it is an account of how Jane Austen has not simply "discarded an ethic of prudence and repression for an ethic of emotional release; she has shifted the axis of her created world". This involves an enthusiastic view of "the new power of the navy" and Captain Wentworth as "a man in harmony with the spirit of the sea, who lives in conjunction with the elements and their motions". Such prattle goes beyond anything even Anne Elliot might feel – sounds like a different kind of fiction, a different sensibility – and is tempered at least, as I shall argue, by Jane Austen's actual dramatic presentation of Wentworth.

Michael Williams in reference to Nina Auerbach in *Six Novels*, 180, and rather in the spirit of 'well, if one's *got* to have Shakespeare...', more plausibly prefers comparison with the *general* structure of the swing from gloom to happiness in *The Winter's Tale* – but again, this is incidental to the present argument.

2   Austen-Leigh/Le Faye, *A Family Record*, xxiii.

3   *The Common Reader*, London, 1925, 142.

4   "Poetry and Drama", reprinted in *On Poetry and Poets*, London, 1957, 86–7. It will be recalled that 'Marina' is one of Eliot's finest poems.

5   For which the present chapters 2, x and xi were substituted. The cancelled chapter is normally printed as an appendix to modern editions (though not, regrettably, to the Virago edition of 1989).

For the tradition about *The Elliots* see, e.g. *A Family Record*, 214. Williams, *Six Novels*, 195, notes that Jane Austen actually wrote down the title *"Persuasion"* in the manuscript of her *Plan of a Novel* (for the text of which see the MW, 428–30) – but, of course, this only makes Henry's decision a reasonable one (as one might indeed expect).

6   In an essay in Juliet McMaster's bicentenary collection *Jane Austen's Achievement*, London and New York, 1976, Professor George Whalley discusses Jane Austen as "poet" to an effect that, unfortunately, only confirms his affable prefatory disclaimers.

7   This is Marilyn Butler's phrase in what is, nevertheless, the most sparkling, though unsympathetic, recent account of the book, in *Jane Austen and the War of Ideas*, 275. Professor Butler argues that *Persuasion* suffers from having a "dual focus": it is torn between Anne's new kind of sensibility and its rendition on the one hand, and an "eighteenth-century" "objective" framework which is too dimly discerned on the other. (Of course, we know that she wants to see Jane Austen as wanting to be a "partisan" conservative.)

Another interesting recent account is by Claude Rawson in his introduction to the World's Classic edition of the novel, Oxford, 1990.

8 A well-known phrase in Jane Austen's letter to Fanny Knight, 23 March 1817, in which also Anne is described as "almost too good for me". (The "almost" seems sometimes to be blurred in people's recollection.) *Letters*, 486–7.

9 Harriet Granville to the Duke of Devonshire (her brother), November 1830, Surtees. *The Second Self*, 237.

10 Introduction to the Penguin edition, Harmondsworth, 1965.

11 A character in one of Alan Bennett's television monologues puts the observation about reader's expectations with wry charm:

> ...they don't ring true. I mean when somebody in a novel says something like "I've never been in an air crash," you know this means that five minutes later they will be...in stories saying it brings it on. So if you get the heroine saying, "I don't suppose I shall ever be happy," then you can bank on it there's happiness round the corner..." (*Talking Heads*, London, 1988)

Indeed, the point of any proposition in a work of fiction is only incidentally its truth in the base sense – its immediate purpose lies in its significance within the work.

12 According to Stephen Howarth writing to the *Independent* (29 November 1989) about Lord Nelson, in 1805 £2,000 = "approximately £56,528.90...in today's terms" (approximately?). This kind of comparison is obviously difficult given the relativity of various types of transaction: e.g. human labour was clearly cheaper then – but was it cheaper than, say, the electricity for a dishwasher? etc. The suggested multiplication by 28 gives Captain Wentworth's (variously estimated in the novel) prize money a value of about £560,000 to £700,000 which makes him quite well off since he's still in business, though nothing like Darcy (£280,000 a year) or Mr. Rushworth (£336,000 a year) from their estates. Even so, my sense is that Howarth's estimate is very low.

13 Usually a man, of course. See, for an account, e.g. Spencer, *The Rise of the Woman Novelist*.

14 For Boswell's attitude see *The Journal of a Tour to the Hebrides*, 1785; ed. R.W. Chapman, 1930. 276. A relevant early twentieth-century Scottish attitude is reflected in John Buchan's *Huntingtower*.

> "Have you considered what day this is? It's the Sabbath, the best of days for an ill deed. There's no kirk hereaways, and everybody in the parish will be sitting indoors by the fire."

And, in case you think this either antique or merely fictional, I remember personally with affection Dorothy Round, the great Wimbledon champion of the 1930s, who was famous not only for her tennis but for her resolute refusal to play it on Sundays.

15 *Jane Austen's Art of Memory*, 202–3.

9 SANDITON

1 For examplifications and variants of the critical climate alluded to by the two friends, see (in chronological order):

R.W. Chapman, Jane Austen: Facts and Problems, 209.

Robert Liddell: *The Novels of Jane Austen*, London, 1963.

B.C. Southam, *Jane Austen's Literary Manuscripts*, ch. 7, 'The Last Work, *Sanditon*', 100–35.

– the same scholar's lively introduction to his facsimile edition: *Sanditon. An Unfinished Novel by Jane Austen*, Oxford, 1975.

John Davie, ed., *Northanger Abbey, Lady Susan, The Watsons, and Sanditon*, Oxford, 1971 and 1980, introduction, xviii–xxi.

J. Lauber, '*Sanditon*, the kingdom of folly', *Studies in the Novel*, IV, 1972.

Margaret Drabble, ed., *Lady Susan. The Watsons. Sanditon*, introduction, 23–31.

Marilyn Butler, *Jane Austen and the War of Ideas*, ch. 12, '*Persuasion* and *Sanditon*', 275–91.

Tony Tanner, *Jane Austen*, ch. 8, 'The Disease of Activity: *Sanditon*', 250–85.

Select Bibliography

The following contains only works considered – or mentioned for some illustrative purpose – in the text, and does not offer a comprehensive list of writings on Jane Austen. No annotation is attempted here either, save an occasional star (*) in the fourth section – intended to alert the reader to a critical work of special importance (and partly to supplement the local comment in text or note).

I have not thought it necessary to include a list of the other works of art whose aid has been invoked from time to time in defining the main subjects – work by Richardson and Flaubert, Maria Edgeworth and Mrs. Gaskell, and so on. References to all these are to be found either in text or note. Nor have I listed completions or continuations of Jane Austen (which exist for *The Watsons*, *Sanditon*, and even *Mansfield Park*).

JANE AUSTEN'S WORKS

The standard edition is: *The Works of Jane Austen*, ed. R.W. Chapman, 6 vols., Oxford, 1923–54, illustrated; revised Mary Lascelles, 1965–7. This includes the 'Minor Works'.

There are good reprints of the novels and *Sanditon*, including the Penguin and World's Classics editions (the latter being reproductions of the Oxford English Novels series, 1970–1). But some paperback issues, e.g. the Pandora edition, have introduced new errors and have no apparatus, besides being poor value for money. Penguin publish also the *Juvenilia* (1986, ed. Frances Beer – together, oddly, with those of Charlotte Brontë).

Also:

The Manuscript Chapters of 'Persuasion', ed. R.W. Chapman, Oxford, 1926; new edn. London, 1985.

Sanditon: An Unfinished Novel by Jane Austen, a facsimile edn., ed. B.C. Southam, Oxford and London, 1975.

Jane Austen's 'Sir Charles Grandison', ed. B.C. Southam. Oxford, 1980.

BIBLIOGRAPHY, ETC.

De Rose, Peter L. and McGuire, S.W., *A Concordance of the Works of Jane Austen*, 3 vols., New York, 1982.

Gilson, David, *A Bibliography of Jane Austen*. Oxford, 1982.

Select Bibliography

BIOGRAPHY

Jane Austen's Letters, collected and ed. R.W. Chapman, Oxford, 1932; 2nd edn., 1952.

Austen, Henry, *Biographical Notice of the Author*, December 1817 (published prefatory to *Northanger Abbey and Persuasion*, 1818).

Austen-Leigh, the Revd. J.E., *Memoir of Jane Austen*, 1871 (reprinted in Penguin edn. of *Persuasion*).

Austen-Leigh, William and Richard Arthur, *Jane Austen: A Family Record*, 1913; revised and enlarged by Deirdre Le Faye, London, 1989.

Chapman, R.W., *Jane Austen: Facts and Problems*, Oxford, 1948.

Hodge, Jane Aiken, *The Double Life of Jane Austen*, London, 1972.

Honan, Park, *Jane Austen: Her Life*, London, 1987.

CRITICISM OF JANE AUSTEN

1 Collections

Grey, J. David, Southam, B.C., and Litz, A. Walton, eds., *The Jane Austen Handbook*, New York, 1986.

Grey, J. David, ed., *Jane Austen's Beginnings: the Juvenilia and 'Lady Susan'*, Ann Arbor and London, 1989.

Halperin, John, ed., *Jane Austen: Bicentenary Essays*, Cambridge, 1975.

Lodge, David, *Jane Austen: 'Emma'. A Casebook*, London, 1968.

McMaster, Juliet, ed., *Jane Austen's Achievement*, London and New York, 1976.

*Southam, B.C., ed., *Jane Austen: The Critical Heritage*, Vol. 1: to 1870, London, 1968; Vol. 2: 1870–1940, 1987.

——, ed., *Critical Essays on Jane Austen*, London, 1968.

——, ed., *Jane Austen: 'Northanger Abbey' and 'Persuasion'. A Casebook*, London, 1976.

——, ed., *Jane Austen: 'Sense and Sensibility', 'Pride and Prejudice' and 'Mansfield Park'. A Casebook*, London, 1976.

Todd, Janet, ed., *Jane Austen: New Perspectives. Women and Literature*, Vol. 3, N.S., New York and London, 1983.

*Watt, Ian, ed., *Jane Austen: Twentieth Century Views*, Englewood Cliffs, N.J., 1963.

2 Monographs

Armstrong, Isobel, *'Mansfield Park'*, Harmondsworth, 1988.

Babb, Howard S., *Jane Austen's Novels: the Fabric of Dialogue*, Columbus, Ohio, 1962.

Bradbrook, Frank, *Jane Austen and her Predecessors*, Cambridge, 1967.

Burrows, J.F., *Jane Austen's 'Emma'*, Sydney, 1968.

*——, *Computation into Criticism: A Study of Jane Austen's Novels and an Experiment in Method*, Oxford, 1987.

Select Bibliography

Bush, Douglas, *Jane Austen*, London and New York, 1975.

*Butler, Marilyn, *Jane Austen and the War of Ideas*, Oxford, 1975; new edn. 1988.

Cecil, Lord David, *A Portrait of Jane Austen*, London, 1978.

De Rose, Peter L., *Jane Austen and Samuel Johnson*, Washington, 1980.

Duckworth, Alisdair M., *The Improvement of the Estate: A Study of Jane Austen's Novels*, Baltimore and London, 1971.

Dussinger, John A., *In the Pride of the Moment: Encounters in Jane Austen's World*, Columbus, Ohio, 1990.

Evans, Mary, *Jane Austen and the State*, London and New York, 1987.

Fergus, Jan, *Jane Austen and the Didactic Novel*, Totowa, New Jersey, 1983.

Fleishman, Avrom, *A Reading of 'Mansfield Park': An Essay in Critical Synthesis*, Minneapolis, 1967.

Gard, Roger, *'Emma' and 'Persuasion'*, Harmondsworth, 1985.

Gillie, Christopher, *A Preface to Jane Austen*, London 1974; revised edn. 1985.

Handler, Richard and Segal, Daniel, *Jane Austen and the Fiction of Culture*, Tucson, 1990.

*Hardy, Barbara, *A Reading of Jane Austen*, London, 1975.

Hardy, John, *Jane Austen's Heroines*, London and New York, 1984.

Harris, Jocelyn, *Jane Austen's Art of Memory*, Cambridge, 1989.

Johnson, Claudia, *Jane Austen: Women, Politics and the Novel*, Chicago, 1988.

*Kirkham, Margaret, *Jane Austen: Feminism and Fiction*, Brighton, 1983.

Lascelles, Mary, *Jane Austen and her Art*, Oxford, 1939.

Liddell, Robert, *The Novels of Jane Austen*, London, 1963.

Litz, A. Walton, *Jane Austen: A Study in her Artistic Development*, London, 1965.

MacDonagh, Oliver, *Jane Austen: Real and Imagined Worlds*, New Haven and London, 1991.

Moler, Kenneth J., *Jane Austen's Art of Allusion*, Lincoln, Nebraska, 1968.

Mooneyham, Laura G., *Romance, Language, and Education in Jane Austen's Novels*, New York, 1988.

Morgan, Susan, *In the Meantime: Character and Perception in Jane Austen's Fiction*, Chicago, 1980.

Morris, Ivor, *Mr. Collins Considered: Approaches to Jane Austen*, London and New York, 1987.

*Mudrick, Marvin, *Jane Austen: Irony as Defense and Discovery*, Princeton and London, 1952.

*Page, Norman, *The Language of Jane Austen*, Oxford, 1972.

Paris, Bernard, *Character and Conflict in Jane Austen's Novels*, Detroit, 1978 (Brighton, 1979).

Phillipps, K.C., *Jane Austen's English*, London, 1970.

Poovey, Mary, *The Proper Lady and the Woman Writer: Ideology and Style in the Works of Mary Wollstonecraft, Mary Shelley, and Jane Austen*, Chicago, 1984.

Roberts, Warren, *Jane Austen and the French Revolution*, New York, 1979.

Sadleir, Michael, *The Northanger Novels: A Footnote to Jane Austen*, Eng. Assoc., Oxford, 1927.

Smith, LeRoy W., *Jane Austen and the Drama of Woman*, London, 1983.

Southam, B.C., *Jane Austen's Literary Manuscripts*, Oxford, 1964.

Stokes, Myra, *The Language of Jane Austen: A Study of Some Aspects of her Vocabulary*, Basingstoke and London, 1991.

Tanner, Tony, *Jane Austen*, London, 1988.

Tave, Stuart, *Some Words of Jane Austen*, Chicago and London, 1973.

Ten Harmsel, Henrietta, *Jane Austen: A Study in Fictional Conventions*, The Hague, 1964.

*Thompson, James, *Between Self and World: The Novels of Jane Austen*, Pennsylvania University Park and London, 1988.

Villard, Léonie, *Jane Austen and her Work*, 1915; London, 1924.

Wallace, Robert K., *Jane Austen and Mozart*, Athens, Georgia, 1983.

Weldon, Fay, *Letters to Alice on First Reading Jane Austen*, London, 1984.

Williams, Michael, *Jane Austen: Six Novels and Their Methods*, Basingstoke and London, 1986.

Wilt, Judith, *Ghosts of the Gothic: Austen, Eliot, and Lawrence*, Princeton, New Jersey, 1980.

Wright, Andrew, *Jane Austen's Novels: a Study of Structure*, London, 1954.

3   *Articles or parts of books*

Auerbach, Nina, 'O Brave New World: Evolution and Revolution in *Persuasion*', *English Literary History*, Vol. 39, 1972, 112–28.

*Booth, Wayne C., *The Rhetoric of Fiction*, Chicago, 1961, Part II, ch. 9.

Bowen, Elizabeth, on Jane Austen in *Impressions of English Literature*, ed. W.J. Turner, London, 1944.

Brogan, Hugh, letter on 'ordination', *Times Literary Supplement*, 19 December 1968, 1440

Brower, Reuben, 'Light and bright and sparkling: irony and fiction in *Pride and Prejudice*', in *The Fields of Light: an Experiment in Critical Reading*, New York, 1951

Crook, Nora, letter on 'Gowland's Lotion', *Times Literary Supplement*, 7 October 1983, 1989

Davie, John, introduction to *Northanger Abbey, Lady Susan, The Watsons, and Sanditon*, Oxford, 1971 and 1980.

Drabble, Margaret, introduction to *Lady Susan. The Watsons. Sanditon*, Harmondsworth, 1974.

Select Bibliography

Emden, C.S., 'Northanger Abbey Re-dated', Notes & Queries, 195 (1950), 407–10.

*Farrer, Reginald, 'Jane Austen, ob. July 1817', Quarterly Review, July 1917. Reprinted in Jane Austen: The Critical Heritage, Vol. 2, 1870–1940, ed. B.C. Southam, London, 1987.

Fleishman, Avrom, 'The Socialisation of Catherine Morland', English Literary History, XLIV, 1974, 649–67.

*Fullbrook, Kate, 'Jane Austen and the Comic Negative', in Women Reading Women's Writing, ed. Sue Roe, Brighton, 1987.

*Harding, D.W., 'Regulated Hatred: An Aspect of the Work of Jane Austen', Scrutiny, VIII, March 1940, 346–62.

——, introduction to Persuasion, Harmondsworth, 1965.

*Hough, Graham, 'Narrative and Dialogue in Jane Austen', Critical Quarterly, Vol. 12, No. 3, 1970, 201–29.

James, Henry, 'The Lesson of Balzac', Atlantic Monthly, August 1905.

Kaplan, Deborah, 'Female Friendship and Epistolary Form: Lady Susan and the Development of Jane Austen's Fiction', Criticism, Spring 1987, Vol. 29, No. 2. 163–78.

Kearful, Frank J., 'Satire and the Form of the Novel: the Problem of Aesthetic Unity in Northanger Abbey', English Literary History, XXXII, 1965, 511–27.

*Kettle, Arnold, An Introduction to the English Novel, London, 1951, Vol. 1, Part III, ch. 2.

Lauber, J., 'Sandition, the Kingdom of Folly', Studies in the Novel, IV, 1972.

*Leavis, F.R., The Great Tradition, London, 1948, ch. 1.

*Leavis, Q.D., 'A Critical Theory of Jane Austen's Writings', Scrutiny, X, 1941–2; reprinted in Collected Essays, Vol. 1: The Englishness of the English Novel, ed. G. Singh, Cambridge, 1983.

——, 'Jane Austen: Novelist of a Changing Society' (1980), in Collected Essays, Vol. 1: The Englishness of the English Novel, ed. G. Singh, Cambridge, 1983.

Levine, Jay Arnold, 'Lady Susan: Jane Austen's character of the Merry Widow', Studies in English Literature, Vol. 1, No. 4, 1961, 23–4.

Lodge, David, 'Composition, Distribution, Arrangement: Form and Structure in Jane Austen's Novels', in The Jane Austen Handbook, ed. D. Griey, B.C. Southam, and A.W. Litz, New York, 1986; reprinted in After Bakhtin, London, 1990, 116–28.

Lundeen, Kathleen, 'Jane Austen's Proposal Scenes', Review of English Studies, Vol. 11, No. 161, 65–75, February 1990.

Lynch, P.R., 'Speculation at Mansfield Park', Notes & Queries, N.S. XIV, 1 (January 1967), 21–2.

Mathison, John K., 'Northanger Abbey and Jane Austen's Conception of the Value of Fiction', English Literary History, XXIV, 1957, 138–52.

Mudrick, Marvin, on Mansfield Park and Persuasion in Books are not Life But Then What Is?, New York, 1979.

Select Bibliography

*Nabokov, Vladimir, section 2 on *Mansfield Park*, in *Lectures in Literature*, London, 1980.

Phillipps, K.C., 'Lucy Steele's English', *English Studies*, Vol. 50, Amsterdam, 1969, lv–lxi.

*Rawson, Claude, introduction to *Persuasion*, Oxford, 1990.

Spacks, Patricia Meyer, on *Lady Susan*, in *Persuasions: Journal of the Jane Austen Society of North America*, 16 December 1987, 88–98.

Teyssandier, Hubert, 'On *Mansfield Park*' in *The Nineteenth Century Novel: Critical Essays and Documents*, ed. Arnold Kettle, London, 1981.

LITERARY/HISTORICAL, MISCELLANEOUS

1 Literary/Historical

Brombert, Victor, *The Novels of Flaubert*, Princeton, 1966.

Butler, Marilyn, *Maria Edgeworth*, Oxford, 1972.

Cannon, John, *Aristocratic Century*, Cambridge, 1984.

Davis, Lennard J., *Resisting Novels*, New York and London, 1987.

Day, Geoffrey, *From Fiction to the Novel*, London and New York, 1987.

Gilbert, Sandra M., and Gubar, Susan, *The Madwoman in the Attic*, New Haven and London, 1979.

Gilmour, Robin, *The Idea of the Gentleman in the Victorian Novel*, London, 1981.

Green, Martin, *Dreams of Adventure, Deeds of Empire*, London and Henley, 1980.

Keen, Maurice, *Chivalry*, New Haven and London, 1984.

Loftus, John, *Comedy and Society from Congreve to Fielding*, Stanford, 1959.

McKeon, Michael, *The Origins of the English Novel 1600–1740*, Baltimore and London, 1987.

Mullan, John, *Sentiment and Sociability: The Language of Feeling in the Eighteenth Century*, Oxford, 1988.

Pascal, Roy, *The Dual Voice*, Manchester, 1977.

Showalter, Elaine, *The Female Malady: Women, Madness and English Culture*, New York and London, 1987.

Smalley, Barbara, *George Eliot and Flaubert*, Athens, Ohio, 1974.

Spencer, Jane, *The Rise of the Woman Novelist*, Oxford, 1986.

Strouse, Jean, *Alice James*, Boston, 1980.

Todd, Janet, *Women's Friendship in Literature*, New York, 1980.

——, *Sensibility: An Introduction*, London, 1986.

Tristram, Philippa, *Living Space in Fact and Fiction*, London, 1989.

Vargas Llosa, Mario, *The Perpetual Orgy*, 1975; trans. and published in New York, 1986.

Watt, Ian, *The Rise of the Novel*, London, 1957.

Würzbach, Natascha, ed., *The Novel in Letters*, London, 1969.

Select Bibliography

2   *Others*

Aristotle, *Poetics*, trans. T.S. Dorsch in *Classical Literary Criticism*, Harmondsworth, 1965.

Bakhtin, M.M., *The Dialogic Imagination*, trans. M. Holquist and C. Emerson, Austin, Texas, 1981.

Booth, Wayne C., *A Rhetoric of Irony*, Chicago, 1974.

Boswell, James, *The Journal of a Tour to the Hebrides*, 1785; ed. R.W. Chapman, 1930.

——, *The Life of Samuel Johnson, LL.D*, 1791 (additions 1793); Oxford edn. ed. R.W. Chapman, 1953.

Brophy, Brigid, *Mozart the Dramatist: the Value of His Operas to Him, to His Age and to Us*, London, 1964; revised edn. 1988.

Eliot, T.S., *On Poetry and Poets*, London, 1957.

Flaubert, Gustave, *Correspondance*, ed. Jean Bruneau, Paris, (Pléiade edn.), 1973–.

The Letters of Gustave Flaubert, selected, ed. and trans. by Francis Steegmuller, Cambridge, Mass and London, 1979 (1830–57); and 1982 (1857–80).

Goncourt, Edmond and Jules de, *Journal* (1851–1896). selected, ed. and trans. as *Pages from the Goncourt Journal* by Robert Baldick, Oxford, 1962.

Granville, Lady Harriet, *A Second Self (1810–45)*, Letters selected and ed. Virginia Surtees, Salisbury, 1990.

James, Henry, *Henry James: Literary Criticism*, 2 vols., ed. Leon Edel and Mark Wilson, Library of America, 1984.

——, *Henry James, Letters*, selected and ed. Leon Edel, Vol. 4, London and Cambridge, Mass., 1984.

Johnson, Samuel, *A Journey to the Western Islands of Scotland*, 1775; ed. R.W. Chapman, Oxford, 1930.

Lawrence, D.H., *Phoenix*, London, 1936.

Macaulay, Thomas, Lord, "Madame D'Arblay", *Edinburgh Review*, January 1843.

Proust, Marcel, *Contre Sainte-Beuve* etc., ed. Clarac and Sandre, Paris (Pléiade edn.), 1971.

Tallis, Raymond, *In Defence of Realism*, London, 1988.

Woolf, Virginia, *The Common Reader*, London, 1925.

Index

NOTE: Works by Jane Austen are entered directly under title; works by others, under authors. Characters in Jane Austen's novels appear in the index, but fictional characters by other authors generally are not listed.

Aiken, Joan: *Mansfield Revisited*, 240n22
Allen, Mrs. (character: *NA*), 51, 56, 68
Amis, Sir Kingsley, 100, 123, 131, 136; 'What Became of Jane Austen', 237n6
Amis, Martin, 144
Anglicanism, 6
Archer, Isabel (character: James's *The Portrait of a Lady*), 128, 200
Aristotle, 160, 166, 231n1
Armstrong, Isobel: '*Mansfield Park*', 237n6
Arnim, Elizabeth von: *Vera*, 110
Ascham, Roger, 98
Auerbach, Nina: 'Jane Austen's Dangerous Charm', 237n6; 'O Brave New World', 244n1
Austen, Cassandra, 124, 138, 186, 235n14, 239n16
Austen, Rear-Admiral Charles, 14
Austen, Admiral Sir Francis, 14
Austen, Henry: publishes *NA*, 26; and JA's admiration for Richardson, 29, 39; on Henry Crawford, 138; chooses title *Persuasion*, 186; and *Sanditon*, 208; *Biographical Notice*, 25
Austen, Jane: moralism, 2; modern popularity, 4, 6, 97; past in, 6; ease in, 9–10, 97, 221; subject limitations, 11; as national figure, 12–14, 17, 104; foreign views of, 13–15; and politics, 15–17; on class, 17–21; affection for, 24; early works and drafts, 25–6; and literary past, 27; epistolary novels, 29–30; narrator's voice, 46, 152; presentation of immediacy in consciousness, 56, 58, 93; defends the novel, 59–62, 65; gentle image, 79–80;

and moral idea, 97–8; male heroes and characters, 104–7; *élite* characters, 113–14, 116–17; uniformity of world, 121–2; as first modern novelist, 122–3, 134, 153; compared with Flaubert, 146–54; linguistic style, 148–9; exclusion and selection in, 149–51, 160–1; dialogue, 170–2; illness and early death, 182–3, 209; *see also* individual novels
Austen-Leigh, Revd. J.E., 223n8; *Memoir of Jane Austen*, 26, 87, 236n4
Austen-Leigh, W. and R.A.: *Jane Austen: a Family Record*, 222n1
authorial voice, 46, 102, 152–3

Bage, Robert: *Hermsprong*, 50, 61
Bakhtin, M.M., 144
Balzac, Honoré de, 14–15, 123; *La Rabouilleuse*, 71
Bates, Miss (character: *E*), 80, 87, 169–72, 179
Bayley, John, 24
Beethoven, Ludwig van, 182
Behn, Aphra, 28
Bennet, Mr. (character: *P & P*), 100, 102–3, 113, 118
Bennet, Mrs. (character: *P & P*), 100, 102–3, 108, 116–18
Bennet, Elizabeth (character: *P & P*): and class, 21; and *Lady Susan*, 28; spirit, 91; and male system, 100, 105–6; as central figure, 102, 117, 120, 173, 177, 178; actions, 103, 111–13, 116, 163; and Darcy, 139, 180; and woman's lot, 174
Bennet, Jane (character: *P & P*), 74, 101–3, 106, 116, 118, 236n4

Index

Index

prose, 47; as heroine, 74, 120, 144;
character, 123–31, 136–7, 173–4, 190,
211; actions, 133, 149; accepts necklace,
134–6; courted by Henry Crawford,
137–41, 143–4; love for Edmund,
139–41; married life, 180
Price, William (character: *MP*), 128, 139
Pride and Prejudice (JA): early draft, 26;
epistolary basis, 71; secondary
characters, 84; popularity, 96–7, 119;
ideas, 97–100; structure, 99; love in,
99–100; dialogues, 99; and male
dominance, 100–1; as entertainment,
101; and marriage, 107–13, 120; speed
and concisions, 115; commonplaces in,
116–17; embarrassing behaviour in,
117–18; feeling in, 119
Proust, Marcel, 15; 'A Propos du "Style"
de Flaubert', 147
Pushkin, Alexander S.: *Eugene Onegin*,
114–15
Putnam, Hilary, 231n1
Pye, Henry, 228n10
Pym, Barbara, 110; *Crampton Hodnet*,
110–11

Quincey, E., 36

Radcliffe, Ann, 64: *The Mysteries of
Udolpho*, 49, 54; *The Romance of the
Forest*, 49, 54
Rawson, Claude, 244n7
Reeve, Clara: *The Old English Baron*, 49
Richardson, Samuel: public, 4; and
epistolary novel form, 29–30, 142; JA
admires, 29, 39, 46, 122; moralising, 49,
117, 136, 230n13; abductions in, 150;
and *Sanditon*, 214; sentiment, 226n22;
on courtship, 230n15; *Clarissa*, 29, 41,
47, 60, 130, 139, 177; *Pamela*, 29,
39–40, 136, 230n13; *Sir Charles
Grandison*, 29–32, 49, 63, 123, 200,
205
Robespierre, Maximilien, 18
Roth, Philip: *When She Was Good*, 149
Round, Dorothy, 245n14
Rousseau, Jean-Jacques, 75, 161, 233n3;
La Nouvelle Heloïse, 40
Rushworth, James (character: *MP*), 18,
125, 245n12
Rushworth, Maria (character: *MP*): *see*
Bertram, Maria
Russell, Lady (character: *P*), 187–8, 199
Russell, Bertrand, 64

Sade, marquis de, 130

Sanders, Wilbur: *The Dramatist and the
Received Idea*, 223n5
Sanditon (JA): tone, 208–9, 213, 216;
title, 208; dates, 209; endings, 210,
213–14; literary pastiche in, 214; mist
in, 216–18, 221; vocabulary, 220
Scott, Sir Walter, 98, 126, 214, 236
Sense and Sensibility (JA): early drafts, 26,
70; as eighteenth-century novel, 26;
epistolary bedrock, 29; title, 70–2;
explanatory nature, 72–5; heroines,
74–6, 92–4; harshness and suffering in,
80–2, 88–91, 95; ill-natured characters
in, 83–7; morality, 92–4, 101; opening,
155; structure, 212
Seronsay, Cecil: 'Jane Austen's Technique',
233n6
Seward, Anna, 229n10
Shaftesbury, Anthony Ashley Cooper, 3rd
Earl of, 233n3
Shakespeare, William, 11, 13–14; *Henry
VIII*, 139; *King Lear*, 77–8; *The
Merchant of Venice*, 152, 164; *Much
Ado about Nothing*, 23, 109; *Othello*,
164; *Pericles*, 183, 184–5; *Romeo and
Juliet*, 23; *Twelfth Night*, 205, 236n3
Sheridan, Richard Brinsley, 227n4
Showalter, Elaine: *The Female Malady*,
239n15
Sidney, Sir Philip, 166
Smith, Mrs. (character: *P*), 20–1, 151, 201
Smith, Charlotte, 48, 73, 117, 160
Smith, Harriet (character: *E*), 66, 136,
160–1, 164, 168–9, 174–5, 177–8,
180–1, 204
Smith, LeRoy: *Jane Austen and the Drama
of Woman*, 231n17
Smollett, Tobias: *Humphry Clinker*, 213
Southam, Brian C., 211–12; *Jane Austen's
Literary Manuscripts*, 224nn2 and 3;
'"Regulated Hatred" Revisited',
227–8n7.
Spacks, Patricia Meyer, 225n14
speech: *see* dialogue
Spender, Dale: *Mothers of the Novel*,
224n4
Staël, Anne-Louise-Germaine Necker,
madame de, 219
Steele, Anne (character: *S & S*), 86, 94
Steele, Lucy (character: *S & S*), 80, 86, 90,
94
Steiner, George, 7–9
Stendhal (Marie-Henri Beyle), 15, 99;
Lucien Leuwen, 127
Sterne, Laurence, 50
Stokes, Myra: *The Language of Jane*

Index